.

Dramatic and miscellaneous poems

George MacDonald

BIBLIOLIFE

DRAMATIC

AND

MISCELLANEOUS POEMS.

BY

GEORGE MACDONALD, LL. D.,

AUTHOR OF "WILFRID CUMBERMEDE," ETC.

I
WITHIN AND WITHOUT.

II.
THE HIDDEN LIFE AND OTHER POEMS.

NEW YORK:

SCRIBNER, ARMSTRONG AND COMPANY.

WITHIN AND WITHOUT.

BY

GEORGE MACDONALD, LL. D.

AUTHOR OF " WILFRID CUMBERMEDE," "ANNALS OF A QUIET NEIGHBOR
HOOD," ETC.

NEW YORK:

SCRIBNER, ARMSTRONG, & CO.

TO

L. P. M. D.

RECEIVE thine own ; for I and it are thine.
   Thou know'st its story ; how for forty days —
   Weary with sickness and with social haze,
(After thy hands and lips with love divine
Had somewhat soothed me, made the glory shine,
   Though with a watery lustre,) more delays
   Of blessedness forbid — I took my ways
Into a solitude, Invention's mine ;
   There thought and wrote afar, and yet with thee.
Those days gone past, I came, and brought a book ;
My child, developed since in limb and look
   It came in shining vapors from the sea,
   And in thy stead sung low sweet songs to me,
When the red life-blood labor would not brook.

                      G M D.

May, 1855.

WITHIN AND WITHOUT.

PART I.

Go thou into thy closet; shut thy door;
  And pray to Him in secret: He will hear.
  But think not thou, by one wild bound, to clear
The numberless ascensions, more and more,
Of starry stairs that must be climbed, before
  Thou comest to the Father's likeness near,
  And bendest down to kiss the feet so dear
That, step by step, their mounting flights passed o'er.
  Be thou content if on thy weary need
There falls a sense of showers and of the spring;
A hope that makes it possible to fling
  Sickness aside, and go and do the deed;
  For highest aspiration will not lead
Unto the calm beyond all questioning.

PART I.

SCENE I. — *A cell in a convent.* JULIAN *alone.*

Julian.　EVENING again, slow creeping like a
　　　　　　　death!
And the red sunbeams fading from the wall,
On which they flung a sky, with streaks and bars,
Of the poor window-pane that let them in,
For clouds and shadings of the mimic heaven!
Soul of my cell, they part, no more to come.
But what is light to me, while I am dark!
And yet they strangely draw me, those faint hues,
Reflected flushes from the Evening's face,
Which as a bride, with glowing arms outstretched,
Takes to her blushing heaven him who has left
His chamber in the dim deserted east.
Through walls and hills I see it!　The rosy sea!
The radiant head half-sunk!　A pool of light,
As the blue globe had by a blow been broken,
And the insphered glory bubbled forth!

Or the sun were a splendid water-bird,

That flying furrowed with its golden feet

A flashing wake over the waves, and home !

Lo there ! —— Alas, the dull blank wall ! — High up,

The window-pane a dead gray eye !   And night

Come on me like a thief ! —— 'Tis best ; the sun

Has always made me sad.   I'll go and pray .

The terror of the night begins with prayer.

    (*Vesper bell.*) Call them that need thee ; I need not

        thy summons ;

My knees would not so pain me when I kneel,

If only at thy voice my prayer awoke.

I will not to the chapel.   When I find Him,

Then will I praise Him from the heights of peace ;

But now my soul is as a speck of life

Cast on the deserts of eternity ;

A hungering and a thirsting, nothing more.

I am as a child new-born, its mother dead,

Its father far away beyond the seas.

Blindly I stretch my arms and seek for him ·

He goeth by me, and I see him not.

I cry to him : as if I sprinkled ashes,

My prayers fall back in dust upon my soul.

(*Choir and organ-music.*) I bless you, sweet sounds,
    for your visiting.
What friends I have! Prismatic harmonies
Have just departed in the sun's bright car,
And fair, convolved sounds troop in to me,
Stealing my soul with faint deliciousness.
Would they took shapes! What levees I should hold!
How should my cell be filled with wavering forms!
Louder they grow, each swelling higher, higher;
Trembling and hesitating to float off,
As bright air-bubbles linger, that a boy
Blows, with their interchanging, wood-dove hues,
Just throbbing to their flight, like them to die.
—Gone now! Gone to the Hades of dead loves!
  Is it for this that I have left the world?
Left what, poor fool? Is this, then, all that comes
Of that night when the closing door fell dumb
On music and on voices, and I went
Forth from the ordered tumult of the dance,
Under the clear cope of the moonless night,
Wandering away without the city-walls,
Between the silent meadows and the stars,
Till something woke in me, and moved my spirit,

And of themselves my thoughts turned towards God ;
When straight within my soul I felt as if
An eye was opened ; but I knew not whether
'Twas I that saw, or God that looked on me ?
It closed again, and darkness fell ; but not
To hide the memory ; that, in many failings
Of spirit and of purpose, still returned ;
And I came here at last to search for God.
Would I could find Him !   O, what quiet content
Would then absorb my heart, yet leave it free.

A knock at the door.   Enter Brother ROBERT *with a light.*

Robert.   Head in your hands as usual !   You will fret
Your life out, sitting moping in the dark.
Come, it is supper-time.

Julian.   I will not sup to-night.

Robert   Not sup !   You'll never live to be a saint.

Julian. A saint !   The devil has me by the heel.

Robert. So has he all saints ; as a boy his kite,
Which ever struggles higher for his hold
It is a silly devil to gripe so hard ; —
He should let go his hold, and then he has you.
If you'll not come, I'll leave the light with you.
Hark to the chorus !   Brother Stephen sings.

Chorus.   *Always merry, and never drunk,*
            That's the life of the jolly monk.

·SONG.

They say the first monks were lonely men,
Praying each in his lonely den,
Rising up to kneel again,
Each a skinny male Magdalen,
Peeping scared from out his hole
Like a burrowing rabbit or a mole;
But years ring changes as they roll.

Cho.   *Now always merry, &c.*

When the moon gets up with her big round face,
Like Mistress Poll's in the market-place,
Down to the village below we pace; —
We know a supper that wants a grace:
Past the curtseying women we go,
Past the smithy, all a-glow,
To the snug little houses at top of the row.

Cho.   *For always merry, &c.*

And there we find, amongst the ale,
The fragments of a floating tale:
To piece them together we never fail;
And we fit them rightly, I'll go bail.
And so we have them all in hand,
The lads and lasses throughout the land,
And we are the masters, — you understand?

Cho.   *So always merry, &c.*

Last night we had such a game of play
With the nephews and nieces over the way,

All for the gold that belonged to the clay
That lies in lead till the judgment-day.
The old man's soul they'd leave in the lurch ;
But we saved her share for old Mamma Church.
How they eyed the bag as they stood in the porch !

Cho.   *O ! always merry, and never drunk,*
        That's the life of the jolly monk !

Robert. The song is hardly to your taste, I see.
Where shall I set the light ?

Julian.   I do not need it.

Robert.   Come, come !   The dark is a hot-bed for
        fancies.
I wish you were at table, were it only
To stop the talking of the men about you.
You in the dark are talked of in the light.

Julian. Well, brother, let them talk ; it hurts not me.

Robert. No ; but it hurts your friend to hear them
        say,
You would be thought a saint without the trouble.
You do no penance that they can discover ;
You keep shut up, say some, eating your heart,
Possessed with a bad conscience, the worst demon.
You are a prince, say others, hiding here,
Till circumstance that bound you, set you free.

To-night, there are some whispers of a lady
That would refuse your love.

Julian.   Aye! What of her?

Robert. I hear no more than so; and that you came
To seek the next best service you could find:
Turned from the lady's door, and knocked at God's.

Julian. One part at least is true: I knock at God's;
He has not yet been pleased to let me in.
As for the lady — that is — so far true,
But matters little.   Had I less to do,
This talking might annoy me; as it is,
Why, let the wind set there, if it pleases it;
I keep in-doors.

Robert.   Gloomy as usual, brother!
Brooding on fancy's eggs.   God did not send
The light that all day long gladdened the earth,
Flashed from the snowy peak, and on the spire
Transformed the weathercock into a star,
That you should gloom within stone walls all day.
At dawn to-morrow, take your staff, and come:
We will salute the breezes, as they rise
And leave their lofty beds, laden with odors
Of melting snow, and fresh damp earth, and moss;

Imprisoned spirits, which life-waking Spring
Lets forth in vapor through the genial air.
Come, we will see the sunrise ; watch the light
Leap from his chariot on the loftiest peak,
And thence descend triumphant, step by step,
The stairway of the hills.   Free air and action
Will soon dispel these vapors of the brain.

 Julian. My friend, if one should tell a homeless
   boy,
"There is your father's house : go in and rest ; "
Through every open room the child would go,
Timidly looking for the friendly eye ;
Fearing to touch, scarce daring even to wonder
At what he saw, until he found his sire.
But gathered to his bosom, straight he is
The heir of all ; he knows it 'midst his tears.
And so with me : not having seen Him yet,
The light rests on me with a heaviness ;
All beauty wears to me a doubtful look ;
A voice is in the wind I do not know ;
A meaning on the face of the high hills
Whose utterance I cannot comprehend.
A something is behind them : that is God.

These are his words, I doubt not, language strange ;

These are the expressions of his shining thoughts ;

And He is present, but I find Him not.

I have not yet been held close to his heart.

Once in his inner room, and by his eyes

Acknowledged, I shall find my home in these,

'Mid sights familiar as a mother's smiles,

And sounds that never lose love's mystery.   ·

Then they will comfort me.   Lead me to Him !

   Robert (pointing to the Crucifix in a recess).   See,

       there is God revealed in human form !

   Julian (kneeling and crossing).   Alas, my friend ! —

       revealed — but as in nature :

I see the man ; I cannot find the God.

I know his voice is in the wind, his presence

Is in the Christ.   The wind blows where it listeth ;

And there stands Manhood: and the God is there,

Not here, not here.

      [*Pointing to his bosom.   Seeing* ROBERT'S *bewildered look,*
        and changing his tone.

         You understand me not.

Without my need, you cannot know my want.

You will all night be puzzling to determine

2

With which of the old heretics to class me.

But you are honest ; will not rouse the cry

Against me. I am honest. For the proof,

Such as will satisfy a monk, look here !

Is this a smooth belt, brother ? And look here !

Did one week's scourging seam my side like that ?

I am ashamed to speak thus, and to show

Things rightly hidden ; but in my heart I love you,

And cannot bear but you should think me true.

Let it excuse my foolishness. They talk

Of penance ! Let them talk when they have tried,

And found it has not even unbarred heaven's gate,

Let out one stray beam of its living light,

Or humbled that proud *I* that knows not God.

You are my friend : — if you should find this cell

Empty some morning, do not be afraid

That any ill has happened

 Robert.   Well, perhaps

"Twere better you should go. I cannot help you,

But I can keep your secret. God be with you. [*Goes.*

 Julian. Amen. — A good man ; but he has not
   waked,

And seen the Sphinx's stony eyes fixed on him.

God veils it.   He believes in Christ, he thinks ,

And so he does, as possible for him.

How he will wonder when he looks for heaven !

He thinks me an enthusiast, because

I seek to know God, and to hear his voice

Talk to my heart in silence , as of old

The Hebrew king, when, still, upon his bed,

He lay communing with his heart ; and God

With strength in his soul did strengthen him, until

In his light he saw light.   God speaks to men.

My soul leans towards him , stretches forth its arms,

And waits expectant.   Speak to me, my God ;

And let me know the living Father cares

For me, even me ; for this one of his children. —

Hast thou no word for me ?   I am thy thought.

God, let thy mighty heart beat into mine,

And let mine answer as a pulse to thine.

See, I am low ; yea, very low; but thou

Art high, and thou canst lift me up to thee.

I am a child, a fool before thee, God ;

But thou hast made my weakness as my strength.

I am an emptiness for thee to fill ;

My soul, a cavern for thy sea.   I lie

Diffused, abandoning myself to thee. . . . .

———— I will look up, if life should fail in looking.

Ah me !   A stream cut from my parent-spring !

Ah me !   A life lost from its father-life !

SCENE II. — *The refectory   The monks at table.   A buzz of conversation.*   ROBERT *enters, wiping his forehead, as if he had just come in*

Stephen (*speaking across the table*). You see, my
        friend, it will not stand to logic ;

Or, if you like it better, stand to reason ;

For in this doctrine is involved a *cause*

Which for its very being doth depend

Upon its own *effect.*   For, don't you see,

He tells me to have faith and I shall live?

Have faith for what?   Why, plainly, that I shall

Be saved from hell by Him, and ta'en to heaven ;

What is salvation else ?   If I believe,

Then He will save me. . . But this his *will*

Has no existence till that I believe ;

So there is nothing for my faith to rest on,

No object for belief.   How can I trust

In that which is not ?   Send the salad, Cosmo.

Besides, 'twould be a plenary indulgence ;

To all intents save one, most plenary —

And that the Church's coffer.   'Tis absurd.

   Monk. 'Tis most absurd, as you have clearly shown.

And yet I fear some of us have been nibbling

At this same heresy.   'Twere well that one

Should find it poison.   I have no pique at him —

But there's that Julian —

   Stephen.   Hush ! speak lower, friend.

    Two Monks further down the table — in a low tone.

   1st Monk. Where did you find her?

   2d Monk.   She was taken ill

At the Star-in-the-East.   I chanced to pass that way,

And so they called me in.   I found her dying.

But ere she would confess and make her peace,

She begged to know if I had ever seen

About this neighborhood, a tall dark man,

Moody and silent, with a little stoop

As if his eyes were heavy for his shoulder,

And a strange look of mingled youth and age, —

   1st Monk. Julian, by ———

   2d Monk. 'St — no names !   I had not seen him.

I saw the death-mist gathering in her eye,

And urged her to proceed ; and she began ;

But went not far before delirium came,

With endless repetitions, hurryings forward,

Recoverings like a hound at fault.   The past

Was running riot in her conquered brain ;

And there, with doors thrown wide, a motley group

Held carnival ; went freely out and in,

Meeting and jostling.   But withal it seemed

As some confused tragedy went on ;

Till suddenly the lights sunk out , the pageant

Went like a ghost , the chambers of her brain

Lay desolate and silent.   I can gather

This much, and nothing more.   This Julian

Is one of some distinction ; probably rich,

And titled *Count*.   He had a love-affair,

In good-boy, layman fashion, seemingly.

Give me the woman ; love is troublesome.

She loved him too, but false play came between,

And used this woman for her minister ;

Who never would have peached, but for a witness

Hidden behind some curtains in her heart

Of which she did not know.   That same, her con-
    science,

Has waked and blabbed so far ; but must conclude

Its story to some double-ghostly father,

For she is ghostly penitent by this.

Our consciences will play us no such tricks ;

They are the Church's, not our own.   We must

Keep this small matter secret.   If it should

Come to his ears, he'll soon bid us good-by —

A lady's love before ten heavenly crowns !

And so the world will have the benefit

Of the said wealth of his, if such there be.

I have told you, old Godfrey ; I tell none else

Until our Abbot comes.

    1st Monk.   That is to-morrow.

    Another group near the bottom of the table, in which is ROBERT.

    1st Monk. 'Tis very clear there's something wrong

        with him.

Have you not marked that look, half scorn, half pity,

Which passes like a thought across his face,

When he has listened, seeming scarce to listen,

A while to our discourse ? — he never joins.

    2d Monk. I know quite well.   I stood beside him

        once,

Some of the brethren near ; Stephen was talking.

He chanced to say the words, *Our Holy Faith.*
"Faith indeed! poor fools!" fell from his lips,
Half-muttered, and half-whispered, as the words
Had wandered forth unbidden. I am sure
He is an atheist at the least.

   3d Monk (pale-faced and large eyed). And I
Fear he is something worse. I had a trance
In which the devil tempted me : the shape
Was Julian's to the very finger-nails.
Non nobis, Domine! I overcame.
I am sure of one thing — music tortures him :
I saw him once, amidst the *Gloria Patri,*
When the whole chapel trembled in the sound,
Rise slowly as in ecstasy of pain,
And stretch his arms abroad, and clasp his hands,
Then slowly, faintingly, sink on his knees.

   2d Monk. He does not know his rubric ; stands
      when others
Are kneeling round him. I have seen him twice
With his missal upside down.

   4th Monk (plethoric and husky). He blew his nose
Quite loud on last Annunciation-day,
And choked our Lady's name in the Abbot's throat.

Robert. When he returns, we must complain ; and
    beg
He'll take such measures as the case requires.

Scene III. —*Julian's cell. An open chest. The lantern on a stool,
its candle nearly burnt out* Julian *lying on his bed, looking
at the light.*

Julian. And so all growth that is not towards God
Is growing to decay.   All increase gained
Is but an ugly, earthy, fungous growth.
'Tis aspiration as that wick aspires,
Towering above the light it overcomes,
But ever sinking with the dying flame.
O let me *live*, if but a daisy's life !
No toadstool life-in-death, no efflorescence !
Wherefore wilt thou not hear me, Lord of me?
Have I no claim on thee? True, I have none
That springs from me, but much that springs from
    thee.
Hast thou not made me? Liv'st thou not in me?
I have done nought for thee, am but a want ;
But thou who art rich in giving, canst give claims ,
And this same need of thee, which thou hast given,
Is a strong claim on thee to give thyself,

And makes me bold to rise and come to thee.

Through all my sinning thou hast not recalled

This witness of thy fatherhood, to plead

For thee with me, and for thy child with thee.

   Last night, as now, I seemed to speak with Him;

Or was it but my heart that spoke for Him?

" Thou mak'st me long," I said, " therefore wilt give;

My longing is thy promise, O my God.

If, having sinned, I thus have lost the claim,

Why doth the longing yet remain with me,

And make me bold thus to besiege thy doors?"

   I thought I heard an answer: " Question on.

Keep on thy need; it is the bond that holds

Thy being yet to mine.   I give it thee,

A hungering and a fainting and a pain,

Yet a God-blessing.   Thou art not quite dead

While this pain lives in thee.   I bless thee with it.

Better to live in pain than die that death."

   So I will live, and nourish this my pain;

For oft it giveth birth unto a hope

That makes me strong in prayer.   He knows it too.

Softly I'll walk the earth; for it is his,

Not mine to revel in.   Content I wait.

A still small voice I cannot but believe,

Says on within : God *will* reveal himself.

  I must go from this place.   I cannot rest.

It boots not staying.   A desire like thirst

Awakes within me, or a new child-heart,

To be abroad on the mysterious earth,

Out with the moon in all the blowing winds.

  'Tis strange that dreams of her should come again.

For many months I had not seen her form,

Save phantom-like on dim hills of the past,

Until I laid me down an hour ago ;

When twice through the dark chamber, full of eyes,

The dreamful fact passed orderly and true.

Once more I see the house ; the inward blaze

Of the glad windows half-quenched in the moon ;

The trees that, drooping, murmured to the wind,

" Ah ! wake me not," which left them to their sleep,

All save the poplar : it was full of joy,

So that it could not sleep, but trembled on.

Sudden as Aphrodite from the sea,

She issued radiant from the pearly night.

It took me half with fear — the glimmer and gleam

Of her white festal garments, haloed round

With denser moonbeams.   On she came — and there
I am bewildered.   Something I remember
Of thoughts that choked the passages of sound,
Hurrying forth without their pilot-words ;
Of agony, as when a spirit seeks
In vain to hold communion with a man ;
A hand that would and would not stay in mine ;
A gleaming of her garments far away ;
And then I know not what.   The moon was low,
When from the earth I rose ; my hair was wet,
Dripping with dew —

Enter ROBERT *cautiously.*

Why, how now, Robert ?

[*Rising on his elbow.*

Robert (*glancing at the chest*).   I see ; that's well.
   Are you nearly ready ?
Julian.   Why ?   What's the matter ?
Robert.   You must go this night,
If you would go at all.

Julian.   Why must I go ?
Robert (*turning over the things in the chest*).
   Here, put this coat on.   Ah ! take that thing too.
No more such head-gear !   Have you not a hat,

[*Going to the chest again.*

Or something for your head ?   There 's such a hubbub

Got up about you !   The Abbot comes to-morrow.

    Julian. Ah, well ! I need not ask.   I know it all.

    Robert. No, you do not.   Nor is there time to tell

    you.

Ten minutes more, they will be round to bar

The outer doors ; and then — good-by, poor Julian !

      JULIAN is rapidly changing his clothes.

    Julian. Now I am ready, Robert.   Thank you,

    friend.

Farewell ! God bless you ! We shall meet again.

    Robert. Farewell, dear friend !   Keep far away from

    this.   *[Goes.*

      JULIAN follows him out of the cell, steps along a narrow
        passage to a door, which he opens slowly.   He goes out,
        and closes the door behind him.

  SCENE IV. — *Night.   The court of a country-inn.   The* ABBOT,
      while his horse is brought out.

    Abbot. Now for a shrine to house this rich Ma

    donna,

Within the holiest of the holy place !

I'll have it made in fashion as a stable,

With porphyry pillars to a marble stall ;

And odorous woods, shaved fine like shaken hay

Shall fill the silver manger for a bed,

Whereon shall lie the ivory Infant carved

By shepherd hands on plains of Bethlehem,

And o'er him shall bend the Mother mild,

In silken white, and coroneted gems.

Glorious ! But wherewithal I see not now —

The Mammon of unrighteousness is scant ;

Nor know I any nests of money-bees

That would yield half-contentment to my need.

Yet will I trust and hope ; for never yet

In journeying through this vale of tears have I

Projected pomp that did not blaze anon.

SCENE V —*After midnight* JULIAN *seated under a tree on the roadside*

Julian So lies my journey — on into the dark.

Without my will I find myself alive,

And must go forward   Is it God that draws

Magnetic all the souls unto their home,

Travelling, they know not how, but unto God ?

It matters little what may come to me

Of outward circumstance, as hunger, thirst,
Social condition, yea, or love or hate ;
But what shall *I* be, fifty summers hence ?
My life, my being, all that meaneth *me*,
Goes darkling forward into something — what ?
O God, thou knowest.   It is not my care.
If thou wert less than truth, or less than love,
It were a fearful thing to be and grow
We know not what.   My God, take care of me.
Pardon and swathe me in an infinite love
Pervading and inspiring me, thy child.
And let thy own design in me work on,
Unfolding the ideal man in me!
Which being greater far than I have grown,
I cannot comprehend.   I am thine, not mine.
One day, completed unto thine intent,
I shall be able to discourse with thee ;
For thy Idea, gifted with a self,
Must be of one with the mind where it sprang,
And fit to talk with thee about thy thoughts.
Lead me, O Father, holding by thy hand ;
I ask not whither, for it must be on.
This road will lead me to the hills, I think ;
And there I am in safety and at home.

SCENE VI. — *The Abbot's room   The* ABBOT *and one of the*
                                    Monks.

Abbot. Did she say *Julian?*   Did she say the
   name?

Monk. She did.

Abbot. What did she call the lady?   What?

Monk I could not hear.

Abbot   Nor where she lived?

Monk   Nor that.

She was too wild for leading where I would

Abbot So.   Send Julian.   One thing I need not
   ask :

You have kept this matter secret?

Monk.   Yes, my lord.

Abbot Well, go, and send him hither.

                                        [MONK *goes.*

                              Said I well,

That wish would burgeon into pomp for me?

That God will hear his own elect who cry?

Now for a shrine, so glowing in the means

That it shall draw the eyes by power of light !

So tender in conceit, that it shall draw

The heart by very strength of delicateness,

And move proud thought to worship !

                                   I must act

With caution now ; must win his confidence ;

Question him of the secret enemies

That fight against his soul ; and lead him thus

To tell me, by degrees, his history.

So shall I find the truth, and lay foundation

For future acts, as circumstance requires.

For if the tale be true that he is rich,

And ——

     Reënter MONK *in haste and terror.*

    Monk. He's gone, my lord !   His cell is empty.

    Abbot (starting up). What ! You are crazy ! Gone !

      His cell is empty !

    Monk. 'Tis true as death, my lord.

    Abbot. Heaven and hell ! It shall not be, I swear !

There is a plot in this !   You, sir, have lied !

Some one is in his confidence — who is it?

Go rouse the convent.   [MONK *goes.*

                        He must be followed, found.

Hunt's up, friend Julian !   First your heels, old stag !

But by and by your horns, and then your side !

     3

'Tis venison much too good for the world's eating.

I'll go and sift this business to the bran.

Robert and him I have sometimes seen together.

God's curse ! it shall fare ill with any man

That has connived at this, if I detect him.

SCENE VII. — *Afternoon.   The mountains.*   JULIAN.

Julian. Once more I tread thy courts, O God of

    heaven !

I lay my hand upon a rock, whose peak

Is miles away, and high amidst the clouds.

Perchance I touch the mountain whose blue summit,

With the fantastic rock upon its side,

Stops the eye's flight from that high chamber-window

Where, when a boy, I used to sit and gaze

With wondering awe upon the mighty thing,

Terribly calm, alone, self-satisfied,

The *hitherto* of my child thoughts.   Beyond,

A sea might roar around its base.   Beyond,

Might be the depths of the unfathomed space,

This the earth's bulwark over the abyss.

Upon its very point I have watched a star

For a few moments crown it with a fire,

As of an incense-offering that blazed

Upon this mighty altar high uplift,

And then float up the pathless waste of heaven.

From the next window I could look abroad

Over a plain unrolled, which God had painted

With trees, and meadow-grass, and a large river,

Where boats went to and fro like water-flies,

In white and green ; but still I turned to look

At that one mount, aspiring o'er its fellows :

All here I saw — I knew not what was there.

O love of knowledge and of mystery,

Striving together in the heart of man !

" Tell me, and let me know ; explain the thing." —

Then when the courier-thoughts have circled round :

" Alas ! I know it all ; its charm is gone ! "

But I must hasten ; else the sun will set

Before I reach the smoother valley-road.

I wonder if my old nurse lives ; or has

Eyes left to know me with.   Surely, I think,

Four years of wandering since I left my home,

In sunshine and in snow, in ship and cell,

Must have worn changes in this face of mine

Sufficient to conceal me, if I will.

SCENE VIII — *A dungeon in the monastery. A ray of the moon
on the floor.* ROBERT.

Robert. One comfort is, he's far away by this.
Perhaps this comfort is my deepest sin.
Where shall I find a daysman in this strife
Between my heart and holy Church's words?
Is not the law of kindness from God's finger,
Yea, from his heart, on mine?   But then we must
Deny ourselves ; and impulses must yield,
Be subject to the written law of words ;
Impulses made, made strong, that we might have
Within the temple's court live things to bring
And slay upon his altar , that we may,
By this hard penance of the heart and soul,
Become the slaves of Christ. — I have done wrong;
I ought not to have let poor Julian go.
And yet that light upon the floor says, yes —
Christ would have let him go.   It seemed a good,
Yes, self-denying deed, to risk my life
That he might be in peace.   Still up and down
The balance goes, a good in either scale ;
Two angels giving each to each the lie,

And none to part them or decide the question.

But still the *words* come down the heaviest

Upon my conscience as that scale descends ;

But that may be because they hurt me more,

Being rough strangers in the feelings' home.

Would God forbid us to do what is right,

Even for his sake?   But then Julian's life

Belonged to God, to do with as He pleases.

I am bewildered.   'Tis as God and God

Commanded different things in different tones.

Ah! then, the tones are different: which is likest

God's voice?   The one is gentle, loving, kind,

Like Mary singing to her mangered child ;

The other like a self-restrained tempest ;

Like — ah, alas ! — the trumpet on Mount Sinai,

Louder and louder, and the voice of *words*.

O for some light !   Would they would kill me ; then

I would go up, close up, to God's own throne,

And ask, and beg, and pray, to know the truth ;

And He would slay this ghastly contradiction.

I should not fear, for He would comfort me,

Because I am perplexed, and long to know.

But this perplexity may be my sin,

And come of pride that will not yield to Him.

O for one word from God! his own, and fresh

From Him to me! Alas! what shall I do?

END OF PART I.

WITHIN AND WITHOUT.

PART II.

HARK, hark, a voice amid the quiet intense !
It is thy Duty waiting thee without.
Rise from thy knees in hope, the half of doubt ;
A hand doth pull thee — it is Providence ;
Open thy door straightway, and get thee hence ;
Go forth into the tumult and the shout ;
Work, love, with workers, lovers, all about :
Of noise alone is born the inward sense
Of silence ; and from action springs alone
The inward knowledge of true love and faith.
Then, weary, go thou back with failing breath,
And in thy chamber make thy prayer and moan :
One day upon *His* bosom, all thine own,
Thou shalt lie still, embraced in holy death.

PART II.

Julian.   NEMBRONI?   Count Nembroni? —
I remember :
A man about my height, but stronger built?
I have seen him at her father's.   There was something
I did not like about him. — Ah ! I know ·
He had a way of darting looks at one,
As if he wished to know you, but by stealth.

Nurse.   The same, my lord.   He is the creditor.
The common story is, he sought his daughter,
But sought in vain : the lady would not wed.
'Twas rumored soon they were in grievous trouble,
Which caused much wonder, for the family
Was always counted wealthy.   Count Nembroni
Contrived to be the only creditor,
And so imprisoned him.

Julian.   Where is the lady ?

Nurse. Down in the town.

Julian.   But where ?

Nurse.   If you turn left,
When you go through the gate, 'tis the last house
Upon this side the way.   An honest couple,
Who once were almost pensioners of hers,
Have given her shelter, till she find a home
With distant friends.   Alas, poor lady! 'tis
A wretched change for her.

Julian.   Hm ! ah ! I see.
What kind of man is this Nembroni, Nurse ?

Nurse. Here he is little known.   His title comes
From an estate, they say, beyond the hills.
He looks ungracious : I have seen the children
Run to the doors when he came up the street.

Julian. Thank you, Nurse ; you may go.   Stay —
       one thing more.
Have any of my people seen me ?

Nurse.   None.
But me, my lord.

Julian.   And can you keep it secret ? —
I know you will for my sake.   I will trust you.
Bring me some supper ; I am tired and faint.

                              [NURSE *goes.*

Poor and alone!   Such a man has not laid

Such plans for nothing further.   I will watch him.

Heaven may have brought me hither for her sake.

Poor child! I would protect thee as thy father,

Who cannot help thee.   Thou wast not to blame,

My love had no claim on like love from thee. —

How the old love comes gushing to my heart!

    I know not what I can do yet but watch.

I have no hold on him.   I cannot go,

Say, *I suspect:* and, *Is it so or not?*

I should but injure them by doing so.

True, I might pay her father's debts; and will,

If Joseph, my old friend, has managed well

During my absence.   *I* have not spent much.

But still she'd be in danger from this man,

If not permitted to betray himself;

And I, discovered, could no more protect.

Or if, unseen by her, I yet could haunt

Her footsteps like an angel, not for long

Should I remain unseen of other eyes,

That peer from under cowls — not angel-eyes —

Hunting me out, over the stormy earth.

    No; I must watch.   I can do nothing better.

SCENE II.— *A poor cottage An old Man and Woman sitting*
together

Man How 's the poor lady now ?

Woman.   She's poorly still
I fancy every day she's growing thinner.
I am sure she's wasting steadily.

Man.   Has the count
Been here again to-day ?

Woman   No. And I think
He will not come again She was so proud
The last time he was here, you would have thought
She was a queen at least.

Man.   Remember, wife,
What she has been. Trouble and that throws down
The common folk like us all of a heap .
With folks like her, that are high bred and blood,
It sets the mettle up.

Woman.   All very right ;
But take her as she was, she might do worse
Than wed the Count Nembroni.

Man.   Possible.
But are you sure there is no other man
Stands in his way ?

Woman.   How can I tell? So be,

He should be here to help her. What she'll do

I am sure I do not know. We cannot keep her.

And for her work, she does it far too well

To earn a living by it. Her times are changed —

She should not give herself such prideful airs.

    Man. Come, come, old wife! you women are so
        hard

On one another! You speak fair for men,

And make allowances; but when a woman

Crosses your way, you speak the worst of her.

But where is this you're going then to-night?

Do they want me to go as well as you?

    Woman. Yes, you must go, or else it is no use.

They cannot give the money to me, except

My husband go with me. He told me so.

    Man. Well, wife, it's worth the going — just to
        see:

I don't expect a groat to come of it.

    Scene III. — *Kitchen of a small inn.* Host *and* Hostess.

    Host. That's a queer customer you've got up stairs;

What the deuce is he?

Hostess.   What is that to us ?

He always pays his way, and handsomely.

I wish there were more like him.

Host.   Has he been

At home all day ?

Hostess.   He has not stirred a foot

Across the threshold.   That's his only fault —

He's always in the way.

Host.   What does he do ?

Hostess. Paces about the room, or sits at the win-
dow.

I sometimes make an errand to the cupboard,

To see what he's about : he looks annoyed,

But does not speak a word

Host.   He must be crazed,

Or else in hiding for some scrape or other.

Hostess. He has a wild look in his eye sometimes ;

But sure he would not sit so much in the dark,

If he were mad, or anything on his conscience ;

And though he does not say much when he speaks

A civiller man ne'er came in woman's way.

Host O ! he's all right, I warrant.   Is the wine
come ?

SCENE IV. — *The inn; a room up stairs.* JULIAN *at the window,*
half hidden by the curtain.

Julian. With what profusion her white fingers spend

Delicate motions on the insensate cloth !

It was so late this morning ere she came !

I fear she has been ill. She looks so pale !

Her beauty is much less, but she more lovely.

Do I not love her more than when that beauty

Beamed out like starlight, radiating beyond

The confines of her wondrous face and form,

And animated with a present power

The outmost folds and waves of drapery?

Ha! there is something now : the old woman drest

In her Sunday clothes, and waiting at the door,

As for her husband. Something will follow this.

And here he comes, all in his best like her.

They will be gone a while. Slowly they walk,

With short steps down the street. Now I must wake

The sleeping hunter-eagle in my eyes !

SCENE V. — *A back street. Two Servants with a carriage and*
pair.

1st Serv. Heavens, what a cloud ! as big as Ætna !

There !

That gust blew stormy. Take Juno by the head,

I'll stand by Neptune.   Take her head, I say ;

We'll have enough to do, if it should lighten.

    2d Serv. Such drops !   That's the first of it.   I
        declare

She spreads her nostrils and looks wild already,

As if she smelt it coming.   I wish we were

Under some roof or other.   I fear this business

Is not of the right sort.

    1st Serv.   He looked as black

As if he too had lightning in his bosom.

There !   Down, you brute !   Mind the pole, Beppo !

SCENE VI. — *Julian's room.* JULIAN *standing at the window,*
    his face pressed against a pane. Storm and gathering dark-
    ness without.

    Julian. Plague on the lamp ! 'tis gone — no, there
        it flares !

I wish the wind would leave or blow it out.

Heavens ! how it thunders !   This terrific storm

Will either cow or harden him.   I'm blind !

That lightning !   O, let me see again, lest he

Should enter in the dark !   I cannot bear

This glimmering longer.   Now that gush of rain

Has blotted all my view with crossing lights.

'Tis no use waiting here.   I must cross over,

And take my stand in the corner by the door.

But if he comes while I go down the stairs,

And I not see?   To make sure, I'll go gently

Up the stair to the landing by her door.

> [*He goes quickly towards the door.*

Hostess (opening the door and looking in)   If you please,

Sir —   [*He hurries past.*

The devil's in the man!

SCENE VII. — *The landing.*

Voice within.   If you scream, I must muffle you.

Julian (rushing up the stair).   He *is* there!

His hand is on her mouth!   She tries to scream!

> [*Flinging the door open, as* NEMBRONI *springs forward on
> the other side.*

Back!

Nembroni.   What the devil! — Beggar!

> [*Drawing his sword, and making a thrust at* JULIAN, *which
> he parries with his left arm, as, drawing his dagger, he
> springs within* NEMBRONI'S *guard.*

Julian (taking him by the throat).   I have faced

worse storms than you   [*They struggle.*

Heart point and hilt strung on the line of force,

> [*Stabbing him*

4

Your ribs will not mail your heart!

[NEMBRONI *falls dead*   JULIAN *wipes his dagger on the
dead man's coat.*

If men *will* be devils,
They are better in hell than here.

[*Lightning flashes on the blade*
What a night
For a soul to go out of doors!   God in heaven!

[*Approaching the lady within*

Ah! she has fainted.   That is well.   I hope
It will not pass too soon.   It is not far
To the half-hidden door in my own fence,
And that is well.   If I step carefully,
Such rain will soon wash out the tell-tale foot-prints.
What! blood!   *He* does not bleed much, I should
      think.
O, I see! it is mine — he has wounded me.
That's awkward now.

[*Taking a handkerchief from the floor by the window.*
Pardon me, dear lady;

[*Tying the handkerchief with hand and teeth round his arm.*
'Tis not to save my blood I would defile
Even your handkerchief.

[*Coming towards the door, carrying her.*

                                  I am pleased to think
Ten monkish months have not ta'en all my strength.

                    [*Looking out of the window on the landing*

For once, thank darkness! 'Twas sent for us, not

    him.   [*He goes down the stair.*

SCENE VIII. — *A room in the castle.*   JULIAN *and the* NURSE.

Julian. Ask me no questions now, my dear old

    Nurse.

You have put your charge to bed ?

    Nurse.   Yes, my dear lord.

    Julian. And has she spoken yet?

    Nurse.   After you left,

Her eyelids half unclosed ; she murmured once :

Where am I, mother ? — then she looked at me,

And her eyes wandered over all my face ;

Till half in comfort, half in weariness,

They closed again.   Bless her, dear soul ! she is

As feeble as a child.

    Julian.   Under your care,

She will recover soon   Let no one know

She is in the house · — blood has been shed for her.

    Nurse. Alas ! I feared it ; for her dress is bloody.

Julian. That's mine, not his.   But put it in the fire

Get her another.   I'll leave a purse with you.

   Nurse. Leave ?

   Julian.   Yes.   I am off to-night, wander

       ing again

Over the earth and sea.   She must not know

I have been here.   You must contrive to keep

My share a secret.   Once she moved and spoke

When a branch caught her ; but she could not see me.

She thought, no doubt, it was Nembroni had her.

Nor would she have known me.   You must hide her

       Nurse.

Let her on no pretense know where she is,

Nor utter word that might awake a guess.

When she is well and wishes to be gone,

Then write to this address — but under cover

                         [*Writing*

To the Prince Calboli at Florence.   I

Will manage all the rest.   But let her know

Her father is set free , assuredly,

Ere you can give the news, it will be so.

   Nurse. How shall I best conceal her, my good lord ?

   Julian. I have thought of that.   There's a deserted

       room

In the old south wing, at the further end
Of the oak gallery.

    Nurse.   Not deserted quite.
I ventured, when you left, to make it mine,
Because you loved it when a boy, my lord.

    Julian. You do not know, Nurse, why I loved it
        though :
I found a sliding panel, and a door
Into a room behind.   I'll show it you.
You'll find some musty traces of me yet,
When you go in.   Now take her to your room,
But get the other ready.   Light a fire,
And keep it burning well for several days.
Then, one by one, out of the other rooms,
Take everything to make it comfortable ;
Quietly, you know.   If you must have your daughter,
Bind her to be as secret as yourself.
Then put her there.   I'll let her father know
She is in safety.   I must change my clothes,
And be far off or ever morning breaks.   [Nurse *goes.*

    My treasure-room ! how little then I thought,
Glad in my secret, one day it would hold
A treasure unto which I dared not come.

Perhaps she'd love me now — a very little ? —
But not with even a heavenly gift would I
Go beg her love ; that should be free as light,
Cleaving unto myself even for myself.
I have enough to brood on, joy to turn
Over and over in my secret heart :
She lives, and is the better that I live.

Reënter NURSE

Nurse. My lord, her mind is wandering; she is
    raving ;
She's in a dreadful fever.   We must send
To Arli for the doctor, else her life
Will be in danger.

Julian (*rising disturbed*).   Go and fetch your daugh-
    ter.

Take her at once to your own room, and there
I'll see her.   Can you manage it between you ?

Nurse. O yes, my lord ; she is so thin, poor child !

[NURSE *goes.*

Julian. I ought to know the way to treat a fever,
If it be one of twenty.   Hers has come
Of low food, wasting, and anxiety.
I've seen enough of that in Prague and Smyrna.

Scene IX. — *The Abbot's room in the monastery.   The* Abbot.

Abbot. 'Tis useless all.   No trace of him found yet.
One hope remains : we'll see what Stephen says.

Enter Stephen.

Stephen, I have sent for you, because I am told
You said to-day, if I commissioned you,
You'd scent him out, if skulking in his grave.

   Stephen. I did, my lord.

   Abbot.   How would you do it,
     Stephen ?

   Stephen. Try one plan till it failed ; then try another ;
Try half a dozen plans at once ; keep eyes
And ears wide open, and mouth shut, my lord :
Your bull-dog sometimes makes the best retriever.
I have no plan ; but, give me time and money,
I'll find him out.

   Abbot.   Stephen, you're just the man
I have been longing for.   Get yourself ready.

SCENE X — *Towards morning The Nurse's room* LILIA *in bed.*
JULIAN *watching.*

Julian. I think she sleeps. Would God it were so ;
   then
She would do well.   What strange things she has
   spoken !
My heart is beating as if it would spend
Its life in this one night, and beat it out
No wonder ! there is more of life's delight .
In one hour such as this than many years ;
For life is measured by intensity,
Not by the how much of the crawling clock.
   Is that a bar of moonlight stretched across
The window-blind ? or is it but a band
Of whiter cloth my thrifty dame has sewed
Upon the other ?   No , it is the moon
Low down in the west.   'Twas such a moon as this —
   Lilia (half asleep, wildly).   If Julian had been here,
      you dared not do it —
Julian ! Julian !   [*Half rising*
   Julian (forgetting his caution, and going up to her)
         I am here, my Lilia.   No.

Put your head down, my love.   'Twas all a dream,
A terrible dream.   Gone now — is it not?

> [*She looks at him with wide restless eyes ; then sinks back on
> the pillow.   He leaves her.*

How her dear eyes bewildered looked at me !
But her soul's eyes are closed.   If this last long
She'll die before my sight, and Joy will lead
In by the hand her sister, Grief, pale-faced,
And leave her to console my solitude.
Ah, what a joy ! I dare not think of it !
And what a grief ! I will not think of that !
Love ? and from her ? my beautiful, my own !
O God, I did not know thou wert so rich
In making and in giving.   I knew not
The gathered glory of this earth of thine.
O ! wilt thou crush me with an infinite joy ?
Make me a god by giving — making mine
Thy centre-thought of living beauty ? — sprung
From thee, and coming home to dwell with me !

> [*He leans on the wall.*

   Lilia (softly). Am I in heaven ? There's some-
      thing makes me glad,
As if I were in heaven ! Yes, yes, I am.

I see the flashing of ten thousand glories ;

I hear the trembling of a thousand wings,

That vibrate music on the murmuring air !

Each tiny feather-blade crushes its pool

Of circling air to sound, and quivers music.

What is it, though, that makes me glad like this ?

I knew, but cannot find it — I forget.

It must be here — what was it ?   Hark ! the fall,

The endless going of the stream of life !

Ah me ! I thirst, I thirst, — I am so thirsty !

[Querulously.

[JULIAN *gives her drink, supporting her. She looks at him
again, with large wondering eyes*

Ah ! now I know — I was so very thirsty !

[*He lays her down.   She is comforted, and falls asleep.
He extinguishes the light, and looks out of the window*

Julian.   The gray earth dawning up, cold, comfort-
less,

With an obtrusive *I am* written large

Upon its face !

[*Approaching the bed, and gazing on* LILIA *silently with
clasped hands ; then returning to the window*

She sleeps so peacefully ?

O God, I thank thee ; thou hast sent her sleep.

Lord, let it sink into her heart and brain.

Enter NURSE

O Nurse, I'm glad you're come.   She is asleep.

You must be near her when she wakes again.

I think she'll be herself.   But do be careful —

Right cautious how you tell her I am here.

Sweet woman-child, may God be in your sleep!

[JULIAN *goes.*

Nurse.   Bless her white face!   She looks just like
       my daughter,

That's now a saint in heaven   Just those thin cheeks,

And eyelids hardly closed over her eyes!

Go on, poor darling! you are drinking life

From the breast of Sleep.   And yet I fain would see

Your shutters open, for I then should know

Whether the soul had drawn her curtains back,

To peep at morning from her own bright windows.

Ah, what a joy is ready, waiting her,

To break her fast upon, if her wild dreams

Have but betrayed her secrets honestly!

Will he not give thee love as dear as thine?

SCENE XI. — *A hilly road.* STEPHEN, *trudging alone, pauses to look around him.*

Stephen Not a footprint! not a trace that a blood-hound would nose at! But Stephen shall be acknowl-edged a good dog and true. If I had him within stick-length — mind thy head, brother Julian! Thou hast not hair enough to protect it, and thy tonsure shall not. Neither shalt thou tarry at Jericho. It is a poor man that leaves no trail ; and if thou wert poor, I would not follow thee.

[Sings

O! many a hound is stretching out
  His two legs or his four,
Where the saddled horses stand about
  The court and the castle door ;
Till out comes the baron, jolly and stout,
  To hunt the bristly boar.

The emperor, he doth keep a pack
  In his antechambers standing,
And up and down the stairs, good lack !
  And eke upon the landing :
A straining leash, and a quivering back,
  And nostrils and chest expanding !

The devil a hunter long has been,
  Though Doctor Luther said it :

Of his canon-pack he was the dean,
 And merrily he led it :
To fatten them up, when game is lean
 He keeps his dogs on credit

Each man is a hunter to his trade,
 And they follow one another ;
But such a hunter never was made
 As the monk that hunted his brother !
And the runaway pig, alive or dead,
 Shall be eaten by its mother.

Better hunt a flea in a woolly blanket, than a leg-bail monk in this wilderness of mountains, forests, and precipices!   But the flea *may* be caught, and so *shall* the monk.   I have said it.   He is well spotted, with his silver crown, and his uncropped ears.   The rascally vow-breaker!   But his vows shall keep him, whether he keep them or not.   The whining, blubbering idiot!   Gave his plaything, and wants it back! — I wonder whereabouts I am.

SCENE XII. — *The Nurse's room   LILIA sitting up in bed. JU-LIAN seated by her ; an open note in his hand*

Lilia. Tear it up, Julian.

Julian.   No ; I'll treasure it
As the remembrance of a by-gone grief :
I love it well, because it is *not* yours.

Lilia. Where have you been these long, long years
   away?
You look much older.   You have suffered, Julian!

Julian. Since that day, Lilia, I have seen much,
   thought much;
Suffered perhaps a little.   But of this
We'll say no more.   When you are quite yourself,
I'll tell you all you want to know about me.

Lilia. Do tell me something now.   I feel quite
   strong;
It will not hurt me.

Julian.   Wait a day or two.
Indeed 'twould weary you to tell you all.

Lilia. And I have much to tell you, Julian.   I
Have suffered too — not all for my own sake.

                              [*Recalling something.*
O what a dream I had!   O Julian! —
I don't know when it was.   It must have been
Before you brought me here   I am sure it was.

Julian. Don't speak about it.   Tell me afterwards.
You must keep quiet now.   Indeed you must.

Lilia. I will obey you, and not speak a word.

Enter NURSE.

Nurse. Blessings upon her ! She's near well already.

Who would have thought, three days ago, to see

You look so bright ? My lord, you have done wonders.

  Julian. 'Tis not my work, dame.   I must leave

      you now.

To please me, Lilia, go to sleep awhile.

                                    [JULIAN *goes.*

Lilia. Why does he always wear that curious cap ?

Nurse. I don't know.   You must sleep.

Lilia.   Yes.   I forgot.

SCENE XIII — *The Steward's room*   JULIAN *and the* STEWARD.
Papers on the table, which JULIAN *has just finished examining*

  Julian. Thank you much, Joseph ; you have done

      well for me.

You sent that note privately to my friend ?

  Steward. I did, my lord ; and have conveyed the

      money,

Putting all things in train for his release,

Without appearing in it personally,

Or giving any clew to other hands.

He sent this message by my messenger :

His hearty thanks, and God will bless you for it.

He will be secret.   For his daughter, she
Is safe with you as with himself ; and so
God bless you both !   He will expect to hear
From both of you from England.

  Julian.   Well, again.
What money is remaining in your hands ?

  Steward. Two bags, three hundred each ; that's all.
   I fear
To wake suspicion, if I call in more.

  Julian. Quite right.   One thing besides : lest a
   mischance
Befall us, though I do not fear it much, —
We have been very secret, — is that boat
I had before I left, in sailing trim ?

  Steward I knew it was a favorite with my lord ;
I've taken care of it.   A month ago
With my own hands I painted it all fresh,
Fitting new oars and rowlocks.   The old sail
I'll have replaced immediately ; and then
'Twill be as good as new.

  Julian.   That's excellent.
Well, launch it in the evening.   Make it fast
To the stone steps behind my garden study.

Stow in the lockers some sea-stores, and put

The money in the old desk in the study.

   Steward. I will, my lord.   It will be safe enough.

SCENE XIV. — *A road near the town. A* WAGONER. STEPHEN,
in lay dress, coming up to him.

   Stephen. Whose castle's that upon the hill, good

      fellow ?

Wagoner. It's present owner's of the Uglii ;

They call him Lorenzino.

   Stephen.   Whose is that

Down in the valley?

   Wagoner.   That is Count Lamballa's.

   Stephen What is his Christian name ?

   Wagoner.   Omfredo.   No.

That was his father's ; his is Julian

   Stephen. Is he at home ?

   Wagoner.   No, not for many a day.

His steward, honest man, I know is doubtful

Whether he be alive ; and yet his land

Is better farmed than any in the country.

   Stephen. He is not married, then ?

   Wagoner   No.   There's a gossip

Amongst the women — but who would heed their
    talking ? —
That love half crazed, then drove him out of doors,
To wander here and there, like a bad ghost,
Because a silly wench refused him — fudge !

   Stephen. Most probably. I quite agree with you.
Where do you stop ?

   Wagoner.   At the first inn we come to ,
You'll see it from the bottom of the hill.
There is a better at the farther end,
But then the stabling is not near so good.

   Stephen. I must push on. Four legs can never go
Down hill so fast as two. Good-morning, friend.

   Wagoner. Good-morning, sir.

   Stephen (aside).   I take the other inn.

SCENE XV. — *The Nurse's room.* JULIAN *and* LILIA *standing
near the window.*

   Julian. But do you really love me, Lilia ?

   Lilia. Why do you make me say it so often, Julian ?
You make me say *I love you,* oftener far
Than you say you love me.

   Julian.   Because mine seems

So much a love of mere necessity.

I can refrain from loving you no more

Than keep from waking when the sun shines full

Upon my face.

  Lilia.   And yet I love to say

How, how I love you, Julian !

   [*Leans her head on his arm.* JULIAN *winces a little. She raises her head and looks at him.*

        Did I hurt you ?

Would you not have me lean my head on you ?

 Julian. Come on this side, my love ; 'tis a slight hurt

Not yet quite healed

  Lilia.   Ah, my poor Julian ! how ?

I am so sorry !· O ! I do remember !

I saw it all quite plain !   It was no dream !

I saw you fighting !   But you did not kill him ?

 Julian (calmly, but drawing himself up) I killed him

  as I would a dog that bit you.

 Lilia (turning pale, and covering her face with her

  hands). O, that is dreadful ; there is blood

  on you !

 Julian. Shall I go, Lilia ?

Lilia.   O no, no, no, do not.
I shall be better presently.

Julian.   You shrink
As from a murderer.

Lilia.   O no, I love you —
Will never leave you.   Pardon me, my Julian ,
But blood is very dreadful.

Julian (*drawing her close to him*).   My sweet Lilia,
'Twas justly shed, for your defense and mine,
As it had been a tiger that I killed.
He had no right to live.   Be at peace, darling ;
His blood lies not on me, but on himself ;
I do not feel its stain upon my conscience.

                               [*A tap at the door.*

Enter NURSE.

Nurse. My lord, the steward waits on you, below.

                               [JULIAN *goes.*
You have been standing till you're faint, my lady.
Lie down a little.   There — I'll fetch you something.

SCENE XVI. — *The Steward's room*   JULIAN.   *The* STEWARD.

Julian.   Well, Joseph, that will do.   I shall expect
To hear from you soon after my arrival.
Is the boat ready?

Steward.   Yes, my lord ; afloat
Where you directed.

Julian.   A strange feeling haunts me,
As of some danger near.   Unlock it, and cast
The chain around the post.   Muffle the oars.

Steward. I will, directly.   [*Goes.*

Julian.   How shall I manage it?
I have her father's leave, but have not dared
To tell her all ; and she must know it first.
She fears me half, even now : what will she think
To see my shaven head?   My heart is free —
I know that God absolves mistaken vows.
I looked for help in the high search from those
Who knew the secret place of the Most High.
If I had known, would I have bound myself
Brother to men from whose low, marshy minds
Never a lark springs to salute the day?
The loftiest of them dreamers ; and the best

Content with goodness growing like moss on stones.

It cannot be God's will I should be such.

But there was more : they virtually condemned

Me in my quest ; would have had me content

To kneel with them around a wayside post,

Nor heed the pointing finger at its top?

It was the dull abode of foolishness.

Not such the house where God would train his chil-
dren.

My very birth into a world of men

Shows me the school where He would have me learn ;

Shows me the place of penance ; shows the field

Where I must fight and die victorious,

Or yield and perish.   True, I know not how

This will fall out : He must direct my way.

But then for her — she cannot see all this ;

Words will not make it plain ; and if they would,

The time is shorter than the words would need :

This overshadowing bodes nearing ill.

It *may* be only vapor, of the heat

Of too much joy engendered ; sudden fear

That the fair gladness is too good to live :

The wider prospect from the steep hill's crest,

The deeper to the gulf the cliff goes down.

But how will she receive it?   Will she think

I have been mocking her?   How could I help it?

Her illness and my danger!   But, indeed,

So strong was I in truth, I never thought

Her doubts might prove a hindrance in the way.

My love did make her so a part of me,

I never dreamed she might judge otherwise,

Until our talk of yesterday.   And now

Her horror at Nembroni's death confirms me:

To wed a monk will seem to her the worst

Of crimes which in a fever one might dream.

I cannot take the truth, and, bodily,

Hold it before her eyes.   She is not strong.

She loves me not as I love her.   But always —

There's Robert for an instance — I have loved

A life for what it might become, far more

Than for its present: there's a germ in her

Of something noble, much beyond her now:

Chance gleams betray it, though she knows it not.

This evening must decide it, come what will.

SCENE XVII. — *The inn ; the room which had been Julian's.*
STEPHEN, HOST, *and* HOSTESS. *Wine on the table.*

Stephen. Here, my good lady, let me fill your glass
Then pass it to your husband, if you please.

Hostess. I thank you, sir, I hope it's to your taste ;
My husband's choice is praised. I cannot say
I am a judge myself.

Host.   I'm confident
It needs but to be tasted.

Stephen (*tasting critically, then nodding*). That is
      wine.
I quite congratulate you, my good sir,
Upon your exquisite judgment.

Host.   Thank you, sir.

Stephen (*to the* HOSTESS). And so this man, you say,
      was here until
The night the Count was murdered : did he leave
Before or after that ?

Hostess.   I cannot tell.
He left before it was discovered though.
In the middle of the storm, like one possessed,
He rushed into the street, half tumbling me

Headlong down stairs.   He never came again.

He had paid his bill that morning, luckily ;

So joy go with him !   Well, he was an odd one.

   Stephen. What was he like, fair Hostess ?

   Hostess.   Tall and dark

And with a lowering look about his brows.

He seldom spoke, but, when he did, was civil.

One queer thing was, he always wore his hat,

In-doors as well as out.   I dare not say

He murdered Count Nembroni ; but it was strange

He always sat at that same window there,

And looked into the street.   'Tis not as if

There were much traffic in this village now ;

These are changed times ; but I have seen the day —

   Stephen. Excuse me ; you were saying that the man

Sat at the window —

   Hostess.   Yes ; even after dark

He would sit on, and never call for lights.

The first night, I brought candles, as of course ;

He let me set them on the table, true ;

But soon's my back was turned, he put them out.

   Stephen. Where is the lady ?

   Hostess.   That's the strangest thing

Of all the story : she has disappeared,

As well as he.   There lay the Count, stone-dead,

White as my apron.   The whole house was empty,

Just as I told you.

   Stephen.   Has no search been made ?

   Host. The closest search ; a thousand pieces offered

For any information that should lead

To the murderer's capture.   I believe his brother,

Who is his heir, they say, is still in town,

Seeking in vain for some intelligence.

   Stephen. 'Tis very odd ; the oddest thing I've heard

For a long time.   Send me a pen and ink ;

I have to write some letters.

   Hostess (*rising*).   Thank you, sir,

For your kind entertainment.   You'll find ink

And paper on that table near the window.

                    [*Exeunt* HOST *and* HOSTESS.

   Stephen. We've found the badger's hole ; we'll draw

him next.   He couldn't have gone far with her and

not be seen.   My life on it, there are plenty of holes

and corners in the old house over the way.   Run off

with a wench !   Holy brother Julian !   Contemptuous

brother Julian !   Stand-by-thyself brother Julian !   Run

away with a wench at last !   Well, there's a downfall !
He'll be for marrying her on the sly, and away ;— I
know the old fox ;— for her conscience-sake, probably
not for his.   Well, one comfort is, it's damnation and
no reprieve.   The ungrateful, atheistical heretic !   As
if the good old mother wasn't indulgent enough to the
foibles of her children !   The worthy lady has winked
so hard at her dutiful sons, that she's nearly blind with
winking.   There's nothing in a little affair with a girl
now and then ; but to marry, and knock one's vows on
the head !   Therein is displayed a little ancestral fact,
as to a certain respectable progenitor, commonly por-
trayed as the knight of the cloven foot.   *Keep back thy
servant*, etc. — Purgatory couldn't cleanse that ; and
more, 'twill never have the chance.   Heaven be about
us from harm !   Amen.   I'll go find the new Count.
The Church shall have the castle and estate ; Re-
venge, in the person of the new Count, the body of
Julian ; and Stephen may as well have the thousand
pieces as not.

SCENE XVIII. — *Night. The Nurse's room.* LILIA; *to her* JULIAN.

Lilia. How changed he is! Yet he looks very no-
ble.

Enter JULIAN.

Julian. My Lilia, will you go to England with me?

Lilia. Julian, my father!

Julian.   Not without his leave.
He says, God bless us both.

Lilia.   Leave him in prison?

Julian. No, Lilia; he's at liberty and safe,
And far from this ere now.

Lilia.   You have done this,
My noble Julian.   I will go with you
To sunset, if you will.   My father gone!
Julian, there's none to love me now but you.
You *will* love me, Julian? — always?

Julian.   I but fear
That your heart, Lilia, is not big enough
To hold the love wherewith my heart would fill it.

Lilia. I know why you think that; and I deserve it.
But try me, Julian.   I was very silly.

I could not help it.   I was ill, you know ;

Or weak at least.   May I ask you, Julian,

How your arm is to-day ?

  Julian.   Almost well, child.

'Twill leave an ugly scar, though, I'm afraid.

  Lilia. Never mind that, if it be well again.

  Julian. I do not mind it ; but when I remember

That I am all yours, then I grudge that scratch

Or stain should be upon me — soul, body, yours.

And there are more scars on me now than I

Should like to make you own, without confession.

  Lilia. My poor, poor Julian !   Never think of it ;

        [*Putting her arms round him.*

I will but love you more.   I thought you had

Already told me suffering enough ;

But not the half, it seems, of your adventures.

You have been a soldier !

  Julian.   I have fought, my Lilia.

I have been down amongst the horses' feet ;

But strange to tell, and harder to believe,

Arose all sound, unmarked with bruise, or blood

Save what I lifted from the gory ground

          [*Sighing*

My wounds are not of such.

[LILIA, *loosening her arms, and drawing back a little with a kind of shrinking, looks a frightened interrogation.*

No.   Penance, Lilia ;

Such penance as the saints of old inflicted

Upon their quivering flesh.   Folly, I know ;

As a lord would exalt himself, by making

His willing servants into trembling slaves.

Yet I have borne it.

Lilia (*laying her hand on his arm*).   Ah, alas, my
    Julian !

You have been guilty.

Julian.   Not what men call guilty,

Save it be now ; now you will think I sin.

Alas, I have sinned much ! but not in this.

Lilia, I have been a monk.

Lilia.   A monk !   [*Turning pale*

I thought —   [*Faltering.*

Julian, — I thought you said . . . did you not

    say . . ?   [*Very pale, brokenly.*

I thought you said . . .   [*With an effort.*

I was to be your wife !

[*Covering her face with her hands, and bursting into tears.*

Julian (*speaking low and in pain*).   And so I did.

Lilia (*hopefully and looking up*).   Then you've had

dispensation ?

Julian. God has absolved me, though the Church

will not.

He knows it was in ignorance I did it.

Rather would He have men to do his will,

Than keep a weight of words upon their souls,

Which they laid there, not graven by his finger.

The vow was made to him — to him I break it.

Lilia (*weeping bitterly*).   I would . . . your words

were true . . . but I do know . . .

It never can . . . be right to break a vow ;

If so, men might be liars every day ;

You'd do the same by me, if we were married.

Julian (*in anguish*).   'Tis ever so.   Words are the

living things !

There is no spirit — save what's born of words !

Words are the bonds that of two souls make one !

Words the security of heart to heart !

God, make me patient !   God, I pray thee, God !

Lilia (*not heeding him*). Besides, we dare not ; you

would find the dungeon

Gave late repentance ; I should weep away
My life within a convent.

Julian   Come to England,
To England, Lilia.

Lilia.   Men would point, and say :
There go the monk and his wife ; if they, in truth,
Called me not by a harder name than that.

Julian. There are no monks in England.

Lilia.   But will that
Make right what's wrong ?

Julian.   Did I say so, my Lilia ?
I answered but your last objections thus ;
I had a different answer for the first.

Lilia No, no, I cannot, cannot, dare not do it.

Julian. Lilia, you will not doubt my love ; you
        cannot

I would have told you all before, but thought,
Foolishly, you would feel the same as I , —
I have lived longer, thought more, seen much mo e ;
I would not hurt your body, less your soul,
For all the blessedness your love can give :
For love's sake weigh the weight of what I say.
Think not that *must* be right which you have heard
From infancy — it *may* ——

Enter the STEWARD *in haste, pale, breathless, and bleeding.*

Steward. My lord, there's such an uproar in the
    town !

They call you murderer and heretic.

The officers of justice, with a monk,

And the new Count Nembroni, accompanied

By a fierce mob with torches, howling out

For justice on you, madly cursing you !

They caught a glimpse of me as I returned,

And stones and sticks flew round me like a storm ;

But I escaped them, old man as I am,

And was in time to bar the castle-gates.

Would Heaven we had not cast those mounds, and
    shut

The river from the moat !   [*Distant yells and cries.*

                    Escape, my lord !

Julian (calmly). Will the gates hold them out awhile,
    my Joseph ?

Steward. A little while, my lord ; but those damned
    torches !

O for twelve feet of water round the walls !

Julian. Leave us, good Joseph ; watch them from a
    window,

And tell us of their progress.

> [JOSEPH *goes.   Sounds approach*

Farewell, Lilia !

> [*Putting his arm round her.   She stands like stone.*

Fear of a coward's name shall not detain me.

My presence would but bring down evil on you,

My heart's beloved ; yes, all the ill you fear,

The terrible things that you have imaged out

If you fled with me.   They will not hurt you,

If you be not polluted by my presence.

> [*Light from without flares on the wall.*

· They've fired the gate.   [*An outburst of mingled cries.*

   Steward (entering). They've fired the gate, my lord !

   Julian.   Well, put yourself in safety, my dear
      Joseph.

You and old Agata tell all the truth,

And they'll forgive you.   It will not hurt me ;

I shall be safe — you know me — never fear.

   Steward. God grant it may be so.   Farewell, dear
      lord !   [*Is going*

   Julian. But add, it was in vain ; for the signora

Would not consent ; therefore I fled alone.

> [LILIA *stands as before*

Steward. It is too true.   Good-by good-by, my mas-

ter !   [*Goes*

Julian. Put your arms round me once, my Lilia.

What ! not once ? not once at parting ?

> [*Rushing feet up the stairs, and along the galleries.*

O God ! farewell !

> [*He clasps her to his heart ; leaves her ; pushes back the panel,
> flings open the door, enters, and closes them behind
> LILIA starts suddenly from her fixed bewilderment, and
> flies after him, but forgets to close the sliding panel.
> Her voice from the inner room, calling.*

Lilia. Julian ! Julian !

> [*The trampling of feet and clamor of voices.   The door of
> the room is flung open.   Enter the foremost of the
> mob.*

1st. I was sure I saw light here.   There it is, burn-

ing still.

2d. Nobody here !   Praise the devil ! he minds his

own.   Look under the bed, Gian.

3d. Nothing there.

4th. Another door !   Another door !   He'll soon be

in hell if he's there.   (*As he tries to open the door.*)

The devil had better leave him, to make up the fire at

home — he'll be cold by and by.   (*Rushes into the

inner room.*)   Follow me, boys !   [*The rest follow.*

Voices from within. I have him. I have him.
Curse your claws! Why do you fix on me, you crab?
You won't pick up the fiend-spawn so easily, I can tell
you. Bring the light there, will you? (*One runs out
for the light.*) A trap! a trap! and a stair, down in
the wall! the hell-faggot's gone! After him, after him,
like storm-drift!

[*Sound of descending footsteps. Others rush in with torches
and follow*

SCENE XIX. — *The river-side* LILIA *seated in the boat,* JULIAN
handing her the bags.

Julian. There, my love — take care, — 'tis heavy.
Put them right in the middle of the boat:
'Tis excellent ballast.

[*A loud shout He steps in and casts the chain loose, then
pushes gently off.*

Look how the torches gleam
Amongst the trees. Thank God, we have escaped!

[*He rows swiftly off. The torches come nearer, with cries of
search.*

(*In a low tone*) Slip down, my Lilia; lie at full
    length

In the bottom of the boat; your dress is white,

And would return the torches' glare.   I fear

The damp night-air will hurt you, dressed like this.

> [*Pulling off his coat, and wrapping her in it.*

Now for a strong pull with my muffled oars !

The water mutters Spanish in its sleep.

My beautiful ! my bride ! my spirit's wife !

God-given, and God-restored ! my heart exults,

Dancing round thee, my beautiful ! my soul !

Once round the headland, I will set the sail ;

And the fair wind blows right adown the stream.

Dear wind, dear stream, dear stars, dear heart of all,

White angel lying in my little boat !

Strange that my boyhood's skill with sail and helm,

Oft steering safely 'twixt the winding banks,

Should make me rich with womanhood and life !

> [*The boat disappears round the headland.* JULIAN *singing in his heart.*

SONG.

Thou hast been blowing leaves, O wind of strife !
  Wan, curled, boat-like leaves, that ran and fled ;
Unresting yet, though folded up from life ;
  Sleepless, though cast among the unwaking dead.
    Out to the ocean fleet and float ;
    Blow, blow my little leaf-like boat.

O wind of strife ! to us a wedding wind !
  O cover me with kisses of her mouth ;
Blow thou our souls together, heart and mind ,
   To narrowing northern lines, blow from the south.
     Out to the ocean fleet and float ;
     Blow, blow my little leaf-like boat.

Thou hast been blowing many a drifting thing
  From circling cove down to the unsheltered sea ;
Thou blowest to the sea my blue sail's wing,
  Us to a new love-lit futurity.
     Out to the ocean fleet and float,
     Blow, blow my little leaf-like boat.

END OF PART II.

WITHIN AND WITHOUT.

PART III.

AND weep not, though the Beautiful decay
   Within thy heart, as daily in thine eyes;
   Thy heart must have its autumn, its pale skies,
Leading, mayhap, to winter's dim dismay.
Yet doubt not. Beauty doth not pass away;
   Her form departs not, though her body dies.
   Secure beneath the earth the snowdrop lies,
Waiting the spring's young resurrection-day,
Through the kind nurture of the winter cold.
   Nor seek thou by vain effort to revive
   The summer time, when roses were alive;
Do thou thy work — be willing to be old:
Thy sorrow is the husk that doth enfold
   A gorgeous June, for which thou need'st not strive.

PART III.

Time : *Five years later*

SCENE I — *Night. London. A large meanly furnished room ; a single candle on the table ; a child asleep in a little crib. JULIAN sits by the table, reading in a low voice out of a book. He looks older, and his hair is lined with gray ; his eyes look clearer.*

Julian.   WHAT is this ? let me see , 'tis called
                "The Singer : "

"Melchah stood looking on the corpse of his son, and spoke not. At length he broke the silence and said : 'He hath told his tale to the Immortals.' Abdiel, the friend of him that was dead, asked him what he meant by the words ? The old man, still regarding the dead body, spake as follows : —

"Three years ago, I fell asleep on the summit of the hill Ya-rib , and there I dreamed a dream. I thought I lay at the foot of a cliff, near the top of a great mountain , for beneath me were the clouds, and above me, the heavens deep and dark. And I heard voices sweet and strong ; and I lifted up my eyes, and lo ! over against me, on a rocky slope, some seated, each on his own crag, some reclining between the fragments, I saw a hundred majestic forms, as of men who had striven and conquered. Then I heard one say : 'What wouldst thou sing unto us, young man ?' A youthful voice replied, tremblingly · 'A song which

I have made for my singing.' 'Come, then, and I will lead thee
to the hole in the rock: enter and sing.' From the assembly
came forth one whose countenance was calm unto awfulness;
but whose eyes looked in love, mingled with doubt, on the face
of a youth whom he led by the hand towards the spot where I
lay. The features of the youth I could not discern; either it
was the indistinctness of a dream, or I was not permitted to be-
hold them. And lo! behind me was a great hole in the rock,
narrow at the entrance, but deep and wide within; and when
I looked into it I shuddered; for I thought I saw, far down, the
glimmer of a star. The youth entered and vanished. His guide
strode back to his seat, and I lay in terror near the mouth of the
vast cavern. When I looked up once more, I saw all the men
leaning forward, with head aside, as if listening intently to a far-
off sound. I likewise listened; but though much nearer than
they, I heard nothing; but I could see their faces change, like
waters in a windy and half-cloudy day. Sometimes, though I
heard nought, it seemed to me as if one sighed and prayed be-
side me; and once I heard a clang of music triumphant in hope,
but I looked up, and lo! it was the listeners who stood on their
feet and sang. They ceased, sat down, and listened as before.
At last one approached me, and I ventured to question him.
'Sir,' I said, 'wilt thou tell me what it means?' And he an-
swered me thus 'The youth desired to sing to the Immortals.
It is a law with us that no one shall sing a song who cannot be
the hero of his tale — who cannot live the song that he sings;
for what right hath he else to devise great things, and to take
holy deeds in his mouth? Therefore he enters the cavern where
God weaves the garments of souls, and there he lives in the
forms of his own tale; for God gives them being that he may be
tried. The sighs which thou didst hear were his longings after
his own Ideal; and thou didst hear him praying for the Truth
he beheld, but could not reach We sang, because in his first
great battle, he strove well and overcame We await the next.'

A deep sleep seemed to fall upon me ; and when I awoke, I saw the Immortals standing with their eyes fixed on the mouth of the cavern   I arose and turned towards it likewise.   The youth came forth.   His face was worn and pale, as that of the dead man before me ; but his eyes were open, and tears trembled within them.   Yet not the less was it the same face, the face of my son, I tell thee ; and in joy and fear I gazed upon him With a weary step he approached the Immortals   But he who had led him to the cave hastened to meet him, spread forth his arms and embraced him, and said unto him : ‘ Thou hast told a noble tale ; sing to us now what songs thou wilt.’   Therefore said I, as I gazed on my son : ‘ He hath told his tale to the Immortals.’ ”

[*He puts the book down ; meditates awhile ; then rises and walks up and down the room.*

And so five years have poured their silent streams,

Flowing from fountains in eternity,

Into my soul, which, as an infinite gulf,

Hath swallowed them ; whose living caves they feed ;

And time to spirit grows, transformed and kept.

And now the day draws nigh when Christ was
     born ;

The day that showed how like to God himself

Man had been made, since God could be revealed

By one that was a man with men, and still

Was one with God the Father ; that men might

By drawing nigh to Him draw nigh to God,

Who had come near to them in tenderness.

O God! I thank thee for the friendly eye,

That oft hath opened on me these five years;

Thank thee for those enlightenings of my spirit,

That let me know thy thought was towards me;

Those moments fore-enjoyed from future years,

Telling what converse I should hold with God.

I thank thee for the sorrow and the care,

Through which they gleamed, bright phosphorescent

     sparks

Crushed from the troubled waters, borne on which

Through mist and dark my soul draws nigh to thee.

Five years ago, I prayed in agony

That thou wouldst speak to me. Thou wouldst not

     then,

With that close speech I craved so hungrily.

Thy inmost speech is heart embracing heart;

And thou wert all the time instructing me

To know the language of thy inmost speech.

I thought thou didst refuse, when every hour

Thou spakest every word my heart could hear,

Though oft I did not know it was thy voice.

My prayer arose from lonely wastes of soul;

As if a world far-off in depths of space,

Chaotic, had implored that it might shine

Straightway in sunlight as the morning star.

My soul must be more pure, ere it could hold

With thee communion.   'Tis the pure in heart

That shall see God.   As if a well that lay

Unvisited, till water-weeds had grown

Up from its depths, and woven a thick mass

Over its surface, could give back the sun !

Or, dug from ancient battle-plain, a shield

Could be a mirror to the stars of heaven !

And though I am not yet come near to Him,

I know I am more nigh ; and am content

To walk a long and weary road to find

My Father's house once more.   Well may it be

A long and weary — I had wandered far.

My God, I thank thee, thou dost care for me.

I am content, rejoicing to go on,

Even when my home seems very far away ;

For over grief, and aching emptiness,

And fading hopes, a higher joy arises.

In cloudiest nights, one lonely spot is bright,

High overhead, through folds and folds of space ;

It is the earnest-star of all my heavens;

And tremulous in the deep well of my being

Its image answers, gazing eagerly.

Alas, my Lilia! But I'll think of Jesus,

Not of thee now; Him who hath led my soul

Thus far upon its journey home to God.

By poor attempts to do the things He said,

Faith has been born; free will become a fact;

And love grown strong to enter into his,

And know the spirit that inhabits there.

One day his truth will spring to life in me,

And make me free, as God says " I am free."

When I am like Him, then my soul will dawn

With the full glory of the God revealed —

Full as to me, though but one beam from Him;

The light will shine, for I shall comprehend it:

In his light I shall see light. God can speak,

Yea, *will* speak to me then, and I shall hear.

Not yet like Him, how can I hear his words?

[*Stopping by the crib, and bending over the child.*

My darling child! God's little daughter, drest

In human clothes, that light may thus be clad

In shining, so to reach my human eyes!

Come as a little Christ from heaven to earth,

To call me *father*, that my heart may know

What *father* means, and turn its eyes to God !

Sometimes I feel, when thou art clinging to me,

How all unfit this heart of mine to have

The guardianship of a bright thing like thee,

Come to entice, allure me back to God

By flitting round me, gleaming of thy home,

And radiating of thy purity

Into my stained heart ; which unto thee

Shall ever show the father, answering

The divine childhood dwelling in thine eyes.

O how thou teachest me with thy sweet ways,

All ignorant of wherefore thou art come,

And what thou art to me, my heavenly ward,

Whose eyes have drunk that secret place's light,

And pour it forth on me !   God bless his own !

> [*He resumes his walk, singing in a low voice*

> My child woke crying from her sleep :
>   I bended o'er her bed,
> And soothed her, till in slumber deep
>   She from the darkness fled.

And as beside my child I stood,
A still voice said in me, —
"Even thus thy Father, strong and good,
Is bending over thee."

SCENE II — *Rooms in Lord Seaford's house. A large company ·
dancers ; gentlemen looking on.*

1*st Gentleman.* Henry, what dark-haired queen is
    that ?   She moves
As if her body were instinct with thought,
Moulded to motion by the music's waves,
As floats the swan upon the swelling lake ;
Or as in dreams one sees an angel move,
Sweeping on slow wings through the buoyant air,
Then folding them, and turning on his track.

2*d* You seem inspired . nor can I wonder at it ;
She is a glorious woman ; and such eyes !
Think — to be loved by such a woman now !

1*st.* You have seen her, then, before ; what is her
    name ?

2*d.* I saw her once ; but could not learn her name.

3*d* She is the wife of an Italian count,
Who for some cause, political I think,
Took refuge in this country.   His estates
The Church has eaten up, as I have heard :
Mephisto says the Church has a good stomach.

2*d.* How do they live ?

3*d.*   Poorly, I should suppose ;

For she gives Lady Gertrude music-lessons :

That's how they know her.   Ah, you should hear her

    sing !

2*d.* If she sings as she looks, or as she dances,

It were as well for me I did not hear.

3*d.* If Count Lamballa followed Lady Seaford

To heaven, I know who'd follow her on earth.

Scene III. — *Julian's room*   Julian ; Lily *asleep.*

Julian. I wish she would come home.   When the

    child wakes,

I cannot bear to see her eyes first rest

On me, then wander searching through the room ;

And then return and rest.   And yet, poor Lilia !

'Tis nothing strange thou shouldst be glad to go

From this dull place, and for a few short hours

Have thy lost girlhood given back to thee ;

For thou art very young for such hard things

As poor men's wives in cities must endure.

I am afraid the thought is not at rest,

But rises still, that she is not my wife —
Not truly, lawfully.   I hoped the child
Would kill that fancy ; but I fear instead,
She thinks I have begun to think the same —
Thinks that it lies a heavy weight of sin
Upon my heart.   Alas, my Lilia !
When every time I pray, I pray that God
Would look and see that thou and I be one !

    Lily (starting up in her crib).   O, take me ! take
        me !

    Julian (going up to her with a smile).   What is the
        matter with my little child ?

    Lily.   I don't know, father ; I was very frightened.

    Julian   'Twas nothing but a dream.   Look — I am
        with you

    Lily.   I am wake now ; I know you're there ; but
        then

I did not know it.   [*Smiling.*

    Julian.   Lie down, then, darling.   Go to sleep
        again.

    Lily (beseechingly).   Not yet.   I will not go to sleep
        again ;

It makes me so, so frightened.   Take me up,

And let me sit upon your knee.   Where's mother?

I cannot see her.

 Julian.   She's not at home, my child ;

But soon she will be back.

 Lily.   But if she walk

Out in the dark streets — so dark, it will catch her.

 Julian. She will not walk ; — but what would catch

  her, sweet ?

 Lily. I don't know. Tell me a story till she

  comes.

 Julian (*taking her, and sitting with her on his knees*

  by the fire). Come then, my little Lily, —

  I will tell you

A story I have read this very night.

          [*She looks in his face.*

There was a man who had a little boy,

And when the boy grew big, he went and asked

His father to give him a purse of money.

His father gave him such a large purse full !

And then he went away and left his home.

You see he did not love his father much.

 Lily. O ! didn't he ?   If he had he wouldn't have

  gone.

Julian. Away he went, far, far away he went,
Until he could not even spy the top
Of the great mountain by his father's house
And still he went away, away, as if
He tried how far his feet could go away;
Until he came to a city huge and wide,
Like London here.

    Lily.   Perhaps it was London.

    Julian. Perhaps it was, my child.   And   there he
        spent
All, all his father's money, buying things
That he had always told him were not worth,
And not to buy them, but he would and did.

    Lily. How very naughty of him !

    Julian.   Yes, my child.
And so when he had spent his last few pence,
He grew quite hungry.   But he had none left
To buy a piece of bread.   And bread was scarce ;
Nobody gave him any.   He had been
Always so idle, that he could not work.
But at last some one sent him to feed swine.

    Lily. Swine '

    Julian.   Yes, swine: 'twas all that he could do ;

And he was glad to eat some of their food.

[*She stares at him.*

But at the last, hunger and waking love

Made him remember his old happy home.

" How many servants in my father's house

Have plenty, and to spare ! " he said.   " I'll go

And say, ' I have done very wrong, my father ;

I am not worthy to be called your son ;

Put me among your servants, father, please.' "

Then he rose up and went , but thought the road

So much, much farther to walk back again,

When he was tired and hungry.   But at last

He saw the blue top of the great big hill

That stood beside his father's house ; and then

He walked much faster.   But a great way off,

His father saw him coming, lame and weary

With his long walk ; and very different

From what he had been.   All his clothes were hang-

    ing

In tatters, and his toes stuck through his shoes —

[*She bursts into tears.*

Lily (*sobbing*). Like that poor beggar I saw yester-

    day ?

Julian. Yes, my dear child.

Lily.   And was he dirty, too?

Julian. Yes, very dirty; he had been so long
Among the swine.

Lily.   Is it all true though, father?

Julian. Yes, my darling; all true, and truer far
Than you can think.

Lily.   What was his father like?

Julian. A tall, grand, stately man.

Lily.   Like you, dear father?

Julian. Like me, only much grander.

Lily.   I love you
The best though.   [*Kissing him.*

Julian   Well, all dirty as he was,
And thin, and pale, and torn, with staring eyes,
His father knew him, the first look, far off,
And ran so fast to meet him! put his arms
Around his neck and kissed him.

Lily.   O, how dear!
I love him too; — but not so well as you.

                    [*Sound of a carriage drawing up.*

Julian. There is your mother.

Lily.   I am glad, so glad!

Enter LILIA, *looking pale.*

Lilia. You naughty child, why are you not in bed?

Lily (pouting).   I am not naughty.   I am afraid to

    go,

Because you don't go with me into sleep;

And when I see things, and you are not there,

Nor father, I am so frightened, I cry out,

And stretch my hands, and so I come awake.

Come with me into sleep, dear mother; come.

Lilia. What a strange child it is!   There,

    (kissing her) go to bed.   [*Laying her down.*

Julian (gazing on the child).   As thou art in thy

    dreams without thy mother,

So are we lost in life without our God.

SCENE IV. — LILIA *in bed.   The room lighted from a gas-lamp in
the street; the bright shadow of the window on the wall and
ceiling.*   .

Lilia. O, it is dreary, dreary!   All the time

My thoughts would wander to my dreary home.

Through every dance, my soul walked evermore

In a most dreary dance through this same room.

I saw these walls, this carpet; and I heard,

As now, his measured step in the next chamber,

Go pacing up and down, and I shut out!

He is too good for me, I weak for him.

Yet if he put his arms around me once,

And held me fast as then, kissed me as then,

My soul, I think, would come again to me,

And pass from me in trembling love to him.

But he repels me now.   He loves me, true, —

Because I am his wife : he ought to love me ;

Me, the cold statue, thus he drapes with duty.

Sometimes he waits upon me like a maid,

Silent with watchful eyes.   O! would to Heaven,

He used me like a slave bought in the market!

Yes, used me roughly!   So, I were his own ;

And words of tenderness would falter in,

Relenting from the sternness of command.

But I am not enough for him : he needs

Some high-entranced maiden, ever pure,

And thronged with burning thoughts of God and him.

So, as he loves me not, his deeds for me

Lie on me like a sepulchre of stones.

Italian lovers love not so ; but he

Has German blood in those great veins of his.

He never brings me now a little flower.

He sings low wandering sweet songs to the child ;
But never sings to me what the voice-bird
Sings to the silent, sitting on the nest.
I would I were his child, and not his wife !
How I should love him then !   Yet I have thoughts
Fit to be women to his mighty men ;
And he would love them, if he saw them once.

Ah, there they come, the visions of my land !
The long sweep of a bay, white sands, and cliffs
Purple above the blue waves at their feet.
Down the full river comes a light-blue sail ;
And down the near hill-side come country girls,
Brown, rosy, laden light with glowing fruits ;
Down to the sands come ladies, young, and clad
For holiday ; in whose hearts wonderment
At manhood is the upmost, deepest thought ;
And to their side come stately, youthful forms,
Italy's youth, with burning eyes and hearts :
Triumphant Love is lord of the bright day.
Yet one heart, under that blue sail, would look
With pity on their poor contentedness ;
For he sits at the helm, I at his feet.
He sung a song, and I replied to him.

His song was of the wind that blew us down
From sheltered hills to the unsheltered sea.
Ah ! little thought my heart that the wide sea,
Where I should cry for comforting in vain,
Was the expanse of his wide awful soul,
To which that wind was helpless drifting me !
I would he were less great, and loved me more.
I sung to him a song, broken with sighs,
For even then I feared the time to come :
" O will thine eyes shine always, love, as now ?
And will thy lips for aye be sweetly curved ? "
Said my song, flowing unrhymed from my heart.
" And will thy forehead, ever, sunlike, bend,
And suck my soul in vapors up to thee ?
Ah love ! I need love, beauty, and sweet odors.
Thou livest on the hoary mountains ; I
In the warm valley, with the lily pale,
Shadowed with mountains and its own great leaves ;
Where odors are the sole invisible clouds
Making the heart weep for deliciousness.
Will thy eternal mountain always bear
Blue flowers upspringing at the glacier's foot ?
Alas ! I fear the storms, the blinding snow,

The vapors which thou gatherest round thy head,

Wherewith thou shuttest up thy chamber-door.

And goest from me into loneliness."

Ah me, my song! it is a song no more!

He is alone amidst his windy rocks;

I wandering on a low and dreary plain!

[*She weeps herself asleep.*

SCENE V. — LORD SEAFORD, *alternately writing at a table and composing at his pianoforte.*

SONG.

Eyes of beauty, eyes of light,
Sweetly, softly, sadly bright!
Draw not, ever, o'er my eye,
Radiant mists of ecstasy·

Be not proud, O glorious orbs!
Not your mystery absorbs; .
But the starry soul that lies
Looking through your night of eyes.

One moment, be less perfect, sweet;
Sin once in something small;
One fault to lift me on my feet
From love's too perfect thrall!

For now I have no soul; a sea
Fills up my caverned brain,
Heaving in silent waves to thee,
The mistress of that main.

O angel ! take my hand in thine ;
   Unfold thy shining silver wings ;
Spread them around thy face and mine,
   Close curtained in their murmurings.

But I should faint with too much bliss
   To be alone in space with thee ;
Except, O dread ! one angel-kiss
   In sweetest death should set me free.

O beauteous devil, tempt me, tempt me on,
   Till thou hast won my soul in sighs ;
I'll smile with thee upon thy flaming throne,
   If thou wilt keep those eyes.

And if the moanings of untold desires
   Should charm thy pain of one faint sting ;
I will arise amid the scorching fires,
   I will arise and sing

O what is God to me ?   He sits apart
   Amidst the clear stars, passionless and cold.
Divine ! thou art enough to fill my heart ;
   O fold me in thy heaven, sweet love, enfold.

With too much life, I fall before thee dead.
   With holding thee, my sense consumes in storm.
Thou art too keen a flame, too hallowed
   For any temple but thy holy form.

Scene VI. — *Julian's room next morning; no fire.* Julian *stands at the window, looking into a London fog.*

Julian. And there are mountains on the earth, far-
off ;
Steep precipices laved at morn in wind
From the blue glaciers fresh ; and falls that leap,
Springing from rock to pool abandonedly ;
And all the spirit of the earth breathed out,
Bearing the soul, as on an altar-flame,
Aloft to God.   And there is woman-love —
Far off, ah me !   [*Sitting down wearily.*
        The heart of earth's delight
Withered from mine !   O for a desert sea,
The cold sun flashing on the sailing icebergs !
Where I might cry aloud on God, until
My soul burst forth upon the wings of pain
And fled to Him.   A numbness as of death
Enfolds me.   As in sleep I walk.   I live,
But my dull soul can hardly keep awake.
Yet God is here as on the mountain-top,
Or on the desert sea, or lonely isle ;
And I should know Him here, if Lilia loved me,

As once I thought she did.   But can I blame her?

The change has been too much for her to bear.

Can poverty make one of two hearts cold,

And warm the other with the love of God?

But then I have been silent, often moody,

Drowned in much questioning; and she has thought

That I was tired of her, while more than all

I pondered how to wake her living soul.

She cannot think why I should haunt my chamber,

Except a goaded conscience were my grief;

Thinks not of aught to gain, but all to shun.

Deeming, poor child, that I repent me thus

Of that which makes her mine for evermore,

It is no wonder if her love grow less.

Then I am older much than she, and this

Fever, I think, has made me old indeed

Before my fortieth year; although, within,

I seem as young as ever to myself.

O my poor Lilia! thou art not to blame;

I'll love thee more than ever; I will be

So gentle to thy heart where love lies dead!

For carefully men ope the door, and walk

With silent footfall through the room where lies,

Exhausted, sleeping, with its travail sore,

The body that erewhile hath borne a spirit.

Alas, my Lilia! where is dead Love's child?

   I must go forth and do my daily work.

I thank thee, God, that it is hard sometimes

To do my daily labor; for, of old,

When men were poor, and could not bring thee much,

A turtle-dove was all that thou didst ask ;

And so in poverty, and with a heart

Oppressed with heaviness, I try to do

My day's work well to thee, — my offering :

That He has taught me, who one day sat weary

At Sychar's well.   Then home when I return,

I come without upbraiding thoughts to thee.

Ah! well I see man need not seek for penance —

Thou wilt provide the lamb for sacrifice ;

Thou only wise enough to teach the soul,

Measuring out the labor and the grief,

Which it must bear for thy sake, not its own.

He neither chose his glory, nor devised

The burden He should bear ; left all to God ;

And of them both God gave to Him enough

And see the sun looks faintly through the mist ;

It cometh as a messenger to me.

My soul is heavy, but I will go forth ;

My days seem perishing, but God yet lives

And loves.   I cannot feel, but will believe

> [*He rises and is going.*   LILIA *enters, looking weary.*

Look, my dear Lilia, how the sun shines out !

   Lilia. Shines out indeed !   Yet 'tis not bad for Eng-
land.

I would I were in Italy, my own !   [*Weeps.*

   Julian. 'Tis the same sun that shines in Italy.

   Lilia But never more will shine upon us there.

It is too late ; all wishing is in vain !

But would that we had not so ill deserved

As to be banished from fair Italy !

   Julian. Ah ! my dear Lilia, do not, do not think

That God is angry when we suffer ill.

'Twere terrible indeed, if 'twere in anger.

   Lilia. Julian, I cannot feel as you.   I wish

I felt as you feel.

   Julian   God will hear you, child,

If you will speak to Him.   But I must go.

Kiss me, my Lilia

> [*She kisses him mechanically   He goes with a sigh*

Lilia.   It is plain to see

He tries to love me, but is weary of me.   [*She weeps.*

Enter LILY.

Lily. Mother, have you been naughty? Mother,

dear!   [*Pulling her hand from her face*

SCENE VII. — *Julian's room.   Noon.* LILIA *at work,* LILY
playing in a closet.

Lily (running up to her mother). Sing me a little

song; please, mother dear.

[LILIA, *looking off her work, and thinking with fixed eyes
for a few moments, sings.*

SONG.

Once I was a child,
 Oimè !
Full of frolic wild ;
 Oimè !
All the stars for glancing,
All the earth for dancing ;
 Oimè ! Oimè !

When I ran about,
 Oimè !
All the flowers came out,
 Oimè !
Here and there like stray things,
Just to be my playthings.
 Oimè ! Oimè !

8

Mother's eyes were deep,
    Oimè !
Never needing sleep,
    Oimè !
Morning — they're above me !
Eventide — they love me !
    Oimè ! Oimè !

Father was so tall !
    Oimè !
Stronger he than all !
    Oimè !
On his arm he bore me,
Queen of all before me.
    Oimè ! Oimè !

Mother is asleep :
    Oimè !
For her eyes so deep,
    Oimè !
Grew so tired and aching,
They could not keep waking.
    Oimè ! Oimè !

Father, though so strong,
    Oimè !
Laid him down along —
    Oimè !
By my mother sleeping ;
And they left me weeping,
    Oimè ! Oimè !

Now nor bird, nor bee,
    Oimè !
Ever sings to me !
    Oime !
Since they left me crying,
All things have been dying
    Oimè ! Oimè !

[LILY *looks long in her mother's face, as if wondering what
the song could be about, then turns away to the closet.
After a little she comes running with a box in her hand.*

Lily.   O mother, mother ! there's the old box I had

So long ago, and all my cups and saucers,

And the farm-house and cows.   O, some are broken.

Father will mend them for me, I am sure.

I'll ask him when he comes to night — I will

He can do everything, you know, dear mother.

SCENE VIII. — *A merchant's counting-house.*   JULIAN *preparing
to go home.*

Julian.   I would not give these days of common
        toil,

This murky atmosphere that creeps and sinks

Into the very soul, and mars its hue —

Not for the evenings when with gliding keel

I cut a pale-green track across the west —

Pale-green, and dashed with snowy white, and spotted
With sunset crimson ; when the wind breathed low,
So low it hardly swelled my xebec's sails,
That pointed to the south, and wavered not,
Erect upon the waters   Jesus said
His followers should have a hundred fold
Of earth's most precious things, with suffering.
In all the laborings of a weary spirit,
I have been bless'd with gleams of glorious things.
The sights and sounds of nature touch my soul,
No more look in from far.   I never see
Such radiant, filmy clouds, gathered about
A gently opening eye into the blue,
But swells my heart, and bends my sinking knee,
Bowing in prayer.   The setting sun, before,
Signed only that the hour for prayer was come,
Where now it moves my inmost soul to pray.

On this same earth He walked ; even thus He looked
Upon its thousand glories ; read them all ;
In splendor let them pass on through his soul,
And triumph in their new beatitude,
Finding a heaven of truth to take them in ;
But walked on steadily through pain to death.

Better to have the poet's heart than brain,

Feeling than song ; but better far than both,

To be a song, a music of God's making ;

Or but a table, on which God's finger of flame,

In words harmonious, of triumphant verse,

That mingles joy and sorrow, sets down clear,

That out of darkness He hath called the light.

It may be voice to such is after given,

To tell the mighty tale to other worlds.

O, I am blest in sorrows with a hope

That steeps them all in glory ; as gray clouds

Are bathed in light of roses ; yea, I were

Most blest of men, if I were now returning

To Lilia's heart as presence.   O my God,

I can but look to thee.   And then the child !

Why should my love to her break out in tears ?

Why should she be only a consolation,

And not an added joy, to fill my soul

With gladness overflowing in many voices

Of song, and prayer — and weeping only when

Words fainted 'neath the weight of utterance ?

SCENE IX. — LILIA *preparing to go out.* LILY.

Lily. Don't go to-night again.

Lilia.   Why, child, your father
Will soon be home; and then you will not miss me.

Lily. O, but I shall though; and he looks so sad
When you're not here

Lilia (aside).   He cannot look much sadder
Than when I am.   I am sure 'tis a relief
To find his child alone when he returns.

Lily. Will you go, mother?   Then I'll go and cry
Till father comes   He'll take me on his knee,
And tell such lovely tales : you never do —
Nor sing me songs made all for my own self.
He does not kiss me half so many times
As you do, mother , but he loves me more.
Do you love father, too?   I love him *so!*

Lilia (ready). There's such a pretty book!   Sit on
     the stool,
And look at the pictures till your father comes.
                                        [*Goes.*

Lily (putting the book down, and going to the window).
I wish he would come home.   I wish he would.

                Enter JULIAN.

O, there he is !   [*Running up to him.*

                O, now I am so happy !   [*Laughing.*
I had not time to watch before you came

Julian (taking her in his arms) I am very glad to

    have my little girl ;

I walked quite fast to come to her again.

    Lily. I do, *do* love you   Shall I tell you something ?

Think I should like to tell you.   'Tis a dream

That I went into, somewhere in last night.

I was alone — quite ; — you were not with me,

So I must tell you.   'Twas a garden, like

That one you took me to, long, long ago,

When the sun was so hot.   It was not winter,

But some of the poor leaves were growing tired

With hanging there so long.   And some of them

Gave it up quite, and so dropped down and lay

Quiet on the ground   And I was watching them

I saw one falling — down, down — tumbling down —

Just at the earth — when suddenly it spread

Great wings and flew.   It was a butterfly,

So beautiful with wings, black, red, and white —

                           [Laughing heartily

I thought it was a crackly, withered leaf.

Away it flew !   I don't know where it went.

And so I thought, I have a story now

To tell dear father when he comes to Lily.

Julian. Thank you, my child ; a very pretty dream.
But I am tired — will you go find another —
Another dream somewhere in sleep for me?

  Lily. O yes, I will   Perhaps I cannot find one.

                   [He lays her down to sleep, then sits musing

  Julian. What shall I do to give it life again?
To make it spread its wings before it fall,
And lie among the dead things of the earth?

  Lily. I cannot go to sleep Please, father, sing
The song about the little thirsty lily.

                   [JULIAN *sings.*

SONG.

Little white Lily
  Sat by a stone,
Drooping and waiting
  Till the sun shone
Little white Lily
  Sunshine has fed ;
Little white Lily
  Is lifting her head

Little white Lily
  Said, " It is good
Little white Lily's
  Clothing and food !
Little white Lily
  Drest like a bride !
Shining with whiteness,
  And crowned beside ! "

Little white Lily
    Droopeth in pain,
Waiting and waiting
    For the wet rain.
Little white Lily
    Holdeth her cup;
Rain is fast falling,
    And filling it up·

Little white Lily
    Said, " Good again,
When I am thirsty
    To have nice rain !
Now I am stronger,
    Now I am cool ;
Heat cannot burn me,
    My veins are so full ! "

Little white Lily
    Smells very sweet :
On her head sunshine,
    Rain at her feet
" Thanks to the sunshine !
    Thanks to the rain !
Little white Lily
    Is happy again ! "

[*He is silent for a moment ; then goes and looks at her.*

Julian. She is asleep, the darling !   Easily
Is Sleep enticed to brood on childhood's heart.
Gone home unto thy Father for the night !

[*He returns to his seat.*

I have grown common to her.   It is strange —
This commonness — that, as a blight, eats up
All the heart's springing corn and promised fruit.

[*Looking round.*

This room is very common · everything
Has such a well known look of nothing in it ;
And yet when first I called it hers and mine,
There was a mystery inexhaustible
About each trifle on the chimney-shelf.
But now the gilt is nearly all worn off.
Even she, the goddess of the wonder world,
Seems less mysterious and worshipful:
No wonder I am common in her eyes.
Alas ! what must I think ?   Is this the true ?
Was that the false that was so beautiful ?
Was it a rosy mist that wrapped it round ?
Or was love to the eyes as opium,
Making all things more beauteous than they were ?
And can that opium do more than God
To waken beauty in a human brain ?
Is this the real, the cold, undraperied truth ;
A skeleton admitted as a guest
At life's loud feast, wearing a life-like mask ?

No, no ; my heart would die if I believed it.

A blighting fog uprises with the days,

False, cold, dull, leaden, gray.   It clings about

The present, far dragging like a robe , but ever

Forsakes the past, and lets its hues shine out:

On past and future pours the light of heaven.

The Commonplace is of the present mind.

The Lovely is the True   The Beautiful

Is what God made.   Men from whose narrow bosoms

The great child-heart has withered, backward look

To their first-love, and laugh, and call it folly,

A mere delusion to which youth is subject,

As childhood to diseases.   They know better ;

And proud of their denying, tell the youth,

On whom the wonder of his being shines,

That will be over with him by and by :

" I was so when a boy — look at me now ! "

Youth, be not one of them, but love thy love.

So with all worship of the high and good,

And pure and beautiful.   These men are wiser !

Their god, Experience, but their own decay ;

Their wisdom but the gray hairs gathered on them.

Yea, some will mourn and sing about their loss,

And for the sake of sweet sounds cherish it,

Nor yet believe that it was more than seeming.

But he in whom the child's heart hath not died,

Hath grown a man's heart, loveth yet the Past;

Believes in all its beauty; knows the hours

Will melt the mist; and though this very day

Casts but a dull stone on Time's heaped-up cairn,

A morning light will break one morn and draw

The hidden glories of a thousand hues

Out from its crystal depths and ruby spots

And sapphire veins, unseen, unknown, before.

Far in the future lies his refuge.   Time

Is God's, and all its miracles are his;

And in the Future he overtakes the Past,

Which was a prophecy of times to come ·

There lie great flashing stars, the same that shone

In childhood's laughing heaven; there lies the wonder

In which the sun went down and moon arose;

The joy with which the meadows opened out

Their daisies to the warming sun of spring;

Yea, all the inward glory, ere cold fear

Froze, or doubt shook the mirror of his soul.

To reach it, he must climb the present slope

Of this day's duty — here he would not rest.

But all the time the glory is at hand,

Urging and guiding — only o'er its face

Hangs ever, pledge and screen, the bridal veil:

He knows the beauty radiant underneath ;

He knows that God who is the living God,

The God of living things, not of the dying,

Would never give his child, for God-born love,

A cloud-made phantom, fading in the sun.

Faith vanishes in sight ; the cloudy veil

Will melt away, destroyed of inward light.

If thy young heart yet lived, my Lilia, thou

And I might, as two children, hand in hand,

Go home unto our Father.   I believe

It only sleeps, and may be wakened yet.

SCENE X — *Julian's room   Christmas Day ; early morn.* Ju-
LIAN.

Julian.   The light comes feebly, slowly, to the
world

On this one day that blesses all the year,

Just as it comes on any other day :

A feeble child He came, yet not the less

Brought godlike childhood to the aged earth,

Where nothing now is common any more.

All things had hitherto proclaimed God :

The wide-spread air ; the luminous mist that hid

The far horizon of the fading sea ;

The low persistent music evermore

Flung down upon the sands, and at the base

Of the great rocks that hold it as a cup ;

All things most common ; the furze, now golden, now

Opening dark pods in music to the heat

Of the high summer sun at afternoon ;

The lone black tarn upon the round hill-top,

O'er which the gray clouds brood like rising smoke,

Sending its many rills, o'erarched and hid,

Singing like children down the rocky sides ; —

Where shall I find the most unnoticed thing,

For that sung God with all its voice of song ?

But men heard not, they knew not God in these ;

To their strange speech unlistening ears were strange ;

For with a stammering tongue and broken words,

With mingled falsehoods and denials loud,

Man witnessed God unto his fellow-man :

How then himself the voice of Nature hear ?

Or how himself be heeded, when, the leader,

He in the chorus sang in discord vile?

When prophet lies, how shall the people preach?

But when He came in poverty, and low,

A real man to half-unreal men,

A man whose human thoughts were all divine,

The head and upturned face of human kind —

Then God shone forth from all the lowly earth,

And men began to read their Maker there.

Now the Divine descends, pervading all.

Earth is no more a banishment from heaven;

But a lone field among the distant hills,

Well ploughed and sown, whence corn is gathered
        home.

Now, now we feel the holy mystery

That permeates all being: all is God's;

And my poor life is terribly sublime.

Where'er I look, I am alone in God,

As this round world is wrapt in folding space;

Behind, before, begin and end in Him:

So all beginnings and all ends are hid;

And He is hid in me, and I in Him.

    O what a unity, to mean them all! —

The peach-dyed morn , cold stars in colder blue

Gazing across upon the sun-dyed west ;

While the cold wind is running o'er the graves.

Green buds, red flowers, brown leaves, and ghostly

    snow ;

The grassy hills, breeze-haunted on the brow ;

And sandy deserts hung with stinging stars.

Half vanished hangs the moon, with daylight sick,

Wan-faced and lost and lonely . daylight fades —

Blooms out the pale eternal flower of space,

The opal night, whose odors are gray dreams —

Core of its petal-cup, the radiant moon.

All, all the unnumbered meanings of the earth,

Changing with every cloud that passes o'er ;

All, all, from rocks slow crumbling in the frost

Of Alpine deserts, isled in stormy air,

To where the pool in warm brown shadow sleeps,

The stream, sun-ransomed, dances in the sun ,

All, all, from polar seas of jeweled ice,

To where she dreams out gorgeous flowers — all, all

The unlike children of her single womb —

O, my heart labors with infinitude !

All, all the messages that these have borne

To eyes and ears, and watching, listening souls ;

And all the kindling cheeks and swelling hearts,

That since the first-born, young, attempting day,

Have gazed and worshipped !   What a unity,

To mean each one, yet fuse the each in all !

O centre of all forms ?   O concord's home !

O world alive in one condensed world !

O face of Him, in whose heart lay concealed

The fountain thought of all this kingdom of heaven !

Lord, thou art infinite, and I am thine !

   I sought my God , I pressed importunate ,

I spoke to Him, I cried, and in my heart

It seemed He answered me.   I said, "O, take

Me nigh to thee, thou mighty life of life !

I faint, I die ; I am a child alone

'Mid the wild storm, the brooding desert night "

   " Go thou, poor child, to Him who once, like thee,

Trod the highways and deserts of the world."

   " Thou sendest me then, wretched, from thy sight !

Thou wilt not have me — I am not worth thy care !"

   " I send thee not away ; child, think not so ;

From the cloud resting on the mountain peak,

I call to guide thee in the path by which

Thou mayst come soonest home unto my heart.

I, I am leading thee.   Think not of Him

As He were one and I were one ; in Him

Thou wilt find me, for He and I are one.

Learn thou to worship at his lowly shrine,

And see that God dwelleth in lowliness."

I came to Him ; I gazed upon his face ;

And lo ! from out his eyes God looked on me !

Yea, let them laugh ! I *will* sit at his feet,

As a child sits upon the ground, and looks

Up in his mother's face.   One smile from Him,

One look from those sad eyes, is more to me

Than to be lord myself of hearts and thoughts.

O perfect made through the reacting pain

In which thy making force recoiled on thee !

Whom no less glory could make visible

Than the utter giving of thyself away,

Without a thought of grandeur in the deed,

More than a child embracing from full heart !

Lord of thyself and me through the sore grief,

Which thou didst bear to bring us back to God,

Or rather, bear in being unto us

Thy own pure shining self of love and truth !

When I have learned to think thy radiant thoughts,

To love the truth beyond the power to know it,

To beaɪ my light as thou thy heavy cross,

Nor ever feel a martyr for thy sake,

But an unprofitable servant still, —

My highest sacrifice my simplest duty

Imperative and unavoidable,

Less than which *All*, were nothingness and waste ;

When I have lost myself in other men,

And found myself in thee — the Father then

Will come with thee, and will abide with me.

SCFNE XI — LILIA *teaching* LADY GERTRUDE.   *Enter* LORD
   SEAFORD.   LILIA *rises. He places her a chair, and seats him-
   self at the instrument; plays a low, half-melancholy, half-de-
   fiant prelude, and sings.*

SONG.

" Look on the magic mirror ;
   A glory thou wilt spy :
Be with thine heart a sharer,
   But go not thou too nigh ;
Else thou wilt rue thine error,
   With a tear-filled, sleepless eye."

The youth looked on the mirror,
   And he went not too nigh ;

And yet he rued his error,
　With a tear-filled, sleepless eye ;
For he could not be a sharer
　Of what he there did spy.

He went to the magician,
　Upon the morrow morn.
" Mighty," was his petition,
　" Look not on me in scorn ,
But one last gaze elysian,
　Lest I should die forlorn ! "

He saw her in her glory,
　Floating upon the main.
Ah me ¹ the same sad story !
　The darkness and the rain !
If I live till I am hoary,
　I shall never laugh again.

She held the youth enchanted,
　Till his trembling lips were pale,
And his full heart heaved and panted
　To utter all its tale :
Forward he rushed, undaunted —
　And the shattered mirror fell.

　　　[*He rises and leaves the room.* LILIA *weeping*

END OF PART III.

WITHIN AND WITHOUT.

PART IV.

AND should the twilight darken into night,
   And sorrow grow to anguish, be thou strong;
   Thou art in God, and nothing can go wrong
Which a fresh life-pulse cannot set aright.
That thou dost know the darkness, proves the light
   Weep if thou wilt, but weep not all too long;
   Or weep and work, for work will lead to song.
But search thy heart, if, hid from all thy sight,
There lie no cause for beauty's slow decay;
   If for completeness and diviner youth,
   And not for very love, thou seek'st the truth;
If thou hast learned to give thyself away
For love's own self, not for thyself, I say:
   Were God's love less, the world were lost, in sooth.

PART IV.

SCENE I — *Summer. Julian's room.* JULIAN *is reading out of a book of poems.*

LOVE me, beloved : the thick clouds lower ;
  A sleepiness filleth the earth and air ;
The rain has been falling for many an hour ;
  A weary look the summer doth wear ·
Beautiful things that cannot be so ;
Loveliness clad in the garments of woe·

Love me, beloved · I hear the birds ;
  The clouds are lighter ; I see the blue ;
The wind in the leaves is like gentle words
  Quietly passing 'twixt me and you ;
The evening air will bathe the buds
With the soothing coolness of summer floods

Love me, beloved : for, many a day,
Will the mist of the morning pass away ;
Many a day will the brightness of noon
Lead to a night that hath lost her moon ,
And in joy or in sadness, in autumn or spring,
Thy love to my soul is a needful thing

Love me, beloved : for thou mayest lie
Dead in my sight, 'neath the same blue sky ;

Love me, O love me, and let me know
The love that within thee moves to and fro ;
That many a form of thy love may be
Gathered around thy memory.

Love me, beloved : for I may lie
Dead in thy sight, 'neath the same blue sky ;
The more thou hast loved me, the less thy pain,
The stronger thy hope till we meet again ;
And forth on the pathway we do not know,
With a load of love, my soul would go.

Love me, beloved : for one must lie
Motionless, lifeless, beneath the sky ;   .
The pale stiff lips return no kiss
To the lips that never brought love amiss ;
And the dark brown earth be heaped above
The head that lay on the bosom of love.

Love me, beloved ; for both must lie
Under the earth and beneath the sky ;
The world be the same when we are gone ;
The leaves and the waters all sound on ;
The spring come forth, and the wild flowers live,
Gifts for the poor man's love to give ;
The sea, the lordly, the gentle sea,
Tell the same tales to others than thee ;
And joys, that flush with an inward morn,
Irradiate hearts that are yet unborn ;
A youthful race call our earth their own,
And gaze on its wonders from thought's high throne,
Embraced by fair Nature, the youth will embrace
The maid beside him, his queen of the race .

When thou and I shall have passed away
Like the foam-flake thou lookedst on yesterday.

Love me, beloved . for both must tread
On the threshold of Hades, the house of the dead ;
Where now but in thinkings strange we roam,
We shall live and think, and shall be at home ,
The sights and the sounds of the spirit land
No stranger to us than the white sea-sand,
Than the voice of the waves, and the eye of the moon,
Than the crowded street in the sunlit noon.
I pray thee to love me, beloved of my heart ;
If we love not truly, at death we part ,
And how would it be with our souls to find
That love, like a body, was left behind !

Love me, beloved : Hades and Death
Shall vanish away like a frosty breath ;
These hands, that now are at home in thine,
Shall clasp thee again, if thou still art mine ,
And thou shalt be mine, my spirit's bride,
In the ceaseless flow of eternity's tide,
If the truest love that thy heart can know
Meet the truest love that from mine can flow.
Pray God, beloved, for thee and me,
That our souls may be wedded eternally.

[*He closes the book, and is silent for some moments.*

Ah me, O Poet ! did *thy* love last out

The common life together every hour ?

The slumber side by side with wondrousness

Each night after a day of fog and rain ?

Did thy love glory o'er the empty purse,

And the poor meal sometimes the poet's lot?

Is she dead, Poet? Is thy love awake?

   Alas! and is it come to this with me?

I might have written that; where am I now?

Yet let me think: I love less passionately,

But not less truly; I would die for her—

A little thing, but all a man can do.

O my beloved, where the answering love?

Love me, beloved; whither art thou gone?

SCENE II. — *Lilia's room.* LILIA.

Lilia. He grows more moody still, more self-with-
   drawn.

Were it not better that I went away,

And left him with the child; for she alone

Can bring the sunshine on his cloudy face?

Alas! he used to say to me, *my child.*

Some convent would receive me in my land,

Where I might weep unseen, unquestioned;

And pray that God, in whom he seems to dwell,

To take me likewise in, beside him there.

   Had I not better make one trial first

To win again his love to compass me?

Might I not kneel, lie down before his feet,

And beg and pray for love as for my life?

Clasping his knees, look up to that stern heaven,

That broods above his eyes, and pray for smiles?

What if endurance were my only meed?

He would not turn away, but speak forced words,

Soothing with kindness me who thirst for love,

And giving service where I wanted smiles;

Till by degrees all had gone back again

To where it was, a slow dull misery.

No.   'Tis the best thing I can do for him —

And that I will do — free him from my sight.

In love I gave myself away to him;

And now in love I take myself again.

He will not miss me; I am nothing now.

SCENE III.— *Lord Seaford's garden.*   LILIA; LORD SEAFORD.

Lord S. How the white roses cluster on the trellis!

They look in the dim light as if they floated

Within the fluid dusk that bathes them round.

One could believe that those far distant sounds

Of scarce-heard music, rose with the faint scent,

Breathed odorous from the heart of the pale flowers,

As the low rushing from a river-bed,

Or the continuous bubbling of a spring

In deep woods, turning over its own joy

In its own heart luxuriously, alone.

'Twas on such nights, after such sunny days,

The poets of old Greece saw beauteous shapes

Sighed forth from out the rooted, earth-fast trees,

With likeness undefinable retained

In higher human form to their tree-homes,

Which fainting let them forth into the air,

And lived a life in death till they returned.

The large-limbed, sweepy-curved, smooth-rinded beech

Gave forth the perfect woman to the night ;

From the pale birch, breeze-bent and waving, stole

The graceful, slight-curved maiden, scarcely grown.

The hidden well gave forth its hidden charm,

The Naiad with the hair that flowed like streams,

And arms that gleamed like moonshine on wet sands.

The broad-browed oak, the stately elm, gave forth

Their inner life in shapes of ecstasy.

All varied, loveliest forms of womanhood

Dawned out in twilight, and athwart the grass

Half danced with cool and naked feet, half floated
Borne on winds dense enough for them to swim.
O what a life they lived ! in poet's brain —
Not on this earth, alas !   But you are sad ;
You do not speak, dear lady.

   Lilia.   Pardon me.
If such words make me sad, I am to blame.

   Lord S. Sad !   True, I spoke of lovely, beauteous
          things ;
Beauty and sadness always go together.
Nature thought Beauty too rich to go forth
Upon the earth without a meet alloy.
If Beauty had been born the twin of Gladness,
Poets had never needed this dream-life ;
Each blessed man had but to look beside him,
And be more blest.   How easily could God
Have made our life one consciousness of joy !
It is denied us.   Beauty flung around
Most lavishly, to teach our longing hearts
To worship her ; then when the soul is full
Of lovely shapes, and all sweet sounds that breathe,
And colors that bring tears into the eyes —
Steeped until saturated with her essence ;

And, faint with longing, gasps for some one thing
More beautiful than all, containing all,
Essential Beauty's self, that it may say:
"Thou art my Queen — I dare not think to crown
        thee,
For thou art crowned already, every part,
With thy perfection ; but I kneel to thee,
The utterance of the beauty of the earth,
As of the trees the Hamadryades ;
I worship thee, intense of loveliness!
Not sea-born only ; sprung from Earth, Air, Ocean,
Star-fire ; all elements and forms commingling
To give thee birth, to utter each its thought
Of beauty held in many forms diverse,
In one form, holding all, a living Love,
Their far-surpassing child, their chosen queen
By virtue of thy dignities combined ! "
And when in some great hour of wild surprise
She floats into his sight ; and, rapt, entranced,
At last he gazes, as I gaze on thee,
And, breathless, his full heart stands still for joy,
And his soul thinks not, having lost itself
In her, pervaded with her being; strayed

Out from his eyes, and gathered round her form,

Clothing her with the only beauty yet

That could be added, ownness unto him :

Then falls the sternest *No* with thunder tone.

Think, lady, — the poor unresisting soul

Clear-burnished to a crystalline abyss

To hold in central deep the ideal form ;

Led then to Beauty, and one glance allowed

From heart of hungry, vacant, waiting shrine,

To set it on the Pisgah of desire —

Lo, the black storm ! the slanting, sweeping rain !

Gray distances of travel to no end !

And the dim rush of countless years behind !

[He sinks at her feet.

Yet for this moment, let me worship thee !

   Lilia (agitated). Rise, rise, my lord ; this cannot be

      indeed.

I pray you, cease ; I will not listen to you.

Indeed it must not, cannot, must not be !

[Moving as to go.

   Lord S. (rising). Forgive me, madam.   Let me cast

      myself

On your good thoughts.   I had been thinking thus,

All the bright morning, as I walked alone ;
And when you came, my thoughts flowed forth in
    words.
It is a weakness with me from my boyhood,
That if I act a part in any play,
Or follow, merely intellectually,
A passion or a motive — ere I know,
My being is absorbed, my brain on fire ;
I am possessed with something not my own,
And live and move and speak in foreign forms.
Pity my weakness, madam ; and forgive
My rudeness with your gentleness and truth.
That you are beautiful is simple fact ;
And when I once began to speak my thoughts,
The wheels of speech ran on, till they took fire,
And in your face flung foolish sparks and dust.
I am ashamed ; and but for dread of shame,
I should be kneeling now to beg forgiveness.

    Lilia. Think nothing more of it, my lord, I pray.
What is this purple flower with the black spot
In its deep heart?   I never saw it before.

SCENE IV. — Julian's room.   The dusk of evening. JULIAN standing with his arms folded, and his eyes fixed on the floor.

Julian. I see her as I saw her then.   She sat
On a low chair, the child upon her knees,
Not six months old.   Radiant with motherhood,
Her full face beamed upon the face below,
Bent over, as with love to ripen love ;
Till its intensity, like summer heat,
Gathered a mist across her heaven of eyes,
Which grew until it dropt in large slow tears,
Rich human rain on furrows of the heart !

> [*He walks towards the window, seats himself at a little table, and writes.*

THE FATHER'S HYMN FOR THE MOTHER TO SING.

> My child is lying on my knees ;
>   The signs of heaven she reads ;
> My face is all the heaven she sees,
>   Is all the heaven she needs.
>
>
> And she is well, yea, bathed in bliss,
>   If heaven is in my face —
> Behind it all is tenderness,
>   And truthfulness and grace.

10

I mean her well so earnestly,
  Unchanged in changing mood;
My life would go without a sigh
  To bring her something good.

I also am a child, and I
  Am ignorant and weak;
I gaze upon the starry sky,
  And then I must not speak;

For all behind the starry sky,
  Behind the world so broad,
Behind men's hearts and souls doth lie
  The Infinite of God.

If true to her, though troubled sore,
  I cannot choose but be,
Thou, who art peace for evermore,
  Art very true to me.

If I am low and sinful, bring
  More love where need is rife;
Thou knowest what an awful thing
  It is to be a life.

Hast thou not wisdom to enwrap
  My waywardness about,
In doubting safety on the lap
  Of Love that knows no doubt?

Lo! Lord, I sit in thy wide space,
  My child upon my knee;
She looketh up unto my face,
  And I look up to thee.

Scene V. — *Lord Seaford's house; Lady Gertrude's room.* Lady Gertrude *lying on a couch;* Lilia *seated beside her, with the girl's hand in both hers.*

Lady Gertrude. How kind of you to come! And
    you will stay
And be my beautiful nurse till I grow well?
I am better since you came. You look so sweet,
It brings all summer back into my heart.

Lilia. I am very glad to come. Indeed, I felt
No one could nurse you quite so well as I.

Lady Gertrude. How kind of you! Do call me
    sweet names now;
And put your white cool hands upon my head,
And let me lie and look in your great eyes:
'Twill do me good; your very eyes are healing.

Lilia. I must not let you talk too much, dear
    child.

Lady Gertrude. Well, as I cannot have my music-
    lesson,
And must not speak much, will you sing to me?
Sing that strange ballad you sang once before;
'Twill keep me quiet.

Lilia.   What was it, child?

Lady Gertrude.   It was

Something about a race — Death and a lady —

Lilia. O, I remember.   I would rather sing

Some other though.

Lady Gertrude.   No, no, I want that one.

Its ghost walks up and down inside my head,

But won't stand long enough to show itself.

You must talk Latin to it — sing it away,

Or when I'm ill, 'twill haunt me.

Lilia.   Well, I'll sing it.

SONG.

Death and a lady rode in the wind,
  In a starry midnight pale ,
Death on a bony horse behind,
  With no footfall upon the gale.

The lady sat a wild-eyed steed ;
  Eastward he tore to the morn
But ever the sense of a noiseless speed,
  And the sound of reaping corn !

All the night through, the headlong race
  Sped to the morning gray ;
The dewdrops lay on her cold white face —
  From Death or the morning ? say.

Her steed's wide knees began to shake,
  As he flung the road behind ;

The lady sat still, but her heart did quake,
    And a cold breath came down the wind.

When, lo ! a fleet bay horse beside,
    With a silver mane and tail ;
A knight, bareheaded, the horse did ride,
    With never a coat of mail.

He never lifted his hand to Death,
    And he never couched a spear ;
But the lady felt another breath,
    And a voice was in her ear.

He looked her weary eyes through and through,
    With his eyes so strong in faith :
Her bridle-hand the lady drew,
    And she turned and laughed at Death.

And away through the mist of the morning gray,
    The spectre and horse rode wide ;
The dawn came up the old bright way,
    And the lady never died.

Lord Seaford (*who has entered during the song*). De-
lightful ! Why, my little pining Gertrude,
With such charm-music you will soon be well.
Madam, I know not how to speak the thanks
I owe you for your kindness to my daughter :
She looks as different from yesterday
As sunrise from a fog.

Lilia.   I am but too happy
To be of use to one I love so much.

SCENE VI. — *A rainy day*   LORD SEAFORD *walking up and down
his room, murmuring to himself.*

O, my love is like a wind of death,
    That turns me to a stone !
O, my love is like a desert breath,
    That burns me to the bone !

O, my love is a flower with a purple glow,
    And a purple scent all day '
But a black spot lies at the heart below,
    And smells all night of clay.

O, my love is like the poison sweet
    That lurks in the hooded cell !
One flash in the eyes, one bounding beat,
    And then the passing bell '

O, my love she's like a white, white rose '
    And I am the canker-worm :
Never the bud to a blossom blows ;
    It falls in the rainy storm.

SCENE VII. — JULIAN *reading in his room.*

" And yet I am not alone, because the Father is with me."

                    [*He closes the book and kneels.*

SCENE VIII. — *Lord Seaford's room*   LILIA *and* LORD SEA-
FORD   *Her hand lies in his.*

Lilia. It may be true.   I am bewildered, though.
I know not what to answer.

Lord S.   Let me answer :
You would it were so — you would love me then ?

[*A sudden crash of music from a brass band in the street,
melting away in a low cadence.*

Lilia (*starting up*). Let me go, my lord !

Lord S. (*retaining her hand*). Why, sweetest ! What
    is this ?

Lilia (*vehemently, and disengaging her hand*). Let
    me go !   O my husband ! my pale child !
                    [*She hurries to the door, but falls*

Lord S. (*raising her*). I thought you trusted me, yes,
    loved me, Lilia !

Lilia. Peace ! that name is his ! Speak it again — I
    rave.
He thought I loved him — and I did — I do.
Open the door, my lord !

[*He hesitates   She draws herself up erect, with flashing
    eyes.*

Once more, my lord —

Open the door, I say.

> [*He still hesitates. She walks swiftly to the window, flings
> it wide, and is throwing herself out.*

Lord S.   Stop, madam ! I will.

> [*He opens the door. She leaves the window, and walks slowly
> out. He hears the house-door open and shut, flings him-
> self on the couch, and hides his face.*

Enter LADY GERTRUDE.

Lady Gertrude. Dear father, are you ill? I knocked

three times ,

You did not speak.

Lord S   I did not hear you, child.

My head aches rather ; else I am quite well.

Lady Gertrude. Where is the Countess ?

Lord S.   She is gone.   She had

An urgent message to go home at once

But, Gertrude, now you seem so well, why not

Set out to-morrow ?   You can travel now ;

And for your sake the sooner that we breathe

Italian air the better.

Lady Gertrude.   This is sudden !

I scarcely can be ready by to-morrow.

Lord S. It will oblige me, child. Do what you can.

Just go and order everything you want.

I will go with you.   Ring the bell, my love;

I have a reason for my haste.   We'll have

The horses to at once.   Come, Gertrude, dear.

SCENE IX. — *Evening.   Hampstead Heath.*   LILIA *seated.*

Lilia. The first pale star of night! the trembling
    star!

And all heaven waiting till the sun has drawn

His long train after! then a new creation   .

Will follow their queen-leader from the depths.

O leader of new worlds!   O star of love!

Thou hast gone down in me, gone down forever;

And left my soul in such a starless night,

It has not love enough to weep thy loss.

O fool! to know thee once, and, after years,

To take a gleaming marsh-light for thy lamp

How could I for one moment hear him speak!

O Julian! for my last love-gift I thought

To bring that love itself, bound and resigned,

And offering it a sacrifice to thee,

Lead it away into the wilderness;

But one slow spot hath tainted this my lamb;

Unoffered it must go, footsore and weary,

Not flattering itself to die for thee.

And yet, thank God, it was one moment only,

That, lapt in darkness and the loss of thee,

Sun of my soul, and half my senses dead

Through very weariness and lack of love,

My heart throbbed once responsive to a ray

That glimmered through its gloom from other eyes,

And seemed to promise rest and hope again.

My presence shall not grieve thee any more,

My Julian, my husband.   I will find

A quiet place where I will seek thy God.

And — in my heart it wakens like a voice

From Him — the Saviour — there are other worlds

Where all gone wrong in this may be set right;

Where I, made pure, may find thee, purer still,

And thou wilt love the love that kneels to thee.

I'll write and tell him I have gone, and why.

But what to say about my late offense,

That he may understand just what it was?

For I must tell him, if I write at all.

I fear he would discover where I was;

Pitiful duty would not let him rest

Until he found me ; and I fain would free

From all the weight of mine, that heart of his.

> [*Sound of a coach-horn.*

It calls me to rise up and go to him,

Leading me further from him and away.

The earth is round ; God's thoughts return again ;

And I will go in hope.   Help me, my God !

SCENE X — *Julian's room   JULIAN reading   A letter is brought in.   He reads it, turns deadly pale, and leans his arms and head on the table, almost fainting   This lasts some time ; then starting up, he paces through the room, his shoulders slightly shrugged, his arms rigid by his sides, and his hands clinched hard, as if a net of pain were drawn tight around his frame. At length he breathes deep, draws himself up, and walks erect, his chest swelling, but his teeth set.*

Julian. Me !   My wife !   Insect, did'st thou say

    my wife ?

> [*Hurriedly turning the letter on the table to see the address.*

Why, if she love him more than me, why then

Let her go with him ! Gone to Italy !

Pursue, says he ?   *Revenge ?*   Let the corpse crush

The slimy maggot with its pulpy fingers !

What if I stabbed —

> [*Taking his dagger, and feeling its point.*

    Whom ?   Her — what then ?   Or him —

What yet?   Would that give back the life to me?

There is one more — myself!   O, peace! to feel

The earthworms crawling through my mouldering
      brain!

But to be driven along the windy wastes —

To hear the tempests, raving as they turn,

Howl *Lilia, Lilia* — to be tossed about

Beneath the stars that range themselves forever

Into the burning letters of her name —

'Twere better creep the earth down here than that ;

For pain's excess here sometimes deadens pain.

                        [*He throws the dagger on the floor*

Have I deserved this?   Have I earned it?   I?

A pride of innocence darts through my veins.

I stand erect.   Shame cannot touch me.   Ha!

I laugh at insult   *I?*   I am myself —

Why starest thou at me?   Well, stare thy fill ;

When devils mock, the angels lend their wings : —

But what their wings?   I have nowhere to fly.

Lilia! my worship of thy purity!

Hast thou forgotten — ah! thou didst not know

How, watching by thee in thy fever-pain,

When thy white neck and bosom were laid bare,

I turned my eyes away and turning drew

With trembling hand white darkness over thee,

Because I knew not thou didst love me then.

Love me !   O God in heaven !   Is love a thing

That can die thus ? Love me ! Would, for thy penance,

Thou saw'st but once the heart which thou hast torn —

Shaped all about thy image set within !

But that were fearful !   What rage would not, love

Must then do for thee — in mercy I would kill thee,

To save thee from the hell-fire of remorse.

If blood would make thee clean, then blood should
        flow ;

Eager, unwilling, this hand should make thee bleed,

Till, drop by drop, the taint should drop away.

Clean ! said I ? fit to lie by me in sleep,

My hand upon thy heart ! — not fit to lie,

For all thy bleeding, by me in the grave !

> [*His eye falls on that likeness of Jesus said to be copied from an emerald engraved for Tiberius. He gazes, drops on his knees, and covers his face ; remains motionless a long time ; then rises very pale, his lips compressed, his eyes filled with tears.*]

O my poor Lilia ! my bewildered child !

How shall I win thee, save thee, make thee mine ?

Where art thou wandering? What words in thine
    ears?
God, can she never more be clean? no more,
Through all the terrible years? Hast thou no well
In all thy heaven, in all thyself, that can
Wash her soul clean? Her body will go down
Into the friendly earth — would it were lying
There in my arms ; for there thy rains will come,
Fresh from the sky, slow sinking through the sod,
Summer and winter ; and we two should lie
Mouldering away together, gently washed
Into the heart of earth , and part would float
Forth on the sunny breezes that bear clouds
Through the thin air. But her stained soul, my God !
Canst thou not cleanse it? Then should we, wher
    death
Was gone, creep into heaven at last, and sit
In some still place together, glory-shadowed.
None would ask questions there. And I should be
Content to sorrow a little, so I might
But see her with the darling on her knees,
And know that must be pure that dwelt within
The circle of thy glory. Lilia! Lilia!

I scorn the shame rushing from head to foot;
I would endure it endlessly, to save
One thought of thine from his polluting touch;
Saying ever to myself: This is a part
Of my own Lilia; and the world to me
Is nothing since I lost the smiles of her:
Somehow, I know not how, she faded from me,
And this is all that's left of her.   My wife!
Soul of my soul! my oneness with myself!
Come back to me; I will be all to thee;
Back to my heart; and we will weep together,
And pray to God together every hour,
That He would show how strong He is to save.
The One that made is able to renew:
I know not how.   I'll hold thy heart to mine,
So close that the defilement needs must go.
My love shall ray thee round, and, strong as fire,
Dart through and through thy soul, till it be
    cleansed.
But if she love him?   O, my heart — beat! beat!
Grow not so sick with misery and life,
For fainting will not save thee.   O, no! no!
She cannot love him as she must love me.

Then if she love him not, O horrible ! O God !

[He stands in a stupor for some minutes

What devil whispered that vile word, *unclean ?*

I care not — loving more than that can touch.

Let me be shamed, aye, perish in my shame,

As men call perishing, so she be saved.

Saved ! my beloved ! my Lilia ! alas !

Would she were here, and I would make her weep,

Till her soul wept itself to purity.

Far, far away ! where my love cannot reach.

No, no ; she is not gone.

[Starting and pacing wildly through the room

It is a lie —

Deluding blind revenge, not keen-eyed love.

I must do something.   *[Enter LILY.*

Ah ! there's the precious thing

That shall entice her back.

[Kneeling and clasping the child to his heart.

My little Lily,

I have lost your mother.

Lily.   O !   *[Beginning to weep.*

She was so pretty,

Somebody has stolen her.

Julian.   Will you go with me,

And help me look for her?

   Lily.   O yes, I will.

                  [Clasping him round the neck

But my head aches so!   Will you carry me?

   Julian. Yes, my own darling   Come, we'll get

     your bonnet.

   Lily. O! you've been crying, father.   You're so

     white!   *[Putting her finger to his cheek.*

SCENE XI. — *A table in a club-room Several* GENTLEMEN *seated round it.   To them enter another.*

   1st Gentleman. Why, Bernard, you look heated,

     what's the matter?

   Bernard. Hot work, as looked at; cool enough,

     as done.

   2d G. A good antithesis, as usual, Bernard,

But a shell too hard for the vulgar teeth

Of our impatient curiosity.

   Bernard. Most unexpectedly I found myself

Spectator of a scene in a home-drama

Worth all stage tragedies I ever saw.

    11

All. What was it? Tell us, then. Here, take thi·

     seat. [*He sits at the table, and pours out a glass of wine*

Bernard. I went to call on Seaford, and was tolc

He had gone to town. So I, as privileged,

Went to his cabinet to write a note ;

Which finished, I came down, and called his valet.

Just as I crossed the hall I heard a voice —

" The Countess Lamballa — is she here to-day ? "

And looking towards the door I caught a glimpse

Of a tall figure, gaunt and stooping, drest

In a blue shabby frock down to his knees,

And on his left arm sat a little child.

The porter gave short answer, with the door

For period to the same ; when, like a flash,

It flew wide open, and the serving man

Went reeling, staggering backward to the stairs,

'Gainst which he fell, and, rolling down, lay stunned

In walked the visitor ; but in the moment

Just measured by the closing of the door,

Heavens ! what a change ! He walked erect, as if

Heading a column, with an eye and face

As if a fountain-shaft of blood had shot

Up suddenly within his wasted frame.

The child sat on his arm quite still and pale,

But with a look of triumph in her eyes.

Of me he took no notice ; came right on ;

Looked in each room that opened from the hall ,

In every motion calm as glacier's flow,

Save now and then a movement, sudden, quick,

Of his right hand across to his left side:

'Twas plain he had been used to carry arms.

   3d G. Did no one stop him ?

Bernard.   Stop him ? I'd as soon

Have faced a tiger with bare hands.   'Tis easy

In passion to meet passion ; but it is

A daunting thing to look on, when the blood

Is going its wonted pace through your own veins.

Besides, this man had something in his face,

With its live eyes, close lips, nostrils distended,

A self-reliance, and a self-command,

That would go right up to his goal, in spite

Of any *no* from any man.   I would

As soon have stopped a cannon-ball as him.

Over the porter, lying where he fell,

He strode, and up the stairs.   I heard him go —

I listened as it were a ghost that walked

With pallid spectre-child upon its arm —
Along the corridors, from door to door,
Opening and shutting.   But at last a sting
Of sudden fear lest he should find the lady,
And mischief follow, shot me up the stairs
I met him half-way down, quiet as at first ;
The fire had faded from his eyes ; the child
Held in her tiny hand a lady's glove
Of delicate primrose.   When he reached the hall,
He turned him to the porter, who had scarce
Lifted him from the floor, and saying thus :
"The Count Lamballa waited on Lord Seaford,"
Turned him again, and strode into the street.

    1st G. Have you got hold of any clew ?

    Bernard.   Not any.

Of course he had suspicions of his wife ;
For all the gifts a woman has to give,
I would not rouse such blood.   And yet to see
The gentle fairy child fall kissing him,
And, with her little arms grasping his neck,
Peep anxious round into his shaggy face,
As they went down the street ! — it almost made
A fool of me   I'd marry for such a child !

SCENE XII — *A by-street.* JULIAN *walking home very weary. The child in his arms, her head lying on his shoulder.* An OR-GAN-BOY *with a monkey, sitting on a door-step. He sings in a low voice.*

Julian. Look at the monkey, Lily.

Lily.   No, dear father;
I do not like monkeys.

Julian.   Hear the poor boy sing.

                                   [*They listen.   He sings.*

SONG

Wenn ich höre dich mir nah',
Stimmen in den Blättern da ;
Wenn ich fuhl' dich weit und breit,
Vater, das ist Seligkeit.

Nun die Sonne liebend scheint,
Mich mit dir und All vereint ;
Biene zu den Blumen fliegt,
Seel' an Lieb' sich liebend schmiegt.

So mich völlig lieb du hast,
Daseyn ist nicht eine Last ;
Wenn ich seh' und höre dich,
Das genügt mir inniglich.

Lily. It sounds so curious. What is he saying, father ?

Julian. My boy, you are not German ?

Boy.   No , my mother

Came from those parts.   She used to sing the song.

I hardly understand it all myself,

For I was born in Genoa.   Ah ! my mother !   [*Weeps.*

Julian. My mother was a German, my poor boy ;

My father was Italian : I am like you.

[*Giving him money*

You sing of leaves and sunshine, flowers and bees,

Poor child, upon a stone in the dark street?

Boy. My mother sings it in her grave ; and I

Will sing it everywhere, until I die.

SCENE XIII. — LILIA'S *room.*   JULIAN *enters with the child,
     undresses her, and puts her to bed.*

Lily. Father does *all* things for his little Lily.

Julian. Dear, dear Lily !   Go to sleep, my pet

[*Sitting by her.*

     " Wenn ich seh' und höre dich,
          Das genugt mir inniglich. "   [*Falling on his knees.*

I come to thee, and, lying on thy breast,

Father of me, I tell thee in thine ear,

Half-shrinking from the sound, yet speaking free,

That thou art not enough for me, my God.

O, dearly do I love thee !   Look ; no fear
Lest thou shouldst be offended, touches me.
Herein I know thy love ; mine casts out fear.
O give me back my wife ; thou without her
Canst never make me blessed to the full.   [*Silence.*

   O yes , thou art enough for me, my God ;
Part of thyself she is, else never mine
My need of her is but thy thought of me ;
She is the offspring of thy beauty, God ;
Yea of the womanhood that dwells in thee :
Thou wilt restore her to my very soul.   [*Rising.*

   It may be all a lie.   Some needful cause
Keeps her away.   Wretch that I am, to think
One moment that my wife could sin against me !
She will come back to-night.   I know she will.'
How shall I answer for such jealousy !
For that fool-visit to Lord Seaford's house !

     [*His eyes fall on the glove which the child still holds in her*
       sleeping hand   He takes it gently away, and hides it in
       his bosom

   It will be all explained.   To think I should,
Without one word from her, condemn her so !
What can I say to her when she reurns ?

I shall be utterly ashamed before her.

She will come back to-night.   I know she will.

> [*He throws himself wearily on the bed.*

SCENE XIV. — *Crowd about the Italian Opera-House.* JULIAN.
LILY *in his arms.   Three* STUDENTS.

1st Student. Edward, you see that long, lank, thread-
bare man?

There is a character for that same novel

You talk of thunder-striking London with,

One of these days

2d St.   I scarcely noticed him ;

I was so taken with the lovely child.

She is angelic.

3d St.   You see angels always,

Where others, more dim-sighted, see but mortals.

She *is* a pretty child.   Her eyes are splendid.

I wonder what the old fellow is about.

Some crazed enthusiast, music-distract,

That lingers at the door he cannot enter!

Give him an obol, Frank, to pay old Charon,

And cross to the Elysium of sweet sounds.

Here's mine.

1st St. And mine.

2d St.   And mine.

> [*3d* Student *offers the money to* Julian.

Julian (very quietly)   No, thank you, sir.

Lily. O, there is mother !

> |*Stretching her hands towards a lady stepping out of a carriage.*

Julian.   No, no ; hush, my child !

> [*The lady looks round, and* Lily *clings to her father.* Women *talking.*

1st W. I'm sure he's stolen the child.   She can't be

his

2d W. There's a suspicious look about him.

3d W.   True ;

But the child clings to him as if she loved him.

> [Julian *moves on slowly.*

Scene XV.— Julian *seated in his room, his eyes fixed on the floor.* Lily *playing in a corner.*

Julian. Though I am lonely, yet this little child —

She understands me better than the Twelve

Knew the great heart of Him they called their Lord.

Ten times last night I woke in agony,

I knew not why.   There was no comforter.

I stretched my arm to find her, and her place
Was empty as my heart.   Though wide awake,
Sometimes my pain, benumbed by its own being,
Forgets its cause, and I would lay my head
Upon her breast — that promises relief:
I lift my eyes, and lo, the vacant world!

    [*He looks up and sees the child playing with his dagger.*

 You'll hurt yourself, my child; it is too sharp.
Give it to me, my darling.   Thank you, dear.

     [*He breaks the hilt from the blade and gives it her.*

Here, take the pretty part.   It's not so pretty
As it was once —   [*Thinking aloud.*

    I picked the jewels out
To buy your mother the last dress I gave her.
There's just one left, I see, for you, my Lily.

 Why did I kill Nembroni?   Poor saviour I,
Leading thee only to a greater ill!

 If thou wert dead, the child would comfort me;
Is she not part of thee, and all my own?
But now —

 *Lily (throwing down the dagger-hilt, and running up
  to him).*   Father, what is a poetry?

 Julian. A beautiful thing, — of the most beautiful
That God has made.

Lily.   As beautiful as mother?

Julian No, my dear child; but very beautiful.

Lily. Do let me see a poetry.

Julian (opening a book).   There, love.

Lily (disappointedly). I don't think that's so very
  pretty, father.

One side is very well — smooth; but the other

[*Rubbing her finger up and down the ends of the lines.*

Is rough, rough, just like my hair in the morning,

[*Smoothing her hair down with both hands.*

Before it's brushed. I don't care much about it

*Julian (putting the book down, and taking her on his
  knee).* You do not understand it yet, my child

You cannot know where it is beautiful

But though you do not *see* it very pretty,

Perhaps your little ears could hear it pretty. [*He reads*

Lily (looking pleased). O, that's much prettier, father
  Very pretty.

It sounds so nice! — not half so pretty as mother

Julian There's something in it very beautiful,

If I could let you see it. When you're older,

You'll find it for yourself, and love it well.

Do you believe me, Lily?

Lily.   Yes, dear father.

[*Kissing him, then looking at the book.*

I wonder where its prettiness is, though ;

I cannot see it anywhere at all

[*He sets her down   She goes to her corner.*

Julian (*musing*). True, there's not much in me to

    love, and yet

I feel worth loving.   I am very poor,

But that I could not help ; and I grow old,

But there are saints in heaven older than I.

I have a world within me ; there I thought

I had a wealth of lovely, precious things, —

Laid up for thinking ; shady woods, and grass ,

Clear streams rejoicing down their sloping channels ;

And glimmering daylight in the cloven east ;

There morning sunbeams stand, a vapory column,

'Twixt the dark boles of solemn forest trees ;

There, spokes of the sun-wheel, that cross their

    bridge,

Break through the arch of the clouds, fall on the

    earth,

And travel round, as the wind blows the clouds :

The distant meadows and the gloomy river

Shine out as over them the ray-pencil sweeps.

Alas ! where am I ?   Beauty now is torture :

Of this fair world I would have made her queen ;

Then led her through the shadowy gates beyond

Into that farther world of things unspoken,

Of which these glories are the outer stars,

The clouds that float within its atmosphere.

Under the holy might of teaching love,

I thought her eyes would open — see how, far

And near, Truth spreads her empire, widening out,

And brooding, a still spirit, everywhere ;

Thought she would turn into her spirit's chamber,

Open the little window, and look forth

On the wide silent ocean, silent winds,

And see what she must see, I could not tell.

By sounding mighty chords I strove to wake

The sleeping music of her poet-soul :

We read together many magic words ;

Gazed on the forms and hues of ancient art ;

Sent forth our souls on the same tide of sound ;

Worshipped beneath the same high temple-roofs ;

And evermore I talked.   I was too proud,

Too confident of power to waken life,

Believing in my might upon her heart,

Not trusting in the strength of living truth

Unhappy saviour, who by force of self

Would save from selfishness and narrow needs!

I have not been a saviour.   She grew weary.

I began wrong.   The infinitely High,

Made manifest in lowliness, had been

The first, one lesson.   Had I brought her there,

And set her down by humble Mary's side,

He would have taught her all I could not teach.

Yet, O my God! why hast thou made me thus

Terribly wretched, and beyond relief?

> [*He looks up and sees that the child has taken the book to her corner.   She peeps into it; then holds it to her ear: then rubs her hand over it; then puts her tongue on it*

Julian (*bursting into tears*).   Father, I am thy *child*.

    Forgive me this:

Thy poetry is very hard to read.

SCENE XVI — JULIAN *walking with* LILY *through one of the squares*

Lily. Wish we could find her somewhere.   'Tis so sad

Not to have any mother!   Shall I ask

This gentleman if he knows where she is?

Julian. No, no, my love , we'll find her by and
  by.

BERNARD *and another* GENTLEMAN *talking together.*

Bernard. Have you seen Seaford lately ?

Gentleman.   No In fact,
He vanished somewhat oddly, days ago.
Sam saw him with a lady in his cab ,
And if I hear aright, one more is missing —
Just the companion for his lordship's taste.
You've not forgot that fine Italian woman
You met there once, some months ago ?

Bern.   Forgot her !
I have to try though, sometimes — hard enough

Lily. Mother was Italy, father — was she not ?

Julian. Hush, hush, my child ! you must not say a
  word.

Bern Her husband is alive.

Gentleman.   O, yes ! he is ;
But what of that — a poor half-crazy creature !

Bern Something quite different, I assure you,
  Harry.
Last week I saw him — never to forget him —
Ranging through Seaford's house, like the questing
  beast.

Gentleman. Better please two than one, they

> thought, no doubt.

I am not the one to blame him ; she is a prize

Worth sinning for a little more than little.

Lily (whispering) Why don't you ask them whether

> it was mother ?

I am sure it was   I am quite sure of it

Gentleman. Look what a lovely child !

Bern.   Henry ! Good heavens !

It is the Count Lamballa   Come along.

SCENE XVII — *Julian's room.* JULIAN   LILY *asleep*

Julian. I thank thee.   Thou hast comforted me,

> thou,

To whom I never lift my soul, in hope

To reach thee with my thinking, but the tears

Swell up and fill my eyes from the full heart

That cannot hold the thought of thee, the thought

Of Him in whom I live, who lives in me,

And makes me live in Him , by whose one thought,

Alone, unreachable, the making thought,

Infinite and self-bounded, I am here,

A living, thinking will, that cannot know

The power whereby I am — so blest the more

In being thus in thee — Father, thy child.

I cannot, cannot speak the thoughts in me.

My being shares thy glory   lay on me

What thou wouldst have me bear.   Do thou with me

Whate'er thou wilt.   Tell me thy will, that I

May do it as my best, my highest joy ;

For thou dost work in me, I dwell in thee.

　　Wilt thou not save my wife ?   I cannot know

The power in thee to purify from sin.

But Life *can* cleanse the life it lived alive.

Thou knowest all that lesseneth her fault.

She loves me not, I know — ah ! my sick heart !

I will love her the more, to fill the cup ;

One bond is snapped, the other shall be doubled ·

For if I love her not, how desolate

The poor child will be left ! *he* loves her not.

　　I have but one prayer left to pray to thee —

Give me my wife again, that I may watch

And weep with her, and pray with her, and tell

What loving kindness I have found in thee ;

And she will come to thee to make her clean.

Her soul must wake as from a dream of bliss,

To know a dead one lieth in the house :

Let me be near her in that agony,

To tend her in the fever of the soul,

Bring her cool waters from the wells of hope,

Look forth and tell her that the morn is nigh ;

And when I cannot comfort, help her weep.

God, I would give her love like thine to me,

Because I love her, and her need is great.

Lord, I need her far more than thou need'st me,

And thou art Love down to the deeps of hell :

Help me to love her with a love like thine.

　　How shall I find her ?　It were horrible

If the dread hour should come, and I not near.

Yet pray I not she should be spared one pang,

One writhing of self-loathing and remorse ;

For she must hate the evil she has done.

Only take not away hope utterly.

　　Lily (in her sleep)　Lily means me — don't throw it
　　　over the wall.

　　Julian (going to her).　She is so flushed ! I fear the
　　　child is ill.

I have fatigued her too much, wandering restless.

To-morrow I will take her to the sea.　　　[*Returning.*

If I knew where, I'd write to her, and write

So tenderly, she could not choose but come.

I will write now , I'll tell her that strange dream

I dreamed last night. 'twill comfort her as well.

[*He sits down and writes.*

My heart was crushed that I could hardly breathe.

I was alone upon a desolate moor ,

And the wind blew by fits and died away —

I know not if it was the wind or me.

How long I wandered there, I cannot tell ;

But some one came and took me by the hand.

I gazed but could not see the form that led me,

And went unquestioning, I cared not whither.

We came into a street I seemed to know,

Came to a house that I had seen before

The shutters were all closed ; the house was dead.

The door went open soundless   We went in,

And entered yet again an inner room

The darkness was so dense, I shrunk as if

From striking on it.   The door closed behind

And then I saw that there was something black,

Dark in the blackness of the night, heaved up

In the middle of the room   And then I saw

That there were shapes of woe all round the room,
Like women in long mantles, bent in grief,
With long veils hanging low down from their heads,
All blacker in the darkness.   Not a sound
Broke the death-stillness.   Then the shapeless thing
Began to move.   Four horrid muffled figures
Had lifted, bore it from the room.   We followed,
The bending woman-shapes, and I.   We left
The house in long procession.   I was walking
Alone beside the coffin — such it was —
Now in the glimmering light I saw the thing.
And now I saw and knew the woman-shapes :
Undine clothed in spray, and heaving up
White arms of lamentation ; Desdemona
In her night-robe, crimson on the left side ;
Thekla in black, with resolute white face ;
And Margaret in fetters, gliding slow —
That last look, when she shrieked on Henry, frozen
Upon her face.   And many more I knew —
Long-suffering women, true in heart and life ;
Women that make man proud for very love
Of their humility, and of his pride
Ashamed.   And in the coffin lay my wife.

On, on, we went   The scene changed.   For the hills

Began to rise from either side the path.

At last we came into a narrow glen,

From which the mountains rose abrupt to heaven,

Shot cones and pinnacles into the skies.

Upon the eastern side one mighty summit

Shown with its snow faint through the dusky air.

Upon its sides the glaciers gave a tint,

A dull metallic gleam, to the slow night.

From base to top, on climbing peak and crag,

Aye, on the glaciers' breast, were human shapes,

Motionless, waiting ; men that trod the earth

Like gods , or forms ideal that inspired

Great men of old — up, even to the apex

Of the snow-spear-point.   *Morning* had arisen

From Giulian's tomb in Florence, where the chisel

Of Michelagnolo laid him reclining,

And stood upon the crest.

                         A cry awoke

Amid the watchers at the lowest base,

And swelling rose, and sprang from mouth to mouth,

Up the vast mountain, to its aerial top ;

And *"Is God coming ?"* was the cry ; which died

Away in silence ; for no voice said *No.*

The bearers stood and set the coffin down ;
The mourners gathered round it in a group ;
Somewhat apart I stood, I know not why.

So minutes passed Again that cry awoke,
And clomb the mountain-side, and died away
In the thin air, far-lost.   No answer came.

How long we waited thus, I cannot tell —
How oft the cry arose and died again.

At last, from far, faint summit to the base,
Filling the mountain with a throng of echoes,
A mighty voice descended : *"God is coming!"*
O ! what a music clothed the mountain-side,
From all that multitude's melodious throats,
Of joy and lamentation and strong prayer !
It ceased, for hope was too intense for song
A pause.   The figure on the crest flashed out,
Bordered with light.   The sun was rising — rose
Higher and higher still.   One ray fell keen
Upon the coffin 'mid the circling group

What God did for the rest, I know not ; it
Was easy to help them.   I saw them not.
I saw thee at my feet, my wife, my own !
Thy lovely face angelic now with grief ;

But that I saw not first : thy head was bent,

Thou on thy knees, thy dear hands clasped between.

I sought to raise thee, but thou wouldst not rise,

Once only lifting that sweet face to mine,

Then turning it to earth.   Would God the dream

Had lasted ever !   No ; 'twas but a dream ;

Thou art not rescued yet.

Earth's morning came,

And my soul's morning died in tearful gray.

The last I saw was thy white shroud yet steeped

In that sun-glory all-transfiguring.

And as a slow chant blossomed suddenly

Into an anthem, silence took me like sound ·

I had not listened in the excess of joy.

SCENE XVIII. — *Portsmouth.   A bedroom.*   LORD SEAFORD
LADY GERTRUDE.

Lord S. 'Tis for your sake, my Gertrude, I am

sorry.

If you could go alone, I'd have you go.

Lady Gertrude. And leave you ill ? No, you are

not so cruel.

Believe me, father, I am happier

In your sick room, than on a glowing island
In the blue Bay of Naples.

   Lord S.   It was so sudden !
I fear it will not go again as quickly
But have your walk before the sun be hot
Put the ice near me, child.   There, that will do.

   Lady Gertrude. Good-by then, father, for a little
      while.   [*Goes.*

   Lord S. I never knew what illness was before.
O life ! to think a man should stand so little
On his own will and choice, as to be thus
Cast from his high throne suddenly, and sent
To grovel beast-like.   All the glow is gone
From the rich world !   No sense is left me more
To touch with beauty   Even she has faded
Into the far horizon, a spent dream
Of love and loss and passionate despair.

   Is there no beauty?   Is it all a show
Flung outward from the healthy blood and nerves,
A reflex of well-ordered organism ?
Is earth a desert?   Is a woman's heart
No more mysterious, no more beautiful,
Than I am to myself this ghastly moment?

It must be so — it *must*, except God is,

And means the meaning that we think we see,

Sends forth the beauty we are taking in.

O Soul of nature, if thou art not, if

There dwelt not in thy thought the primrose-flower

Before it blew on any bank of spring,

Then all is untruth, unreality,

And we are wretched things ; our highest needs

Are less than we, the offspring of ourselves ;

And when we are sick, they *are* not ; and our hearts

Die with the voidness of the universe.

But if thou art, O God, then all is true ;

Nor are thy thoughts less radiant that our eyes

Are filmy, and the weary, troubled brain

Throbs in an endless round of its own dreams.

And she *is* beautiful — and I have lost her !

O God ! thou art, thou art ; and I have sinned

Against thy beauty and thy graciousness !

That woman-splendor was not mine, but thine.

Thy thought passed into form, that glory passed

Before my eyes, a bright particular star :

Like foolish child, I reached out for the star,

Nor kneeled, nor worshipped.   I will be content

That she, the Beautiful, dwells on in thee,

Mine to revere, though not to call my own.

Forgive me, God ! Forgive me, Lilia !

My love has taken vengeance on my love.

I writhe and moan   Yet I will be content.

Yea gladly will I yield thee, so to find

That thou art not a phantom, but God's child ;

That Beauty is, though it is not for me.

When I would hold it, then I disbelieved :

That I may yet believe, I will not touch it.

I have sinned against the Soul of love and beauty,

Denying Him in grasping at his work.

SCENE XIX. — *A country church-yard.* JULIAN *seated on a tomb-stone.* LILY *gathering flowers and grass among the graves*

Julian. O soft place of the earth ! down-pillowed
    couch,

Made ready for the weary !   Everywhere,

O Earth, thou hast one gift for thy poor children —

Room to lie down, leave to cease standing up,

Leave to return to thee, and in thy bosom

Lie in the luxury of primeval peace,

Fearless of any morn ; as a new babe

Lies nestling in his mother's arms in bed :
That home of blessedness is all there is ;
He never feels the silent rushing tide,
Strong setting for the sea, which bears him on,
Unconscious, helpless, to wide consciousness.
But thou, thank God, hast this warm bed at last
Ready for him when weary : well the green
Close-matted coverlid shuts out the dawn.
O Lilia, would it were our wedding-bed
To which I bore thee with a nobler joy !
Alas ! there's no such rest : I only dream
Poor pagan dreams with a tired Christian brain.

   How couldst thou leave me, my poor child ? my
      heart
Was all so tender to thee !   But I fear
My face was not.   Alas ! I was perplexed
With questions to be solved, before my face
Could turn to thee in peace : thy part in me
Fared ill in troubled workings of the brain.
Ah, now I know I did not well for thee
In making thee my wife.   I should have gone
Alone into eternity.   I was
Too rough for thee, for any tender woman —

Other I had not loved — so full of fancies !

Too given to meditation.   A deed of love

Is stronger than a metaphysic truth ;

Smiles better teachers than the mightiest words.

Thou, who wast life, not thought, how couldst thou

    help it ?

How love me on, withdrawn from all thy sight —

For life must ever need the shows of life ?

How fail to love a man so like thyself,

Whose manhood sought thy fainting womanhood ?

I brought thee pine-boughs, rich in hanging cones,

But never white flowers, rubied at the heart.

O God, forgive me ; it is all my fault.

Would I have had dead Love, pain-galvanized,

Led fettered after me by jailer Duty ?

Thou gavest me a woman rich in heart,

And I have kept her like a caged sea-mew

Starved by a boy, who weeps when it is dead

O God, my eyes are opening — fearfully :

I know it now — 'twas pride, yes, very pride

That kept me back from speaking all my soul.

I was self-haunted, self-possessed — the worst

Of all possessions.   Wherefore did I never

Cast all my being, life and all, on hers,

In burning words of openness and truth?

Why never fling my doubts, my hopes, my love,

Prone at her feet abandonedly?   Why not

Have been content to minister and wait ;

And if she answered not to my desires,

Have smiled and waited patient?   God, they say,

Gives years a hundred to an aloe-flower :

I gave not five years to a woman's soul.

Had I not drunk at last old wine of love?

I flung her love back on her lovely heart ;

I did not shield her in the wintry day ;

And she has withered up and died and gone.

God, let me perish, so thy beautiful

Be brought with gladness and with singing home.

If thou wilt give her back to me, I vow

To be her slave, and serve her with my soul.

I in my hand will take my heart, and burn

Sweet perfumes on it to relieve her pain.

I, I have ruined her — O God, save thou !

> [*He bends his head upon his knees   LILY comes running up
> to him, stumbling over the graves.*

Lily. Why do they make so many hillocks, father?

The flowers would grow without them.

Julian. So they would.

Lily. What are they for, then?

Julian (aside). I wish I had not
   brought her ;

She *will* ask questions. I must tell her all.

(*Aloud.*) 'Tis where they lay them when the story's
   done.

Lily. What I lay the boys and girls?

Julian. Yes, my own child —

To keep them warm till it begin again.

Lily. Is it dark down there?

> [*Clinging to* JULIAN, *and pointing down.*

Julian. Yes, it is dark , but pleasant — O, so
   sweet !

For out of there come all the pretty flowers.

Lily. Did the church grow out of there, with the
   long stalk

That tries to touch the little frightened clouds?

Julian. It did, my darling. There's a door down
   there

That leads away to where the church is pointing

> [*She is silent for some time, and keeps looking first down and
> then up.* JULIAN *carries her away in his arms.*

SCENE XX. — *Portsmouth*.   LORD SEAFORD, *partially recovered*
Enter LADY GERTRUDE *and* BERNARD.

Lady Gertrude. I have found an old friend, father.

Here he is.

Lord S. Bernard ! Who would have thought to see

you here !

Bern. I came on Lady Gertrude in the street.

I know not which of us was more surprised.

[LADY GERTRUDE *goes.*

Bern. Where is the countess ?

Lord S.   Countess ! What do

you mean ?

I do not know.

Bern.   The Italian lady.

Lord S.   Countess

Lamballa, do you mean ? You frighten me !

Bern. I am glad indeed to know your ignorance ;

For since I saw the count, I would not have you

Wrong one gray hair upon his noble head.

[LORD SEAFORD *covers his eyes with his hands.*

You have not then heard the news about yourself ?

Such interesting morsels reach the last

A man's own ear.   The public has decreed
You and the countess run away together.
'Tis certain she has balked the London Argos,
And that she has been often to your house.
The count believes it — clearly from his face :
The man is dying slowly on his feet.

    Lord S. (*starting up and ringing the bell*).   O God !
    what am I ?   My love burns like hate,
Scorching and blasting with a fiery breath !

    Bern. What the deuce ails you, Seaford ?   Are you
    raving?

             Enter WAITER.

    Lord S. Post-chaise for London — four horses —
    instantly.   [*He sinks exhausted in his chair.*

    SCENE XXI — LILY *in bed.* JULIAN *seated by her.*

    Lily. O father, take me on your knee, and nurse me.
Another story is very nearly done.

             [*He takes her on his knees.*

I am so tired !   Think I should like to go
Down to the warm place that the flowers come from,
Where all the little boys and girls are lying
In little beds — white curtains, and white tassels.

No, no, no — it is so dark down there !

Father will not come near me all the night.

    Julian. You shall not go, my darling ; I will keep

      you.

    Lily. O will you keep me always, father dear ?

And though I sleep ever so sound, still keep me ?

I should be so happy, never to move !

'Tis such a dear well place, here in your arms !

Don't let it take me ; do not let me go :

I cannot leave you, father — love hurts so.

    Julian. Yes, darling ; love does hurt.   It is too

      good

Never to hurt.   Shall I walk with you now,

And try to make you sleep ?

    Lily. Yes — no ; for I should leave you then.   O,

      my head !

Mother, mother, dear mother !   Sing to me, father.

                      [He tries to sing

    O the hurt, the hurt, and the hurt of love !
    Wherever the sun shines, the waters go.
    It hurts the snowdrop, it hurts the dove,
    God on his throne, and man below.

    But sun would not shine, nor waters go,
    Snowdrop tremble, nor fair dove moan,

    13

God be on high, nor man below,
But for love — for the love with its hurt alone.

Thou knowest, O Saviour, its hurt and its sorrows,
Didst rescue its joy by the might of thy pain.
Lord of all yesterdays, days, and to-morrows,
Help us love on in the hope of thy gain.

Hurt as it may, love on, love forever ;
Love for love's sake, like the Father above,
But for whose brave-hearted Son we had never
Known the sweet hurt of the sorrowful love.

[*She sleeps at last. He sits as before, with the child leaning
on his bosom, and falls into a kind of stupor, in
which he talks*

Julian. A voice comes from the vacant, wide sea-
vault ·

Man with the heart, praying for woman's love,

Receive thy prayer   be loved, and take thy choice :

Take this or this   O Heaven and Earth ! I see —

What is it ?   Statue trembling into life

With the first rosy flush upon the skin ?

Or woman-angel, richer by lack of wings ?

I see her — where I know not ; for I see

Nought else : she filleth space, and eyes, and brain —

God keep me ! — in celestial nakedness.

She leaneth forward, looking down in space,

With large eyes full of longing, made intense

By mingled fear of something yet unknown ;

Her arms thrown forward, circling half ; her hands

Half lifted, and half circling, like her arms.

O heavenly artist ! whither hast thou gone

To find my own ideal womanhood —

Glory grown grace, divine to human grown !

I hear the voice again : *Speak but the word :*

She will array herself and come to thee.

Lo, at her white foot lie her solar clothes,

Her earthly dress for work and weary rest

I see a woman-form, laid as in sleep,

Close by the white foot of the wonderful.

It is the same shape, line for line, as she.

Green grass and daisies shadow round her limbs.

Why speak I not the word ?   Clothe thee, and come,

O infinite woman ! my life faints for thee.

Once more the voice : *Stay ! look on this side first.*

I spake of choice.   Look here, O son of man !

Choose then between them.   Ah ! ah !   [*Silence.*

Her I knew

Some ages gone ; the woman who did sail

Down a long river with me to the sea ;
Who gave her lips up freely to my lips,
Her body willingly into my arms ;
Came down from off her statue-pedestal,
And was a woman in a common house,
Not beautified by fancy every day,
And losing worship by her gifts to me.
She gave me that white child — what came of her ?
I have forgot   I opened her great heart,
And filled it half-way to the brim with love —
With love half wine, half vinegar and gall —
And so — and so — she — went away and died ?
O God ! what was it ? — something terrible —
I will not stay to choose, nor look again
Upon the beautiful.   Give me my wife,
The woman of the old time on the earth.
O lovely spirit, fold not thy parted hands,
Nor let thy hair weep like a sunset-rain
From thy bent brows, shadowing thy snowy breasts !
If thou descend to earth, and find no man
To love thee purely, strongly, in his *will*,
Even as he loves the truth, because he will,
And when he cannot see it beautiful —

Then thou mayst weep, and I will help thee weep.

Voice, speak again, and tell my wife to come.

 ''Tis she, 'tis she, low-kneeling at my feet !

In the same dress, same flowing of the hair,

As long ago, on earth : is her face changed ?

Sweet, my love rains on thee, like a warm shower ;

My dove descending rests upon thy head ;

I bless and sanctify thee for my own :

Lift up thy face, and let me look on thee.

   Heavens, what a face !   'Tis hers !   It is not hers !

She rises — turns it up from me to God,

With great rapt orbs, and such a brow ! — the stars

Might find new orbits there, and be content.

O blessed lips, so sweetly closed that sure

Their opening must be prophecy or song ;

A high-entranced maiden, ever pure,

And thronged with burning thoughts of God and

        Truth !

Vanish her garments ; vanishes the silk

That the worm spun, the linen of the flax —

O heavens ! she standeth there, my statue-form,

With the rich golden torrent-hair, white feet,

And hands with rosy palms — my own ideal !

The woman of *my* world, with deeper eyes

Than I had power to think — and yet my Lilia,

My wife, with homely airs of earth about her ;

And dearer to my heart as my lost wife,

Than to my soul as its new-found ideal !

O, Lilia ! teach me ; at thy knees I kneel ,

Make me thy scholar ; speak, and I will hear.

Yea, all eternity —   [*He is roused by a cry from the child*

   Lily. O, father ! put your arms close round about

      me.

Kiss me.   Kiss me harder, father dear.

Now ! I am better now.

      [*She looks long and passionately in his face.   Her eyes close ;*
        her head drops backward.   She is dead.

    SCENE XXII. — *A cottage-room.* LILIA *folding a letter.*

Lilia Now I have told him all ; no word kept back

To burn within me like an evil fire.

And where I am, I have told him ; and I wait

To know his will.   What though he love me not,

If I love him !   I will go back to him,

And wait on him submissive.   'Tis enough

For one life, to be servant to that man !

It was but pride — at best, love stained with pride,

That drove me from him.   He and my sweet child

Must miss my hands, if not my eyes and heart

How lonely is my Lily all the day,

Till he comes home and makes her paradise !

  I go to be his servant.   Every word

That comes from him softer than a command,

I'll count it gain, and lay it in my heart,

And serve him better for it.   He will receive me.

  SCENE XXIII — LILY *lying dead*   JULIAN *bending over her.*

  Julian.   The light of setting suns be on thee, child !

Nay, nay, my child ! the light of rising suns

Is on thee.   Joy is with thee — God is Joy ;

Peace to Himself, and unto us deep joy ;

Joy to Himself, in the reflex of our joy.

Love be with thee ! yea God, for He is Love.

Thou wilt need love, even God's, to give thee joy

Children, they say, are born into a world

Where grief is their first portion : thou, I think,

Never hadst much grief — thy second birth

Into the spirit-world has taught thee grief,

If, orphaned now, thou know'st thy mother's story,

And know'st thy father's hardness   O my God,

Let not my Lily turn away from me.

Now I am free to follow and find *her*.

Thy truer Father took thee home to Him,

That He might grant my prayer, and save my wife.

I thank Him for his gift of thee ; for all

That thou hast taught me, blessed little child.

I love thee, dear, with an eternal love.

And now farewell !   [*Kissing her.*

             No, not farewell ; I come.

Years keep not back, they lead me on to thee.

Yes, they will also lead me on to her.

              Enter a JEW.

  Jew. What is your pleasure with me ?   Here I am,
     sir.

  Julian. Walk into the next room ; then look at
     this,

And tell me what you'll give for everything.   [JEW *goes*

My darling's death has made me almost happy.

Now, now I follow, follow.   I'm young again.

When I have laid my little one to rest,

Among the flowers in that same sunny spot,

Straight from her grave I'll take my pilgrim-way ;

And, calling up all old forgotten skill,

Lapsed social claims, and knowledge of mankind,

I'll be a man once more in the loud world

Revived experience in its winding ways,

Senses and wits made sharp by sleepless love,

If all the world were sworn to secrecy,

Will guide me to her, sure as questing Death.

I'll follow my wife, follow until I die.

How shall I face the Shepherd of the sheep.

Without the one ewe-lamb He gave to me?

How find her in great Hades if not here,

In this poor little round O of a world?

I'll follow my wife, follow until I find.

Reënter JEW.

Well, how much?   Name your sum.   Be liberal.

Jew. Let me see this room, too.   The things are all

Old-fashioned and ill-kept.   They're worth but little.

Julian. Say what you will — only make haste and go.

Jew. Say twenty pounds.

Julian.   Well, fetch the money at once,

And take possession.   But make haste, I pray.

SCENE XXIV — *The country church-yard.* JULIAN *standing by*
LILY'S *new-filled grave.   He looks very worn and ill.*

Julian.   Now I can leave thee safely to thy sleep ;
Thou wilt not wake and miss me, my fair child !
Nor will they, for she's fair, steal this ewe-lamb,
Out of this fold, while I am gone to seek
And find the wandering mother of my lamb.
I cannot weep ; I know thee with me still.
Thou dost not find it very dark down there?
Would I could go to thee ; I long to go ;
My limbs are tired ; my eyes are sleepy, too ;
And fain my heart would cease this beat, beat, beat.
O gladly would I come to thee, my child,
And lay my head upon thy little heart,
And sleep in the divine munificence
Of thy great love !   But my night has not come :
She is not rescued yet ; and I must go

> [*He turns, but sinks on the grave.   Recovering and rising.*

Now for the world — that's Italy and her.

SCENE XXV — *The empty room, formerly* LILIA'S   *Enter*
JULIAN.

Julian.   How am I here ?   Alas !   I do not know.
I should have been at sea.   Ah ! now I know !

I have come here to die.   *[Lies down on the floor.*

Where's Lilia ?

I cannot find her.   She is here, I know.

But O these endless passages and stairs,

And dreadful shafts of darkness !   Lilia !

Lilia ! wait for me, child ; I'm coming fast,

But something holds me.   Let me go, devil !

My Lilia, have faith ; they cannot hurt you.

You are God's child — they dare not touch you, wife.

O pardon me, my beautiful, my own !   *[Sings.*

> Wind, wind, thou blowest many a drifting thing
> From sheltering cove, down to the unsheltered sea ;
> Thou blowest to the sea my blue sail's wing —
> Us to a new, love-lit futurity .
>> Out to the ocean fleet and float —
>> Blow, blow my little leaf-like boat.

[While he sings, enter LORD SEAFORD, *pale and haggard.*
    JULIAN *descries him suddenly*

What are you, man ?   O brother, bury me —

There's money in my pocket —

[Emptying the Jew's gold on the floor.

by my child.

[Staring at him.

  O ! you are Death.   Go, saddle the pale horse —

I will not walk — I'll ride What, skeleton !

I cannot sit him! ha! ha!   Hither, brute!

Here, Lilia, do the lady's task, my child,

And buckle on my spurs.   I'll send him up

With a gleam through the blue, snorting white foam-
    flakes.

Ah me! I have not won my golden spurs,

Nor is there any maid to bind them on:

I will not ride the horse, I'll walk with thee.

Come, Death, give me thine arm, poor slave!—we'll go.

    Lord Seaford (stooping over him).   I am Seaford,
    Count.

    Julian. Seaford!   What Seaford?   [*Recollecting*

       Seaford!   [*Springing to his feet.*

        Where is my wife?

      [*He falls into* SEAFORD'S *arms.   He lays him down.*

    Lord S. Had I seen *him*, she had been safe for me.

                              [*Goes.*

    [JULIAN *lies motionless.   Insensibility passes into sleep.*
    He wakes calm, in the sultry dusk of a summer
    evening.

    Julian. Still, still alive!   I thought that I was dead.

I had a frightful dream!   'Tis gone, thank God!

                       [*He is quiet a little.*

So then thou didst not take the child away

That I might find my wife !   Thy will be done
Thou wilt not let me go.   This last desire
I send away with grief, but willingly.
I have prayed to thee, and thou hast heard my prayer:
Take thou thine own way, only lead her home.
Cleanse her, O Lord.   I cannot know thy might ;
But thou art mighty, with a power unlike
All, all that we know by the name of power,
Transcending it as intellect transcends
The stone upon the ground — it may be more ;
For these are both created — thou creator,
Lonely, supreme.
              Now it is almost over,
My spirit's journey through this strange sad world ;
This part is done, whatever cometh next
Morning and evening have made out their day ;
My sun is going down in stormy dark,
But I will face it fearless
                    The first act
Is over of the drama.   Is it so ?
What means the dim dawn of half-memories
Of something I knew once and know not now —
Of something differing from all this earth ?

I cannot tell ; I care not — only know

That God will keep the living thing He made.

How mighty must He be to have the right

Of swaying this great power I feel I am,

Moulding and forming it, as pleaseth Him !

O God, I come to thee, thou art my life ;

O God, thou art my home, I come to thee.

　　Can this be death ?　Lo ! I am lifted up

Large-eyed into the night.　Nothing I see

But that which *is*, the living awful Truth ;

All forms of which are but the sparks flung out

From the luminous ocean clothing round the sun,

Himself all dark.　Ah ! I remember me :

Christ said to Martha — " Whosoever liveth,

And doth believe in me, shall never die."

I wait, I wait, expecting, till the door

Of God's wide theatre be open flung

To let me in.　What wonders I shall see !

The expectation fills me, like new life

Dancing through all my veins.

　　　　　　　　　Once more I thank thee

For all that thou hast made me — most of all,

That thou didst make me wonder and seek thee.

I thank thee for my wife : to thee I trust her ;

Forget her not, my God.   If thou save her,

I shall be able then to thank thee so

As will content thee — with full-flowing song,

The very bubbles on whose dancing waves

Are daring thoughts flung faithful at thy feet.

   My heart sinks in me — I grow faint.   O ! whence

This wind of love that fans me out of life ?

One stoops to kiss me — ah, my lily child !

God hath not flung thee over his garden wall.

> [*Reenter* LORD SEAFORD *with the doctor.* JULIAN *takes no heed of them. The doctor shakes his head.*

My little child, I'll never leave thee more ;

We are both children now in God's big house.

Come, lead me ; you are older here than I

By three whole days, my darling angel-child !

> [*A letter is brought in.* LORD SEAFORD *holds it before* JULIAN'S *eyes. He looks vaguely at it.*

Lord S. It is a letter from your wife, I think.

Julian (*feebly*). A letter from my Lilia !   Bury it

   with me —

I'll read it in my chamber, by and by :

Dear words should not be read with others nigh.

Lilia, my wife ! I am going home to God.

Lord S. (bending over him). I'll pledge my soul your

wife is innocent.

> [J<small>ULIAN</small> *gazes at him blankly. A light begins to grow in his
> eyes. It grows till his face is transfigured. It vanishes.
> He dies.*

END OF PART IV.

WITHIN AND WITHOUT.

PART V.

AND do not fear to hope.   Can poet's brain
More than the father's heart rich good invent?
Each time we smell the autumn's dying scent,
We know the primrose time will come again ;
Not more we hope, nor less would soothe our pain.
Be bounteous in thy faith, for not misspent
Is confidence unto the Father lent :
Thy need is sown and rooted for his rain.
His thoughts are as thine own . nor are his ways
Other than thine, but by their loftier sense
Of beauty infinite and love intense.
Work on.   One day, beyond all thoughts of praise,
A sunny joy will crown thee with its rays ;
Nor other than thy need, thy recompense.

PART V.

A DREAM.

SCENE I. — *" A world not realized."* LILY. *To her,* JULIAN

Lily. **O**FATHER, come with me! I have found her — mother

SCENE II. —*A room in a cottage* LILIA *on her knees before a crucifix. Her back only is seen, for the Poet dares not look on her face On a chair beside her lies a book, open at CHAPTER VIII. Behind her stands an* ANGEL, *bending forward, as if to protect her with his wings partly expanded Appear* JULIAN, *with* LILY *in his arms LILY looks with love on the angel, and a kind of longing fear on her mother.*

Julian. Angel, thy part is done ; leave her to me.

Angel Sorrowful man, to thee I must give place ;
Thy ministry is stronger far than mine ;
Yet have I done my part.   She sat with him.
He gave her rich white flowers with crimson scent,
The tuberose and datura ever burning
Their incense to the dusky face of night.
He spoke to her pure words of lofty sense,

But tinged with poison for a tranced ear.

He bade low music sound of faint farewells,

Which fixed her eyes upon a leafy picture,

Wherein she wandered through an amber twilight

Towards a still grave in a sleepy nook.

And ever and anon she sipped pale wine,

Rose-tinged, rose-odored, from a silver cup.

He sang a song, each pause of which closed up,

Like a day-wearied daisy for the night,

With these words falling like an echo low:

" Love, let us love and weep and faint and die "

With the last pause the tears flowed at their will,

Without a sob, down from their cloudy skies.

He took her hand in his, and it lay still.

A blast of music from a wandering band

Billowed the air with sudden storm that moment.

The visible rampart of material things

Was rent — the vast eternal void looked in

Upon her awe-struck soul   She cried and fled.

It was the sealing of her destiny.

A wild convulsion shook her inner world ;

Its lowest depths were heaved tumultuously ;

Far unknown molten gulfs of being rushed

Up into mountain-peaks, rushed and remained.

The soul that led a fairy life, athirst

For beauty only, passed into a woman's:

In pain and tears was born the child-like need

For God, for Truth, and for essential Love.

But first she woke in terror, was alone,

For God she saw not; woke up in the night,

The great wide night.   No mother's hand had she

To soothe her pangs, no father's voice to cheer.

She would not come to thee, for love itself

Too keenly stung her sad, repentant heart,

Giving her bitter names to name herself;

But calling back old words which thou hadst spoken

In other days, by light winds borne away,

Returning in the storm of wretchedness,

Hither she came to seek her Julian's God.

So now farewell!   My care of her is over.

 Julian. A heart that knows what thou canst never

  know,

Fair angel, blesseth thee, and saith, farewell.

> [*The angel goes* JULIAN *and* LILY *take his place.* LILIA
> *is praying, and they hear parts of her prayer.*

Lilia. O Jesus, hear me !   Let me speak to thee.

No fear oppresses me ; for misery

Fills my heart up too full for any fear.

Is there no help, O Holy ?   Am I stained

Beyond release ?

Julian.   Lilia, thy purity

Maketh thy heart abuse thee.   I, thy husband,

Sinned more against thee, in believing ill,

Than thou, by ten times what thou didst, poor child,

Hadst wronged thy husband.

Lilia.   Pardon will not do ;

I need much more, O Master.   That word *go*

Surely thou didst not speak to send away

The sinful wife thou wouldst not yet condemn !

Or was that crime, though not too great for pardon,

Too great for loving-kindness afterwards ?

Certain, she came again behind thy feet,

And weeping, wiped, and kissed them, Mary's son !

Blessed forever with a heavenly grief.

Ah ! she nor I can claim with her who gave

The best she had, her tears, her hair, her lips,

To soothe feet hard with Galilean roads ·

She sinned against herself, not against — Julian.

O God, O God, find some excuse for me

Wilt thou not find something to say for me,

As for the crowd that cried against thee, then,

When heaven was dark, because thy lamp burned

    low ?

   Julian. Not thou, but I am guilty, Lilia.

I made it possible to tempt thee, child.

Thou didst not fall, beloved ; only, one moment

Beauty was queen, and Truth not lord of all.

   Lilia. O Julian, my husband — it is strange —

But when I think of Him, He looks like thee ;

And when He speaks to comfort me, the voice

Is like thy voice, my husband, my beloved !

O ! if I could but lie down at thy feet,

And tell thee all, yes, every word, I know

That thou wouldst think the best that could be

    thought,

And love and comfort me.   O Julian,

I am more thine than ever.   Forgive me, husband,

For calling me, defiled and outcast, thine.

Yet may I not be thine as I am His ?

Would I might be thy servant — yes, thy slave,

To wash thy feet, and dress thy lovely child,

And bring her at thy call — more wife than I.

But I shall never see thee, till the earth

Lies on us both — apart — O, far apart !

How lonely shall I lie the long, long years !

   Lily. O mother, there are blue skies here, and

      flowers,

And blowing winds, and kisses, mother dear.

And every time my father kisses me,

It is not father only, but Another.

Make haste and come.   My head never aches here.

   Lilia. Can it be that they are dead ?   Is it possible?

I feel as if they were near me !   Speak again,

Beloved voices ! comfort me ; I need it.

   Julian (*singing*).

        Come to us ; above the storm
          Ever shines the blue
        Come to us : beyond its form
          Ever lies the True.

   Lily (*singing*).

        Mother, darling, do not weep -
          All I cannot tell
        By and by, you'll go to sleep,
          And you'll wake so well.

   Julian (*singing*)

        There is sunshine everywhere
          For thy heart and mine :

> God, for every sin and care,
>   Is the cure divine.

Lily (*singing*).

> We're so happy all the day,
>   Waiting for another :
> All the flowers and sunshine stay,
>   Waiting for you, mother.

Julian. My maiden ! for true wife is maiden ever

To the true husband : thou art mine forever.

Lilia. What gentle hopes are passing to and fro!

Thou shadowest me with thine own rest, my God ,

A cloud from thee stoops down and covers me.

> [*She falls asleep on her knees.*

SCENE III. — JULIAN *on the summit of a mountain-peak. The stars are brilliant around a crescent moon, hanging half-way between the mountain and the sky. Below lies a sea of vapor. Beyond rises a loftier pinnacle, across which is stretched a bar of cloud.* LILY *lies on the cloud, looking earnestly into the mist below*

Julian (*gazing upwards*). And thou wert with me
    all the time, my God,

Even as now !   I was not far from thee.

Thy spirit spoke in all my wants and fears,

And hopes and longings.   Thou art all in all.

I am not mine, but thine.   I cannot speak

The thoughts that work within me like a sea.

When on the earth I lay, crushed down beneath
The hopeless weight of empty desolation,
Thy sympathizing face was lighted then
With expectation of my joy to come,
When all the realm of possible ill should lie
Under my feet, and I should stand as now
All-sure of thee, true-hearted, only One.
Was ever heart filled to such overflowing
With the pure wine of blessedness, my God?
Filled as the night with stars, am I with joys;
Filled as the heavens with thee, am I with peace;
For now I wait the end of all my prayers,
Of all that have to do with old-world things:
What new things come to wake new prayers, my God,
Thou knowest, and I wait in perfect peace.

> [*He turns his gaze downwards. From the fog-sea below half
> rises a woman-form, which floats towards him.*

Lo, as the lily lifts its shining bosom
Above the couch of waters where it slept,
When the bright morn toucheth and waketh it;
So riseth up my lily from the deep
Where human souls are tried in awful dreams.

> [LILY *spies her mother, darts down into the fog, and is
> caught in her arms. They land on* JULIAN'S *peak,
> and climb,* LILY *leading her mother.*

Lily. Come faster, mother dear ; father is waiting.

Lilia. Have patience with me, darling By and by,
I think I shall do better.   O my Julian!

Julian. I may not help her.   She must climb and
   come.

   [*He reaches his hand, and the three are clasped in infinite
   embrace.*

O God, thy thoughts, thy ways, are not as ours :
They fill our longing hearts up to the brim.

   [*The moon and the stars and the blue night close around
   them , and the Poet awakes from his dream*

THE END.

A HIDDEN LIFE.

CONTENTS.

———◆———

		PAGE
A HIDDEN LIFE		I
POEMS:—		
A STORY OF THE SEA-SHORE . . .	61
TO LADY NOEL BYRON	86
TO THE SAME	86
TO AURELIO SAFFI . . .	87
THE DISCIPLE	89

THE GOSPEL WOMEN :—

I. THE MOTHER MARY	139
II THE WOMAN THAT LIFTED UP HER VOICE	149
III. THE MOTHER OF ZEBEDEE'S CHILDREN .	151
IV THE SYRO-PHŒNICIAN WOMAN . .	153
V. THE WIDOW OF NAIN	155
VI. THE WOMAN WHOM SATAN HAD BOUND .	158
VII THE WOMAN WHO CAME BEHIND HIM IN THE CROWD	160
VIII. THE WIDOW WITH THE TWO MITES . .	161
XI THE WOMEN WHO MINISTERED UNTO HIM .	163
X. PILATE'S WIFE	163
XI THE WOMAN OF SAMARIA	165
XII MARY MAGDALENE	166
XIII. THE WOMAN IN THE TEMPLE . . .	169

THE GOSPEL WOMEN : — *continued.*

PAGE

XIV. MARTHA 172

XV. MARY 174

XVI. THE WOMAN THAT WAS A SINNER . . . 178

A BOOK OF SONNETS : —

THE BURNT OFFERING 185

THE UNSEEN FACE 186

CONCERNING JESUS 187

A MEMORIAL OF AFRICA 201

A. M. D. 203

TO GARIBALDI 204

TO S. F. S. 205

ORGAN SONGS : —

TO A. J. SCOTT 209

LIGHT 211

TO A. J. SCOTT 225

I WOULD I WERE A CHILD 227

A PRAYER FOR THE PAST 230

LONGING 238

I KNOW WHAT BEAUTY IS 241

SYMPATHY 243

THE THANK-OFFERING 245

PRAYER 247

REST 248

O DO NOT LEAVE ME 252

BLESSED ARE THE MEEK, FOR THEY SHALL INHERIT

THE EARTH 253

HYMN FOR A SICK GIRL 255

A CHRISTMAS CAROL FOR 1862 257

CONTENTS.

ORGAN SONGS:—*continued.*   PAGE

    A Christmas Carol 260

    The Sleepless Jesus 262

    The Children's Heaven 264

    Rejoice 267

    The Grace of Grace 269

    Antiphony 270

    Dorcas 273

    Marriage Song 275

    Blind Bartimæus 277

    Come unto Me 279

    Morning Hymn 281

    Noontide 283

    Evening Hymn 284

    The Holy Midnight 285

TO

MY FATHER.

I.

TAKE of the first fruits, Father, of thy care,
  Wrapped in the fresh leaves of my gratitude,
  Late waked for early gifts ill understood;
Claiming in all my harvests rightful share,
Whether with song that mounts the joyful air
  I praise my God, or, in yet deeper mood,
  Sit dumb because I know a speechless good,
Needing no voice, but all the soul for prayer.
  Thou hast been faithful to my highest need;
And I, thy debtor, ever, evermore,
Shall never feel the grateful burden sore.
  Yet most I thank thee, not for any deed,
  But for the sense thy living self did breed
That fatherhood is at the great world's core.

II.

All childhood, reverence clothed thee, undefined,
  As for some being of another race;

Ah ! not with it, departing — grown apace,
As years have brought me manhood's loftier mind
Able to see thy human life behind —

The same hid heart, the same revealing face —
My own dim contest settling into grace
Of sorrow, strife, and victory combined.

So I beheld my God, in childhood's morn,
A mist, a darkness, great, and far apart,
Moveless and dim — I scarce could say *Thou art*.

My manhood came, of joy and sadness born —
Full soon the misty dark, asunder torn,
Revealed man's glory, God's great human heart

G. M. D. J<small>R</small>.

A<small>LGIERS</small>, *April*, 1857.

A HIDDEN LIFE.

——◆——

PROUDLY the youth, sudden with manhood
        crowned,
Went walking by his horses, the first time
That morning, to the plough. No soldier gay
Feels at his side the throb of the gold hilt
(Knowing the blue blade hides within its sheath,
As lightning in the cloud) with more delight,
When first he belts it on, than he that day
Heard still the clank of the plough-chains against
The horses' harnessed sides, as to the field
They went to make it fruitful. O'er the hill
The sun looked down, baptizing him for toil.

    A farmer's son, a farmer's grandson he ;
Yea, his great-grandsire had possessed those fields.
Tradition said they had been tilled by men
Who bore the name long centuries ago,
And married wives, and reared a stalwart race,

And died, and went where all had followed them,
Save one old man, his daughter, and the youth
Who ploughs in pride, nor ever doubts his toil ;
And death is far from him this sunny morn.
Why should we think of death when life is high ?
The earth laughs all the day, and sleeps all night.
The daylight's labor and the night's repose
Are very good, each better in its time.

   The boy knew little ; but he read old tales
Of Scotland's warriors, till his blood ran swift
As charging knights upon their death career.
He chanted ancient tunes, till the wild blood
Was charmed back into its fountain-well,
And tears arose instead.   That poet's songs,
Whose music evermore recalls his name,
His name of waters babbling as they run,
Rose from him in the fields among the kine,
And met the skylark's, raining from the clouds.
But only as the birds he sang as yet,
From rooted impulse of essential song ,
The earth was fair — he knew not it was fair ;
His heart was glad — he knew not it was glad :
He walked as in a twilight of the sense,
Which this one day shall turn to tender light.

Long ere the sun had cleared the feathery tops
Of the fir-thicket on the eastward hill,
His horses leaned and labored. Each great hand
Held rein and plough-stilt in one guiding grasp —
No ploughman there would brook a helper. Proud
With a true ploughman's pride — nobler, I think,
Than statesman's, ay, or poet's, painter's pride,
For little praise will come that he ploughs well :
He did plough well, proud of his work itself,
And not of what would follow. With sure eye,
He saw his horses keep the arrow-track ;
He saw the swift share cut the measured sod ;
He saw the furrow folding to the right,
Ready with nimble foot to aid at need :
Turning its secrets upward to the sun,
And hiding in the dark the sun-born grass,
And daisies dipped in carmine, lay the tilth —
A million graves to nurse the buried grain,
And send a golden harvest up the air.

When the steep sun had clomb to his decline,
And pausing seemed, at edge of slow descent,
Upon the key-stone of his airy bridge,
They rested likewise, half-tired man and horse,

And homeward went for food and courage new.
Therewith refreshed, they turned again to toil,
And lived in labor all the afternoon;
Till, in the gloaming, once again the plough
Lay like a stranded bark upon the lea,
And home with hanging neck the horses went,
Walking beside their master, force by will.
Then through the lengthening shadows came a show.
   It was a lady mounted on a horse,
A slender girl upon a mighty steed,
That bore her with the pride horses must feel
When they submit to women. Home she went,
Alone, or else her groom lagged far behind.
Scarce had she bent simple acknowledgment
Of the hand in silent salutation lifted
To the bowed head, when something faithless yielded,
The saddle slipped, the horse stopped, and the girl
Stood on her feet, still holding fast the reins.
   Three paces bore him bounding to her side,
Her radiant beauty almost fixed him there,
But with main force, as one that grapples fear,
He threw the fascination off, and saw
The work before him Soon his hand and knife

Had set the saddle firmer than before
Upon the gentle horse ; and then he turned
To mount the maiden.   But bewilderment
A moment lasted ; for he knew not how,
With stirrup-hand and steady arm, to throne,
Elastic, on her steed, the ascending maid :
A moment only ; for while yet she thanked,
Nor yet had time to teach her further will,
About her waist he put his brawny hands,
That all but zoned her round ; and like a child
Lifting her high, he set her on the horse ;
Whence like a risen moon she smiled on him,
Nor turned aside, although a radiant blush
Shone in her cheek, and shadowed in her eyes.
But he was never sure if from her heart
Or from the rosy sunset came the flush.
Again she thanked him, while again he stood
Bewildered in her beauty.   Not a word
Answered her words that flowed, folded in tones
Round which dissolving lambent music played,
Like dropping water in a silver cup ;
Till, round the shoulder of the neighboring hill,
Sudden she disappeared.   And he awoke,

And called himself hard names, and turned and went
After his horses, bending too his head.

Ah God! when Beauty passes from the door,
Although she came not in, the house is bare:
Shut, shut the door; there 's nothing in the house.
Why seems it always that she should be ours?
A secret lies behind which thou dost know,
And I can partly guess.

                          But think not then,
The holder of the plough sighed many sighs
Upon his bed that night; or other dreams
Than pleasant rose upon his view in sleep;
Nor think the airy castles of his brain
Had less foundation than the air admits.
But read my simple tale, scarce worth the name;
And answer, if he had not from the fair
Beauty's best gift; and proved her not, in sooth,
An angel vision from a higher world.

Not much of her I tell Her glittering life,
Where part the waters on the mountain-ridge,
Ran down the southern side, apart from his,
Yet was not over-blessed; for, I know,
Her tale wiled many sighs, one summer eve,

From him who in the mysteries of a wood
Walking, received it from beloved lips.
But now she was as God had made her, ere
The world had tried to spoil her; tried, I say,
And half-succeeded, failing utterly.
Fair was she, frank, and innocent as a child
That stares in every eye; fearless of ill,
Because she knew it not; and brave withal,
Because she led a simple country life,
Much in the open air. Her father's house —
A Scottish laird was he, of ancient name —
Was but two miles away among the hills;
Yet often as she passed his father's farm,
The youth had never seen her face before,
And should not twice. Yet was it not enough?
The vision tarried. She, as the harvest-moon
That goeth on her way, and knoweth not
The fields of corn whose ripening grain she fills
With strength of life, and hope, and joy for men,
Went on her way, and knew not of the virtue
Gone out of her; yea, never thought of him,
Save at such times as, all at once, old scenes
Return uncalled, with wonder that they come.

Soon was she orphaned of her parent-haunts,
And rounded with dead glitter, not the shine
Of leaves and waters dancing in the sun;
But he abode in ever-breaking dawns,
Breathed ever new-born winds into his soul;
And saw the aurora of a greater dawn
Climbing the hill-sides of the heapy world.

   Again I say, no fond romance of love,
No argument of possibilities,
If he were some one, and she sought his help,
Turned his clear brain into a nest of dreams
As soon he had sat down and twisted cords
To snare, and carry home for daylight aid,
Some woman-angel, wandering half seen
On moonlight wings, o'er withered autumn fields.
But when he rose next morn, and went abroad
(The exultation of his new-found rank
Already settling into dignity),
He found the earth was beautiful. The sky
Shone with the expectation of the sun.
He grieved him for the daisies, for they fell
Caught in the furrow, with their innocent heads
Just out imploring. A gray hedgehog ran

With tangled mesh of bristling spikes, and face
Helplessly innocent, across the field :
He let it run, and blessed it as it ran.
Returned at noon-tide, something drew his feet
Into the barn : entering, he gazed and stood.
For, through the rent roof lighting, one sunbeam
Blazed on the yellow straw one golden spot,
Dulled all the amber heap, and sinking far,
Like flame inverted, through the loose-piled mound,
Crossed the keen splendor with dark shadow straws,
In lines innumerable. 'Twas so bright,
His eye was cheated with a spectral smoke
That rose as from a fire. He had not known
How beautiful the sunlight was, not even
Upon the windy fields of morning grass,
Nor on the river, nor the ripening corn.
As if to catch a wild live thing, he crept
On tiptoe silent, laid him on the heap,
And gazing down into the glory gulf,
Dreamed as a boy half sleeping by the fire ;
And dreaming rose, and got his horses out.

    God, and not woman, is the heart of all.
But she, as priestess of the visible earth,

Holding the key, herself most beautiful,
Had come to him, and flung the portals wide.
He entered in: each beauty was a glass
That gleamed the woman back upon his view.
Shall I not rather say: each beauty gave
Its own soul up to him who worshipped her,
For that his eyes were opened thus to see?
  Already in these hours his quickened soul
Put forth the white tip of a floral bud,
Ere long to be a crown-like, aureole flower.
His songs unbidden, his joy in ancient tales,
Had hitherto alone betrayed the seed
That lay in his heart, close hidden even from him,
Yet not the less mellowing all his spring:
Like summer sunshine came the maiden's face,
And in the youth's glad heart the seed awoke.
It grew and spread, and put forth many flowers,
And every flower a living open eye,
Until his soul was full of eyes within.
Each morning now was a fresh boon to him;
Each wind a spiritual power upon his life;
Each individual animal did share
A common being with him; every kind

Of flower from every other was distinct,

Uttering that for which alone it was —

Its something human, wrapt in other veil.

   And when the winter came, when thick the snow

Armed the sad fields from gnawing of the frost,

When the low sun but skirted his far realms,

And sank in early night, he drew his chair

Beside the fire; and by the feeble lamp

Read book on book ; and wandered other climes,

And lived in other lives and other needs,

And grew a larger self by other selves.

Ere long, the love of knowledge had become

A hungry passion and a conscious power,

And craved for more than reading could supply.

Then, through the night (all dark, except the moon

Shone frosty o'er the heath, or the white snow

Gave back such motes of light as else had sunk

In the dark earth) he bent his plodding way

Over the moors to where the little town

Lay gathered in the hollow. There the student

Who taught from lingering dawn to early dark,

Had older scholars in the long fore-night ;

For youths who in the shop, or in the barn,

Or at the loom, had done their needful work,
Came gathering through starlight, fog, or snow,
And found the fire ablaze, the candles lit,
And him who knew waiting for who would know.
Here mathematics wiled him to their heights;
And strange consent of lines to form and law
Made Euclid a profound romance of truth.
The master saw with wonder that the youth
So eagerly devoured the offered food;
And longed to lead him further; for fair knowledge
Would multiply like life; and two clear souls
That see one truth, and, turning, also see
Each other's face glow in that truth's delight,
Are something more than lovers. So he offered
To guide him through the narrow ways that lead
To lofty heights of Roman speech. The youth
Caught at the offer; and for many a night,
When others slept, he groped his twilight way
With lexicon and rule, through ancient story,
Or fable fine, embalmed in Latin old;
Wherein his knowledge of the English tongue
(Through reading many books) much aided him, —
For the best is alike in every tongue.

At length his progress, through the master's word,
Proud of such pupil, reached the father's ears.
Great gladness woke within him, and he vowed,
If caring, sparing might accomplish it,
He should to college, and should have his fill
Of that same learning.

                To the plough no more,
All day to school he went ; and ere a year,
He wore the scarlet gown with the closed sleeves.
  Awkward at first, but with a dignity
Soon finding fit embodiment in speech
And gesture and address, he made his way,
Not seeking such, to the full-orbed respect
Of students and professors ; for whose praise
More than his worth, society, so called,
To its rooms in that great city of the North,
Invited him. He entered. Dazzled at first
By brilliance of the outer show, the lights,
The mirrors, gems, white necks, and radiant eyes,
He stole into a corner, and was quiet
Until the vision too had quieter grown.
Bewildered next by many a sparkling word,
Nor knowing the light-play of polished minds,

Which, like rose-diamonds cut in many facets,
Catch and reflect the wandering rays of truth
As if they were home-born and issuing new,
He held his peace, and, silent soon began
To see how little fire it needs to shine.
Hence, in the midst of talk, his thoughts would
        wander
Back to the calm divine of homely toil;
And round him still and ever hung an air
Of breezy fields, and plough, and cart, and scythe —
A kind of clumsy grace, in which gay girls
Saw but the clumsiness — another sort
Saw the grace too, yea, sometimes, when he spoke,
Saw the grace only; and began at last,
For he sought none, to seek him in the crowd,
And find him unexpected, maiden-wise.

But oftener far they sought than found him thus,
For seldom was he drawn away from toil.
Seldomer yet he stinted toil's due time;
For if one eve his panes were dark, the next
They gleamed far into morning. And he won
Honors among the first, each session's close.
Nor think that new familiarity

With open forms of ill, not to be shunned
Where many youths are met, endangered much
A mind that had begun to will the pure.
Oft when the broad rich humor of a jest
With breezy force drew in its skirts a troop
Of pestilential vapors following —
Arose within his sudden silent mind,
The maiden face that once blushed down on him,
That lady face, insphered beyond his earth,
Yet visible as bright, particular star.
A flush of tenderness then glowed across
His bosom — shone it clean from passing harm.
Should that sweet face be banished by rude words?
It could not stay what maidens might not hear.
He almost wept for shame, that face, that jest
Should meet in *his* house: to his love he made
Love's only worthy offering — purity.

And if the homage that he sometimes met,
New to the country lad, conveyed in smiles,
Assents, and silent listenings when he spoke,
Threatened yet more his life's simplicity,
An antidote of nature ever came,
Even Nature's self. For, in the summer months,

His former haunts and boyhood's circumstance
Received him to the bosom of their grace.
And he, too noble to despise the past,
Too proud to be ashamed of manly toil,
Too wise to fancy that a gulf lay wide
Betwixt the laboring hand and thinking brain,
Or that a workman was no gentleman
Because a workman, clothed himself again
In his old garments, took the hoe, the spade,
The sowing sheet, or covered in the grain,
Smoothing with harrows what the plough had ridged.
With ever fresher joy he hailed the fields,
Returning still with larger powers of sight:
Each time he knew them better than before,
And yet their sweetest aspect was the old.
His labor kept him true to life and fact,
Casting out worldly judgments, false desires,
And vain distinctions. Ever, at his toil,
New thoughts arose; which, when still night awoke,
He ever sought, like stars, with instruments;
By science, or by wise philosophy,
Bridging the gulf betwixt the new and old.
Thus labored he with hand and brain at once,

Preparing for the time when Scotland's sons
Reap wisdom in the silence of the year.

His sire was proud of him ; and, most of all,
Because his learning did not make him proud.
A wise man builds not much upon his lore.
The neighbors asked what he would make his son
"I'll make a man of him," the old man said ;
"And for the rest, just what he likes himself.
He is my only son — I think he'll keep
The old farm on, and I shall go content,
Leaving a man behind me, as I say."

So four years long his life went to and fro,
Alternating the red gown and blue coat,
The garret study and the wide-floored barn,
The wintry city and the sunny fields.
In every change his mind was well content,
For in himself he was the growing same.

Nor in one channel flowed his seeking thoughts ,
To no profession did he ardent turn :
He knew his father's wish — it was his own.
"Why should a man," he said, "when knowledge
        grows,
Leave therefore the old patriarchal life,

And seek distinction in the noise of men?"
He turned his asking face on every side;
Went reverent with the anatomist, and saw
The inner form of man laid skillful bare;
Went with the chemist, whose wise-questioning hand
Made Nature do in little, before his eyes,
And momently, what, huge, for centuries,
And in the veil of vastness and lone deeps,
She labors at; bent his inquiring eye
On every source whence knowledge flows for men:
At some he only sipped, at others drank.

At length, when he had gained the master's right —
A custom sacred from of old — to sit
With covered head before the awful rank
Of black-gowned senators; and each of those,
Proud of his pupil, was ready at a word
To speed him on towards any further goal;
He took his books, his well-worn cap and gown,
And, leaving with a sigh the ancient walls,
The grand old crown of stone, unchanging gray
In all the blandishments of youthful spring,
He sought for life the lone ancestral farm.

With simple gladness met him on the road

His gray-haired father — elder brother now.

Few words were spoken, little welcome said,

But on each side the more was understood.

If with a less delight he brought him home

Than he who met the prodigal returned,

It was with more reliance, with more peace;

For with the leaning pride that old men feel

In young strong arms that draw their might from
    them,

He led him to the house. His sister there,

Whose kisses were not many, but whose eyes

Were full of watchfulness and hovering love,

Set him beside the fire in the old place,

And heaped the table with best country fare.

  When the swift night grew deep, the father rose,

And led him, wondering why and where they went,

Through the limpid dark, with tortuous path

Between the corn-ricks, to a loft above

The stable, where the same old horses slept

Which he had guided that eventful morn.

Entering, he saw some plan-pursuing hand

Had been at work. The father, leading on

Across the floor, heaped high with store of grain,

Opened a door. An unexpected light
Flashed on him cheerful from a fire and lamp,
That burned alone, as in a fairy tale.
Behold! a little room, a curtained bed,
An easy-chair, book-shelves, and writing desk,
An old print of a deep Virgilian wood,
And one of choosing Hercules! The youth
Gazed and spoke not. The old paternal love
Had sought and found an incarnation new ;
For, honoring in his son the simple needs
Which his own bounty had begot in him,
He gave him thus a lonely thinking space,
A silent refuge. With a quiet good-night,
He left him dumb with love. Faintly beneath,
The horses stamped and drew the lengthening chain.

   Three sliding years, with slowly blended change,
Drew round their winter, summer, autumn, spring,
Fulfilled of work by hands, and brain, and heart.
He labored as before ; though when he would,
And Nature urged not, he, with privilege,
Would spare from hours of toil,— read in his room,
Or wander through the moorland to the hills ;
There on the apex of the world would stand,

As on an altar, burning, soul and heart,
Himself the sacrifice of faith and prayer ;
Gaze in the face of the inviting blue
That domed him round ; ask why it should be blue ;
Pray yet again ; and with love-strengthened heart
Go down to lower things with lofty cares.

When Sundays came, the father, daughter, son
Walked to the church across their own loved fields.
It was an ugly church, with scarce a sign
Of what makes English churches venerable.
Likest a crowing cock upon a heap
It stood — but let us say — St. Peter's cock ;
For, sure, it lacked not many a holy charm
To whom it was coeval with his being —
Dawning with it from darkness of the unseen.
And the low mounds of monumental grass
Were far more solemn than great marble tombs ;
For flesh is grass, its goodliness the flower.
O, lovely is the face of country graves
On sunny afternoons ! The light itself
Nestles amidst the grass ; and the sweet wind
Says, *I am here*, — no more. With sun and wind
And crowing cocks, who can believe in death ?

He, on such days, when from the church they came,
And through God's ridges took their thoughtful way,
The last psalm lingering lowly in their hearts,
Would look, inquiring where his ridge would rise;
But when it gloomed and rained, he turned aside ·
What mattered it to him?

                    And as they walked
Home from the church, the father loved to hear
The fresh rills pouring from his son's clear well.
For the old man clung not to the old alone;
Nor leaned the young man only to the new:
They would the best, and sought, and followed it.
The pastor's lore was sound, his teaching poor;
The Past alone he cherished, said our friend;
Honored those Jewish times as he were a Jew,
But had no ear for this poor needy hour,
Which wanders up and down the centuries,
Like beggar boy roaming the wintry streets,
With hand held out to any passer by;
And yet God made the voice of its many cries.

  He used to say: "Mine be the work that comes
First ready to my hand. The lever set
I grasp and heave withal. Or let me say,

I love where I live, and let my labor flow
Into the hollows of the neighbor-needs.
Perhaps I like it best: I would not choose
Another than the ordered circumstance.
This farm is God's as much as yonder town;
These men and maidens, kine and horses, his;
For them his laws must be incarnated
In act and fact, and so their world redeemed."
  Though thus he spoke at times, he spake not oft;
But ruled by action — what he said he did.
No grief was suffered there of man or beast
More than was need; no creature fled in fear;
All slaying was with generous suddenness,
Like God's benignant lightning. "For," he said,
"God makes the beasts, and loves them dearly
    well —
Better than any parent loves his child,
It may be," would he say; for still the *may be*
Was sacred with him no less than the *is*, —
In such humility he lived and wrought, —
"Hence are they sacred. Sprung from God as we,
They are our brethren in a lower kind;
And in their face I see the human look."

If any said: "Men look like animals;
Each has his type set in the lower kind;"
His answer was: "The animals are like men.
Each has his true type set in the higher kind,
Though even there only rough-hewn as yet."
He said that cruelty would need no hell
Save that the ghosts of the sad beasts should come,
And crowding, silent, all their centred heads,
Stare the ill man to madness.

                    When he spoke,
His word had all the force of unborn deeds
That lay within him ready to be born.
His goodness ever went beyond his word,
Embodying itself unconsciously
In understanding of the need that prayed,
And help to which he had not pledged himself;
For, like his race, the pledge with him was slow.
  When from great cities came the old sad news
Of crime and wretchedness, and children sore
With hunger, and neglect, and cruel blows,
He would walk sadly all the afternoon,
With head down-bent, and pondering footstep slow;
Arriving ever at the same result, —

Concluding ever: " The best that I can do
For the great world, is the same best I can
For this my world.   What truth may be therein
Will pass beyond my narrow circumstance,
In truth's own right."   When a philanthropist
Said pompously: " It is not for your gifts
To spend themselves on common labors thus:
You owe the world far nobler things than such ; "
He answered him : " The world is in God's hands ;
This part in mine.   Hither my sacred past,
With all its loves inherited, has led ;
Here let me fit.   Shall I judge, arrogant,
Primeval, godlike work in earth and air,
Seed-time and harvest — offered fellowship
With God in nature — unworthy of my hands?
I know what you would say — I know with grief—
The crowds of men, in whom a starving soul
Cries through the windows of their hollow eyes
For bare humanity, and leave to grow : —
Would I could help them !   But all crowds are made
Of individuals ; and their grief, and pain,
And thirst, and hunger, all are of the one,
Not of the many: the true saving power

Enters the individual door, and thence
Issues again in thousand influences
Besieging other doors.   You cannot throw
A mass of good into the general midst
Whereof each man can seize his private share ;
Or if you could, it were of lowest kind,
Not reaching to that hunger of the soul.
Now here I labor whole in the same place
Where they have known me from my childhood up,
And I know them, each individual :
If there is power in me to help my own,
Even of itself it flows beyond my will,
Takes shape in commonest of common acts
Meeting the humble day's necessity:
I would not always consciously do good, —
Not always work from full intent of help, —
Lest I forget the measure heaped and pressed
And running over which they pour for me ,
And never reap the too-much of return
In smiling trust, and wealth of kindly eyes.
But in the city, with a few lame words
And a few wretched coins, sore-coveted,
To mediate 'twixt my *cannot* and my *would*,

My best attempts could hardly strike a root ;

My scattered corn would turn to wind-blown chaff,

And I grow weak, and weary of my kind,

Misunderstood the most where almost known,

Baffled and beaten by their unbelief:

Years could not place me where I stand this day, —

High on the vantage-ground of confidence:

I might for years toil on, and reach no man.

Besides, to leave the thing that nearest lies,

And choose the thing far off, more difficult —

The act, having no touch of God in it,

Who seeks the needy for the pure need's sake,

Must straightway die, choked in its selfishness."

Thus he. The world-wise schemer for the good

Held his poor peace, and went his trackless way.

What of the vision now? the vision fair

Sent forth to meet him, when at eve he went

Home from his first day's ploughing? Oft he

     dreamed

She passed him smiling on her stately horse ;

But never band or buckle yielded more ;

Never again his hands enthroned the maid ;

He only gazed and worshipped and awoke.

Nor woke he then with foolish vain regret;
But, saying, "I have seen the beautiful,"
Smiled with his eyes upon a flower or bird,
Or any living form of gentleness
That met him first; and all that day, his face
Would oftener dawn into a blossomy smile.

And ever when he read a lofty tale,
Or when the storied leaf, or ballad old,
Or spake or sang of woman very fair,
Or wondrous good, he saw her face alone,
The genius henceforth of the tale or song.

Nor did he turn aside from other maids,
But loved their faces pure and faithful eyes.
He may have thought, "One day I wed a maid,
And make her mine;" but never came the maid,
Or never came the hour: he walked alone.

Meantime how fared the lady? She had wed
One of the common crowd. There must be ore
For the gold grains to lie in: virgin gold
Lies by the dross, enriching not the dross.
She was not one who of herself could *be*,
And she had found no heart, that, one with hers,
Would sound accord. She sat alone in the house,

And read the last new novel, vaguely, faintly
Desiring better ; or listlessly conversed
With phantom-visitors — they were no friends,
But spectral forms from fashion's hollow glass.
She haunted gay assemblies, ill-content ;
But, better there than lonely with her mate,
There danced, or sat and talked.

                      What had she felt,
If through the rhythmic motion of fair forms
A vision had arisen — as when, of old,
The minstrel's art laid bare the seer's eye,
And showed him plenteous waters in the waste, —
If the gay dance had vanished from her eyes,
And she had seen her ploughman-lover go
With his great stride across a lonely field,
Under the dark blue vault ablaze with stars,
Lifting his full eyes to the radiant roof?
Or in the emerging vision had she seen
Him, studious, with space-compelling mind,
Bent o'er his slate, pursue some planet's course ;
Or read, and justify the poet's wrath,
Or sage's slow conclusion ? If a voice
Had whispered then : This man in many a dream

3

And many a moment of keen consciousness,
Blesses you for the look that woke his heart,
That smiled him into life, and, still unwithered,
Lies cherished in the cabinet of his soul, —
Would those dark eyes have beamed with darker
      light?
Would that fair soul, half dead with emptiness,
Have risen from the couch of her unrest,
And looked to Heaven again, again believed
In God and the realities of life?
Would not that soul have sung to her lone self:
"I have a friend, a ploughman, who is wise.
He knows what God, and goodness, and fair faith
Mean in the words and books of mighty men.
He little heeds the outer shows of things,
But worships the unconquerable truth.
This man of men loves me: I will be proud
And very humble. If he knew me well,
Would he go on to love me as he loves?"
  In the third year, a heavy harvest fell,
Full filled, before the reaping-hook and scythe.
The men and maidens in the scorching heat
Lightened their toil by merry jest and song;

Rested at mid-day, and from brimming bowl
Drank the brown ale, and white abundant milk;
Until the last ear fell, and stubble stood
Where waved the forests of the murmuring corn,
And o'er the land rose piled the shocks, like tents
Of an encamping army, tent by tent,
To stand until the moon should have her will.

The grain was ripe. The harvest carts went out
Broad-platformed, bearing back the towering load,
With frequent passage 'twixt homeyard and field.
And half the oats already hid their tops,
Their ringing, rustling, wind-responsive sprays,
In the still darkness of the towering stack;
When in the north low billowy clouds appeared,
Blue-based, white-crested, in the afternoon;
And westward, darker masses, plashed with blue,
And outlined vague in misty steep and dell,
Clomb o'er the hill-tops: thunder was at hand.
The air was sultry. But the upper sky
Was clear and radiant.
                    Downward went the sun,
Below the sullen clouds that walled the west,
Below the hills, below the shadowed world.

The moon looked over the clear eastern wall,
And slanting rose and looked, and rose and looked,
Searching for silence in her yellow fields.
There it was not. For there the staggering carts,
Like overladen beasts, crawled homeward still,
Returning light and low. The laugh broke yet,
That lightning of the soul's unclouded skies,
Though not so frequent, now that labor passed
Its natural hour. Yet on the labor went,
Straining to beat the welkin-climbing toil
Of the huge rain-clouds, heavy with their floods.
Sleep, old enchantress, sided with the clouds,
The crawling clouds, and threw benumbing spells
On man and horse. One youth who walked beside
A ponderous load of sheaves, higher than wont,
Which dared the slumbering leven overhead,
Woke with a start, falling against the wheel,
That circled slow after the sleepy horse.
Yet none would yield to soft-suggesting sleep,
Or leave the last few shocks ; for the wild storm
Would catch thereby the skirts of Harvest-home,
And hold her lingering half way in the rain.
    The scholar labored with his men all night.

He did not favor such prone headlong race
With Nature. To himself he said. " The night
Is sent for sleep ; we ought to sleep in it,
And leave the clouds to God. Not every storm
That climbeth heavenward, overwhelms the earth.
And if God wills, 'tis better as He wills ;
What He takes from us never can be lost."
But the old farmer ordered ; and the son
Went manful to the work, and held his peace.

When the dawn blotted pale the clouded east,
And the first drops, o'ergrown and helpless, fell,
Oppressed with sheaves, the last cart home was
        going ;
And by its side, the last in the retreat,
The scholar walked, glad bringing up the rear.
Half distance only had he measured back,
When, on opposing strength of upper winds
Tumultuous borne at last, the laboring racks
Met in the zenith, and the silence ceased·
The lightning brake, and flooded all the world,
Its roar of airy billows following it
The darkness drank the lightning, and again
Lay more unslaked. But ere the darkness came,

In the full revelation of the flash,
Met by some stranger flash from cloudy brain,
He saw the lady, borne upon her horse,
Careless of thunder, as when, years agone,
He saw her once, to see for evermore.
"Ah ha!" he said; "my dreams are come for me;
Now shall they have their time." For, all the night,
He had felt a growing trouble in his frame.
Which might be nothing, or an illness dire.

  Homeward he went, with a pale smile arrived,
Gave up his load, walked softly to his room,
And sought the welcome haven of his bed —
There slept and moaned, cried out, and woke, and
        slept:
Through all the netted labyrinth of his brain
The fever shot its pent malignant fire.
'Twas evening when to passing consciousness
He woke and saw his father by his side.
His guardian form in every vision drear
That followed, watching shone; and the healing face
Of his good sister gleamed through all his pain,
Soothing and strengthening with cloudy hope;
Till, at the weary last of many days,

He woke to sweet quiescent consciousness,
Enfeebled much, but with a new-born life —
His soul a summer evening, after rain.

Slow, with the passing weeks, he gathered strength,
And ere the winter came, seemed half restored,
And hope was busy. But a fire too keen
Burned in his larger eyes; and in his cheek
Too ready came the blood at faintest call,
Glowing a fair, quick-fading, sunset hue.

Before its hour, a biting frost set in.
It gnawed with icy fangs his shrinking life;
And that disease well known in all the land,
That smiling, hoping, wasting, radiant death,
Was born of outer cold and inner heat.

One morn his sister, entering while he slept,
Saw in his listless hand a handkerchief
Spotted with red. Cold with dismay, she stood
Scared, motionless. But catching in a glass
A sudden glimpse of a white ghostly face,
She started at herself, and he awoke.
He understood, and said with smile unsure,
" Bright red was evermore my master-hue;
And see, I have it in me: that is why."

She shuddered, and he saw, nor jested more;
But from that hour looked silent Death in the face.
  When first he saw the red blood outward leap,
As if it sought again the fountain-heart
Whence it had flowed to fill the golden bowl,
No terror seized: a wild excitement swelled
His spirit. Now the pondered mystery
Would fling its portals wide, and take him in,
One of the awful dead them fools conceive
As ghosts that fleet and pine, bereft of weight,
And half their valued lives — he otherwise;
Hoped now, and now expected; and again
Said only, "I will wait for what will come."
So waits a child the lingering curtain's rise,
While yet the panting lights restrained burn
At half height, and the theatre is full.
  But as the days went on, they brought sad hours,
When he would sit, his hands upon his knees,
Drooping, and longing for the wine of life.
For when the ninefold crystal spheres, through which
The outer light sinks in, are rent and shattered,
Yet whole enough to keep the pining life,
Distressing shadows cross the checkered soul:

Poor Psyche trims her irresponsive lamp,
And anxious visits oft her store of oil,
And still the shadows fall — she must go pray.
For God, who speaks to man at door and lattice,
Glorious in stars, and winds, and flowers, and waves,
Not seldom shuts the door and dims the pane,
That, isled in calm, his still small voice may sound
The clearer, by the hearth, in the inner room —
Sound on until the soul, fulfilled of hope,
Look undismayed on that which cannot kill;
And saying in the gloom, *I will the light*,
Glow in the gloom the present will of God —
So melt the shadows of her clouded house.

He, when his lamp shot up a spiring flame,
Would thus break forth and climb the heaven of
      prayer:
" Do with us what thou wilt, all-glorious heart !
Thou God of them that are not yet, but grow !
We trust thee for the thing we shall be yet;
We too are ill content with what we are."
And when the flame sank, and the darkness fell,
He lived by faith which is the soul of sight.

Yet in the frequent pauses of the light,

When all was dreary as a drizzling thaw,
When sleep came not although he prayed for sleep,
And wakeful weary on his bed he lay,
Like frozen lake that has no heaven within;
Then, then the sleeping horror woke and stirred,
And with the tooth of unsure thought began
To gnaw the roots of life. What if there were
No truth in beauty — loveliness a toy
Invented by himself in happier mood?
" For, if my mind can dim or slay the Fair,
Why should it not enhance or make the Fair?"
" Nay," Psyche answered; "for a tired man
May drop his eyelids on the visible world,
To whom no dreams, when fancy flieth free,
Will bring the sunny excellence of day.
'Tis easy to destroy; God only makes.
Could my invention sweep the lucid waves
With purple shadows — next create the joy
With which my life beholds them? Wherefore should
One meet the other without thought of mine?
If God did not mean beauty in them and me,
But dropped them, helpless shadows, from his sun,
There were no God, his image not being mine,

And I should seek in vain for any bliss.

O, lack and doubt and fear can only come

Because of plenty, confidence, and love!

They are the shadow-forms about their feet,

Because they are not perfect crystal-clear

To the all-searching sun in which they live.

Dread of its loss is Beauty's certain seal!"

Thus reasoned mourning Psyche. And suddenly

The sun would rise, and vanish Psyche's lamp,

Absorbed in light, not swallowed in the dark.

It was a wintry time with sunny days,

And visitings of April airs and scents,

That came with sudden presence, unforetold,

As brushed from off the outer spheres of spring

In the great world where all is old and new.

Strange longings he had never known till now,

Awoke within him, flowers of rooted hope.

For a whole silent hour he would sit and gaze

Upon the distant hills whose dazzling snow

Starred the dim blue, or down their dark ravines

Crept vaporous; until the fancy rose

That on the other side those rampart hills

A mighty woman sat, with waiting face,

Calm as the life whose rapt intensity
Borders on death, silent, waiting for him,
To make him grand forever with a kiss,
And send him silent through the toning worlds.
  The father saw him waning. The proud sire
Beheld his pride go drooping in the cold,
Like snow-drop to the earth ; and gave God thanks
That he was old. But evermore the son
Looked up and smiled as he had heard strange news,
Across the waste, of tree-buds and primroses.
And yet again the other mood would come,
And, being a troubled child, he sought his father
For comfort such as fathers only give : —
Sure there is one great Father in the heavens,
Since every word of good from fathers' lips
Falleth with such authority, although
They are but men as we ! This trembling son
Who saw the unknown death draw hourly nigher,
Sought comfort in his father's tenderness,
And made him strong to die.
                          One shining day,
Shining with sun and snow, he came and said,
" What think you, father — is death very sore ? "

"My boy," the father answered, "we will try
To make it easy with the present God.
But, as I judge, though more by hope than sight,
It seems much harder to the lookers on,
Than to the man who dies. Each panting breath,
We call a gasp, may be to him who knows,
A sigh of pleasure ; or, at worst, the sob
With which the unclothed spirit, step by step,
Wades forth into the cool eternal sea.
I think, my boy, death has two sides to it, —
One sunny, and one dark ; as this round earth
Is every day half sunny and half dark.
We on the dark side call the mystery *death* ;
They on the other, looking down in light,
Wait the glad *birth*, with other tears than ours."
"Be near me, father, when I die ; " he said.
" I will, my boy, until a better Father
Draws your hand out of mine. Be near in turn,
When my time comes : you in the light beyond,
And knowing all about it , I all dark."
     The days went on, until the tender green
Shone through the snow in patches. Then the hope
Of life awoke, fair-faintly, in his heart ;

For the spring drew him, warm, soft, budding spring,
With promises.   The father better knew.

He who had strode a king across his fields,
Crept slowly now through softest daisied grass;
And sometimes wept in secret, that so soon
The earth with all its suns and harvests fair
Must lie beyond a sure dividing waste.

But though I lingering listen to the old,
Ere yet I strike new chords that seize the old
And bear their lost souls up the music-stair—
Think not he was too fearful-faint of heart
To look the blank unknown full in the void;
For he had hope in God, the growth of years,
Ponderings, and aspirations from a child,
And prayers and readings and repentances;
For something in him had ever sought the peace
Of other something deeper in him still;
Some sounds sighed ever for a harmony
With other fainter tones, that softly drew
Nearer and nearer from the unknown depths
Where the Individual goeth out in God,
Smoothing the discord ever as they grew:
He sought the way back which the music came,

Hoping at last to find the face of Him
To whom St. John said *Lord* with holy awe,
Yet on his bosom fearless leaned the while.

As the slow spring came on, his swelling life,
The new creation inside of the old,
Pressed up in buds toward the invisible,
And burst the crumbling mould wherein it lay.
He never thought of church-yards, — ever looked
Away from the green earth to the blue sky.

Yet of the earth remained one hurtless stain —
He thanked God that he died not in the cold.
"For," said he, "I would rather go abroad
When the sun shines, and birds are singing blithe.
It may be that we know not any place,
Or sense at all, and only live in thought,
But, knowing not, I cling to warmth and light.
I *may* pass forth into the sea of air
That swings its massy waves around the earth,
And I would rather go when it is full
Of light and blue and larks, than when gray fog
Dulls it with steams of old earth winter-sick.
Now in the dawn of summer I shall die ;
Sinking asleep at sunset, I will hope,

And going with the light. And by the time
When they say: 'He is dead ; his face is changed ;'
I shall be saying: 'Yet, yet, I live, I love.'"

   The weary nights had taught him much ; for all
He knew before seemed as he knew it not,
And he must learn it yet again and better.
The sick half dreaming child will oft forget
In longings for his mother, that her arms
Are all the time holding him to her heart:
Mother he murmuring moans; she wakes him up,
That he may see her face, and sleep in peace.
And God was very good to him, he said.

   Faint-hearted reader, lift thy heart with me.

   Father! we need thy winter as thy spring ;
And thy poor children, knowing thy great heart,
And that thou bearest thy large share of grief,
Because thou lovest goodness more than joy
In them thou lovest — so dost let them grieve,
Will cease to vex thee with our peevish cries,
Will lift our eyes and smile, though sorrowful ;
Yet not the less pray for thy help, when pain
Is overstrong. Remember our poor hearts.
We never grasp the zenith of the time ;

We find no spring except in winter-prayers;
But we believe — nay, Lord, we only hope,
That one day we shall thank thee perfectly
For pain and hope and all that led or drove
Us back into the bosom of thy love.

  One night, as oft, he lay and could not sleep.
His spirit was a chamber, empty, dark,
Through which bright pictures passed of the outer
      world ;
The regnant Will gazed passive on the show.
The tube, as it were, through which the shadows
      came,
Was turned upon the past. One after one,
Glided across the field the things that were,
Silent and sorrowful, like all things old ;
For withered rose-leaves have a mournful scent,
And old brown letters are more sad than graves.

  At length, as ever in such vision-hours,
Came the bright maiden, high upon her horse.
Then, then the passive Will sprang regnant up,
And, like a necromantic sage, compelled
What came unbidden to abide his will.

  Gathered around her form his brooding thoughts:

4

How would she fare, spinning her history
Into a Psyche-cradle? With what wings
Greet the æonian summer? Glistening white,
With feathery dust of silver? or dull red,
Seared with black spots of scorching sulphur-fume?
"I know," he said, "some women fail, and cease.
Men rave of eyes in which I could not rest."
    The fount of possibilities began
To glow ebullient in the hidden part;
Anon the lava-stream burst blasting forth.
For purest souls sometimes have direst fears,
In ghost-hours when the shadow of the earth
Is cast on half her children, and the sun
Is far away and busy with the rest.
"If she be only such as some men say,
Pure in the eyes of poet-boys, who still
Fancy the wavings of invisible wings,
And tremble as they feel the wafted air;
But, private and familiar with their thoughts,
Common as clay, and of the trodden earth!
It cannot, cannot be! She is of God.
And yet fair things will perish, higher life
Gives deeper death; fair gifts make fouler faults:

Women themselves — I dare not think the rest."
Such thoughts went walking up and down his soul,
Until they found a spot wherein to rest,
And build a resolution for the day.

But next day, and the next, he was too worn
To make intent a deed   Besides, there blew
A cold dry wind from out the kindless East,
Withering his life — as if he had come too soon,
Before God's spirit moved on the waters' face,
To make his dwelling ready.   But the next
Morning rose radiant.   A genial wind
Rippled the blue air 'neath the golden sun,
And brought glad news of summer from the South.

He lay now in his father's room ; and there
The growing summer sun poured a steep light.
It fell upon the fire, alive with flames,
And turned it ghostly pale, and would have slain ;
Even as the sunshine of the further life,
Quenching the glow of this, leaves but a coal.
He sat him down 'twixt sun and fire, himself
The meeting point of two conflicting lives,
And half from each forth flowed the written stream :
    " Lady, I owe thee much.   Stay not to look

Upon my name : I write it, but I date
From the church-yard, where it shall lie in peace
When thou art reading, — and thou knowest me not
Nor dared I write, but death is crowning me
Thy equal. If my boldness should offend,
I, pure in my intent, hide with the ghosts ;
Where, when thou com'st, thou hast already known,
As God at first, Death equal makes at last.

   "But pardon, lady. Ere I had begun,
My thoughts moved towards thee with a gentle flow
That bore a depth of waters. When I took
My pen to write, they rushed into a gulf,
Precipitate and foamy. Can it be,
That death who humbles all hath made me proud ?

   "Lady, thy loveliness hath walked my brain,
As if I were thy heritage bequeathed
From many sires ; yet only from afar
I have worshipped thee — content to know the vis-
    ion
Had lifted me above myself who saw,
And taken my angel nigh thee in thy heaven.
Thy beauty, lady, hath overflowed, and made
Another being beautiful beside,

With virtue to aspire and be itself
Afar as angels or the sainted dead,
Yet near as loveliness can haunt a man,
And taking any shape for every need,
Thy form hath put on each revealing diess
Of circumstance and history, high or low,
In which from tale of holy life and thought
Essential womanhood hath shone on me.

"Ten years have passed away since the first time,
Which was the last, I saw thee. What have these
Made or unmade in thee? I ask myself.
O lovely in my memory! art thou
As lovely in thyself? Thy glory then
Was what God made thee; art thou such indeed?
Forgive my boldness, lady, — I am dead:
The dead may cry, their voices are so small.

"I have a prayer to make thee — hear the dead.
Lady, for God's sake be as beautiful
As that white form that dwelleth in my heart;
Yea, better still, as that ideal Pure
That waketh in thee, when thou prayest God,
Or helpest thy poor neighbor. For myself
I pray. For if I die and find that she,

My woman-glory, lives in common air,
Is not so very radiant after all,
My sad face will afflict the calm-eyed ghosts,
Unused to see such rooted sadness there.
With palm to palm, my kneeling ghost implores
Thee, living lady — justify my faith
In womanhood's white-handed nobleness,
And thee, its revelation unto me.

"But I bethink me. If thou turn thy thoughts
Upon thyself, even for that great sake
Of purity and conscious whiteness' self,
Thou wilt but half succeed. The other half
Is to forget the first, and all thyself,
Quenching thy moonlight in the blaze of day,
Turning thy being full unto thy God.
Be thou in Him a pure, twice holy child,
Doing the right with sweet unconsciousness ;
Having God in thee, thy completed soul.

"Lady, I die — the Father holds me up.
It is not much to thee that I should die ;
But it is much to know He holds me up.

"I thank thee, lady, for a gentle look
Which crowned me from thine eyes ten years ago,

Ere, clothed in nimbus of the setting sun,
Thee from my dazzled eyes thy horse did bear,
Proud of his burden.   My dull tongue was mute —
I was a fool before thee ; but my silence
Was the sole homage possible to me then :
That I can speak nor be ashamed, is thine.
The same sweet look be possible to thee
For evermore   I bless thee with thine own,
And say farewell, and go into my grave —
Nay, to the sapphire heaven of all my hopes."

    Followed his name in full, and then the name
Of the green church-yard where his form would lie.
    Back to his couch he crept, weary, and said :
"O God ! I am but an attempt at life
Sleep falls again ere I am full awake.
Life goeth from me in the morning hour.
I have seen nothing clearly ; felt no thrill
Of pure emotion, save in dreams, ah — dreams !
The high Truth has but flickered in my soul —
Save at such times, in lonely midnight hours,
When, dawning sudden on my inner world,
New stars came forth, revealing unknown depths,
New heights of silence, quelling all my sea.

Then only I beheld the formless fact,
Beheld myself a living lonely thought,
Isled in the hyaline of Truth alway.
I have not reaped earth's harvest, O my God;
Have gathered but a few poor wayside flowers, —
Harebells, red poppies, daisies, eyebrights blue, —
Gathered them by the way, for comforting.
Have I aimed proudly, therefore aimed too low,
Striving for something visible in my thought,
And not the unseen thing hid far in thine?
Make me content to be a primrose-flower
Among thy nations, so the fair truth, hid
In the sweet primrose, come awake in me,
And I rejoice, an individual soul,
Reflecting thee — as truly then divine
As if I towered the angel of the sun.
Once, in a southern eve, a glowing worm
Gave me a keener joy than the heaven of stars ·
Thou camest in the worm more near me then;
Nor do I think, were I that green delight,
I'd change to be the shadowy evening star.
Ah, make me, Father, anything thou wilt,
So be thou will it! I am safe with thee.

I laugh exulting. Make me something, God ;
Clear, sunny, veritable purity
Of high existence, in thyself content,
And seeking for no measures. I *have* reaped
Earth's harvest, if I find this holy death.
Now I am ready ; take me when thou wilt."

He laid the letter in his desk, with seal
And superscription. When his sister came,
He told her where to find it — afterwards.

As the slow eve, through paler, darker shades,
Insensibly declines, until at last
The lordly day is but a memory,
So died he. In the hush of noon he died.
The sun shone on — why should he not shine on ?
The summer noises rose o'er all the land.
The love of God lay warm on hill and plain.
'Tis well to die in summer.

                              When the breath,
After a hopeless pause, returned no more,
The father fell upon his knees, and said :
"O God, I thank thee ; it is over now ;
Through this sore time thy hand has led him well.
Lord, let me follow soon, and be at rest."

And then he rose, and comforted the maid,
Who in her brother had lost the pride of life,
And wept as all her heaven were only rain.
  Of the loved lady, little more I know.
I know not if, when she had read the lines,
She rose in haste, and to her chamber went,
And shut the door ; nor if, when she came forth,
A dawn of holier purpose gleamed across
The sadness of her brow. But this I know,
That on a warm autumnal afternoon,
When   headstone-shadows   crossed   three   neighbor
      graves,
And, like an ended prayer, the empty church
Stood in the sunshine, like a cenotaph,
A little boy, who watched a cow near by
Gather her milk where alms of clover-fields
Lay scattered on the sides of silent roads,
All sudden saw — but saw not whence she came —
A lady, closely veiled, alone, and still,
Seated upon a grave. Long time she sat
And moved not, weeping sore, the watcher said.
At length slow-leaning on her elbow down,
She pulled a something small from off the grave —

A shining daisy, or a blade of grass,
And put it in a letter. Then she rose,
And glided silent forth, over the wall,
Where the two steps on this side and on that
Shorten the path from westward to the church.
The clang of hoofs and sound of light, swift wheels
Arose and died upon the listener's ear.

A STORY OF THE SEA-SHORE.

A STORY OF THE SEA-SHORE.

——◆——

INTRODUCTION.

I SOUGHT the long clear twilights of my home,
   Far in the pale-blue skies and slaty seas,
What time the sunset dies not utterly,
But withered to a ghost-like stealthy gleam,
Round the horizon creeps the short-lived night,
And changes into sunrise in a swoon.
I found my home in homeliness unchanged:
The love that made it home, unchangeable,
Received me as a child, and all was well.
My ancient summer-heaven, borne on the hills,
Once more embraced me; and once more the vale,
So often sighed for in the far-off nights,
Rose on my bodily vision, and, behold!
In nothing had the fancy mocked the fact:
The hasting streams went garrulous as of old;

The resting flowers in silence uttered more ;
The blue hills rose and dwelt alone in heaven ;
Householding Nature from her treasures brought
Things old and new, the same yet not the same,
For all was holier, lovelier than before.
And best of all, once more I paced the fields
With him whose love had made me long for God —
So good a father that needs-must I sought
A better still, Father of him and me.

Once on a day, my cousin Frank and I
Sat swiftly borne behind the dear white mare
Which oft had carried me in by-gone days
Along the lonely paths of moorland hills ;
But now we sought the coast, where deep waves foam
'Gainst rocks that lift their dark fronts to the north.
Beside me sat a girl, on whose kind face
I had not looked for many a changeful year,
But the old friendship straightway blossomed new.
The heavens were sunny, and the earth was green ;
The harebells large, in gathered groups along
The grassy borders, of a tender blue
Transparent as the sky, haunted with wings

Of many butterflies, as blue as they;
And as we talked and talked without restraint,
Brought near by memories of days that were
And therefore are forever, by the joy
Of motion through a warm and shining air,
By the glad sense of freedom and like thoughts,
And by the bond of friendship with the dead,
She told the tale which here I tell again.

I had returned to childish memories,
Asking her if she knew a castle old,
Whose masonry, all worn away above,
Yet faced the sea-cliff up, and met the waves:
'Twas one of my child-marvels; for, each year,
We turned our backs upon the ripening corn,
And sought some village on the desert shore;
And nigh this ruin, was that I loved the best.

For O the riches of that little port!
Down almost to the beach, where a high wall
Inclosed them, came the gardens of a lord,
Free to the visitor with foot restrained:
His shady walks, his ancient trees of state;

5

His river, which, outside the wall, with course
Indefinite, went dreaming o'er the sands,
And lost itself in finding out the sea,
But inside, bore grave swans, white splendors — crept
Under the fairy leap of a wire bridge,
Vanished in leaves, and came again where lawns
Lay verdurous, and the peacock's plumy heaven
Bore azure suns with green and golden rays.
It was my childish Eden; for the skies
Were loftier in that garden, and the clouds
More summer-gracious, edged with broader white;
And when they rained, it was a golden rain
That sparkled as it fell — an odorous rain.
And then its wonder-heart! — a little room,
Half hollowed in the side of a steep hill.
The hill was with a circular temple crowned,
A landmark to far seas; the room below
Was clouded ever in the gentle night
Of a luxuriant ivy, and its door,
Half filled with rainbow hues of colored glass,
Opened into the bosom of the hill.
Never to sesame of mine that door
Gave up its sanctuary; but through the glass,

Gazing with reverent curiosity,

I saw a little chamber, round and high,

Which to behold was to escape the heat,

And bathe in coolness of the eye and brain.

All was a dusky green; for on one side,

A window, half blind with ivy manifold,

Whose leaves, like heads of gazers, climbed to the
    top,

Gave all the light; and all the light that came

Through the thick veil, was green, O kindest hue!

But the heart has a heart, and here was one;

For in the midst, the evermore of all,

On a low column stood, white, cold, and clear,

A marble woman. Who she was I know not —

A Psyche, or a Silence, or an Echo.

Pale, undefined, a silvery shadow, still,

In one lone chamber of my memory,

She is a power upon me, as of old.

But ah! to dream there through hot summer days,

In coolness shrouded and sea-murmurings,

Forgot by all till twilight shades grew dark!

To find half hidden in the hollowed wall,

A nest of tales, quaint volumes such as dreams
Hoard up in book-shops dim in tortuous streets!
That wondrous marble woman evermore
Filling the gloom with calm delirium
Of radiated whiteness, as I read!
The fancied joy, too plenteous for its cup,
O'erflowed, and turned to sadness as it fell.

But the gray ruin on the shattered shore,
Not the green refuge in the bowering hill,
Drew forth our talk that day. For, as I said,
I asked her if she knew it. She replied,
"I know it well. A woman used to live
In one of its low vaults, my mother says."
"I came once on a turret stair," I said,
"Leading from level of the ground above
To a low-vaulted room within the rock,
Whence through a small square opening you look
        forth
Wide o'er the sea; but the dim-sounding waves
Are many feet below, and shrunk in size
To a great ripple." — " 'Twas not there," she said, —
"Not in that room half up the cliff, but one

Below, within the margin of spring-tides ;
So that when tides and northern winds are high,
'Tis more an ocean-cave than castle-vault."
And then she told me all she knew of her.

It was a simple tale, with facts but few :
She clomb one sunny hill, gazed once abroad,
Then slowly sank to pace a dreary plain.
Alas! how many such are told by night,
In fisher-cottages along the shore!

Farewell, old summer-day! I turn aside
To tell my story, interwoven with thoughts
Born of its sorrow; for I dare not think
A woman at the mercy of a sea.

THE STORY.

Ay as it listeth blows the listless wind,
Swelling great sails, and bending lordly masts,
Or scaring shadow-waves o'er fields of corn,
And hunting lazy clouds across the sky:
Now, like a white cloud o'er another sky,
It blows a tall brig from the harbor's mouth

Out 'mid the high-tossed heads of broken waves,
And hoverings of long-pinioned arrowy birds
With clouds and birds and sails and broken crests,
All space is full of spots of fluttering white,
And yet one sailor knows that handkerchief
Waved wet with tears, and heavy in the wind.
Blow, wind! draw out the cord that binds the twain;
Draw, for thou canst not break the lengthening cord.
Blow, wind! yet gently; gently blow, fair wind!
And let love's vision slowly, gently die;
Let the bright sails all solemn-slowly pass,
And linger ghost-like o'er the vanished hull,
With a white farewell to her straining eyes;
For nevermore in morning's level beams
Will those sea-shadowing sails, storm-stained and worn,
From the gray-billowed north come dancing in;
And never, gliding home 'neath starry skies,
Over the dark of the dim-glancing sea,
Will the great ship send forth a herald cry
Of home-come sailors, into sleeping streets.
Blow gently, wind! blow slowly, gentle wind!

   Weep not yet, maiden; 'tis not yet thy hour
Why shouldst thou weep before thy time is come?

Go to thy work; break into song sometimes, —
Song dying slow forgotten, in the lapse
Of dreamy thought, ere natural pause ensue;
Or broken sudden when the eager heart
Hurries the ready eye to north and east.
Sing, maiden, while thou canst, ere yet the truth,
Slow darkening on thee, choke the founts of song.

The weeks went by. Oft leaving household work,
With bare arms and uncovered head she clomb
The landward slope of the prophetic hill;
From whose green head, as from the verge of time,
Far out on the eternity of waves,
Shading her hope-rapt eyes, seer-like she gazed,
If from the Hades of the nether world,
Slow climbing up the round side of the earth,
Haply her prayers were drawing his tardy sails
Over the threshold of the far horizon, —
Drawing her sailor home, to celebrate
With holy rites of family and church
The apotheosis of maidenhood.

Months passed; he came not; and a shadowy fear,
Long haunting the horizon of her soul,
In deeper gloom and sharper form drew nigh;

And growing in bulk, possessed her atmosphere,

And lost all shape, because it filled all space,

And reached beyond the bounds of consciousness;

But in sudden incarnations darting swift

From out its infinite a gulfy stare

Of terror blank, and hideous emptiness,

And widowhood or ever wedding-day.

On granite ridge, and chalky cliff, and pier,

Far built into the waves along our shores,

Maidens have stood since ever ships went forth;

The same pain at the heart; the same slow mist

Clouding the eye; the same fixed longing look,

As if the soul had gone out and left the door

Wide open — gone to lean and peep and peer

Over the awful edge where voidness sinks

Sheer to oblivion — that horizon-line

Over whose edge he vanished — came no more.

O God, why are our souls lone, helpless seas,

Tortured with such immitigable storm?

What is this love, that now on angel wing

Sweeps us amid the stars in passionate calm;

And now with demon arms fast cincturing,

Drops us, through all gyrations of keen pain,

Down the black vortex, till the giddy whirl
Gives fainting respite to the ghastly brain?
O happy they for whom the Possible
Opens its gates of madness, and becomes
The Real around them! those to whom henceforth
There is but one to-morrow, the next morn,
Their wedding-day, ever one step removed;
The husband's foot ever upon the verge
Of the day's threshold, in a lasting dream!
Such madness may be but a formless faith, —
A chaos which the breath of God will blow
Into an ordered world of seed and fruit?
Shall not the Possible become the Real?
God sleeps not when He makes his daughters dream.
Shall not the morrow dawn which leads at last
The maiden-ghost, confused and half awake,
Into the land whose shadows are our dreams?
Thus questioning we stand upon the shore,
And gaze across into the Unrevealed.

Upon its visible symbol gazed the girl,
Till earth behind her ceased, and sea was all,
Possessing eyes and brain and shrinking soul;
So smooth, because all mouth to swallow up,

And cover the invisible with blue smile;
A still monotony of greed and loss,
Its only voice an endless dreary song
Of wailing, and of craving from the shore;
A low dull dirge that ever rose and died,
Recurring without pause or change or close
Like one verse chanted ever in sleepless brain.
Down to the shore it drew her, drew her down,
Like witch's spell, that fearful endless moan;
For somewhere in the green abyss below,
His body, in the centre of the moan,
Obeyed the motions whence the moaning grew;
Now in a circle slow revolved, and now
Swaying like wind-swung bell, or swept along
Hither and thither, idly to and fro,
In heedless wandering through the heedless sea.
The fascination drew her onward still;
On to the ridgy rocks that seaward ran,
And out along their furrows and jagged backs,
To the last lonely point where the green mass
Arose and sank, heaved slow and forceful. There
She shuddered and recoiled. Then, for a time
From that hour, to and fro between she went,

'Twixt shore and ocean alternating — ever
Drawn to the greedy lapping lip, and ever
Once more repelled, with terror sudden stung;
For there the heartless, miserable depth
Lay in close wait, with horror's glittering eye
Enticing her to its green gulfing maw.

At length a faint hope grew, that, once the prey
Of the cruel waters, she, death's agony o'er,
Must, in the washing of perennial waves,
In some far century, æons remote,
But in an hour sure-fixed of pitiful fate,
All-conscious still of love, despite the deep,
Float over some stray bone, some particle,
An all-diffused sense would know as his;
Then would she sit her down, and watch the tide,
Slow growing, till it touched at length her feet,
When, terror-stricken, she would spring upright,
And turn, and flee aghast, with white-rimmed eye.

But still, where'er she fled, the strange voice fol-
    lowed;
Whisperings innumerable of water-drops
Growing together to a giant cry;
Which, now in hoarse, half-stifled undertones,

And now in thunderous peals of billowy shouts,

Called after her to come, and make no stay.

From the low mists that mingled with the clouds,

And from the tossings of the lifted waves,

Where plunged and rose the raving wilderness,

Voices, pursuing arms, and beckoning hands

Came shorewards, feeling, reaching after her.

Then would she fling her gaunt wild arms on high,

Over her head, in tossings like the waves,

Or fix them, with clasped hands of prayer intense,

Forward, appealing to the bitter sea ;

Or sudden from her shoulders she would tear

Her garments, one by one, and cast them out

Into the roarings of the heedless surge,

A vain oblation to the hungry waves.

As vain was pity's care to cover her ;

Best gifts but bribed the sea, and left her bare.

But such a fire was burning in her brain,

That all-unheeded, cold winds lapped her round,

And sleet-like spray flashed on her tawny skin.

Even her food she brought and flung it far,

To feed the sea — with naked arms, and hair

Streaming like rooted weed on windy tides,

Coal-black and lustreless. But evermore
Back came the wave, while floated yet at hand
Her sacrifice accepted ; so despair,
Back surging, on her heart rushed ever afresh :
She sickening moaned, — half muttered and half
       moaned, —
" She will not be content ; she'll have me yet."
  But when the night grew thick upon the sea,
Quenching it all, except its quenchless voice,
She, half released until the light, would rise,
And step by step withdraw ; as dreaming man,
With an eternity of slowness, drags
His earth-bound, lead-like, irresponsive feet
Back from a sleeping horror that will wake ;
Until, upon the narrow beach arrived,
She turned her back at last upon her foe ;
Then, clothed in all the might of the Unseen,
Terror grew ghastly, and she shrieked and fled —
Fled to the battered base of the old tower,
And round the rock, and through the arched gap,
Into the opening blackness of the vault,
And sank upon the sand, and gasped, and raved.
There, cowering in a nook, she sat all night,

Her eyes fixed on the entrance of the cave,
Through which a pale light shimmered — from the eye
Of the great sleepless ocean — Argus more dread
Than he with hundred lidless watching orbs;
And when she slept, still saw the sea in dreams.
But in the stormy nights, when all was dark,
And the wild tempest swept with slanting wing
Against her refuge; and the heavy spray
Shot through the doorway serpentine cold arms
To seize the fore-doomed morsel of the sea,
She slept not, evermore stung to new life
By new sea-terrors. Now it was the gull,
Whose clanging pinions darted through the arch,
And flapped about her head, and now a wave
Grown arrogant, that rushed into her vault,
Clasped her waist-high, and out again and away
To swell the devilish laughter in the fog:
It left her clinging to the rocky wall,
Watching with white face lest it came again;
And though the tide were ebbing, she slept not yet,
But sat unmoving, till the low gray dawn
Grew on the misty dance of spouting waves,
Seen like a picture through the arched door;

At which the old fascination woke and drew,
And, rising slowly, forth she went once more
To haunt the border of the dawning sea.

Yet all the time there lay within her soul
An inner chamber, quietest place : her love
Had closed its door, and held her in the storm.
She, entering there, had found a refuge calm
As summer evening, or a mother's arms.
There had she found her lost love, only lost
In that he slept nor yet would be awaked ;
And waiting for her there, watching the lost,
The Love that waits and watches evermore.

Thou too hast such a chamber, quietest place,
Where God is waiting for thee. What is it
That will not let thee enter? Is it care
For the provision of the unborn day,
As if thou wert a God that must foresee?
Is it thy craving for the praise of men?
Ambition to outstrip them in the race
Of wealth or honor? Is it love of self,
The greed that still to have must still destroy? —
Go mad for some lost love ; some voice of old,
Which first thou madest sing, and after sob ;

Some heart thou foundest rich, and leftest bare,
Choking its well of faith with thy false deeds ;
Not like thy God, who keeps the better wine
Until the last, and, if He giveth grief,
Giveth it first, and ends the tale with joy.
Such madness clings about the feet of God,
For love informs it.   Better a thousandfold
Be she than thou ! for though thy brain be strong
And clear and active, hers a withered fruit
That nourishes no seed ; her heart is full
Of that in whose might God did make the world, —
A living well, and thine an empty cup.
It was the invisible unbroken cord
Between the twain, her and her sailor-lad,
That drew her ever to the ocean marge.
Better to die, better to rave for love,
Than never to have loved ; or having sought
The love of love, nor gained responsive boon,
To turn away with sickly sneering heart!
    But if thy heart be noble, think and say
If thou rememberest not one hour of torture,
When, maddened with the thought that could not be,
Thou mightst have yielded to the demon wind

That swept in tempest through thy scorching brain,
And rushed into the night, and howled aloud,
And clamored to the waves, and beat the rocks;
And never found thy way back to the seat
Of conscious self, and power to rule thy pain,
Had not God made thee strong to bear and live;
Then own at least this woman's story fit
For poet's tale; and in her wildest moods,
Acknowledge her thy sister. Then thy love,
In the sad face, whose eyes, like suns too fierce,
Have parched and paled the cheeks — in that spare
    form,
Deformed by tempests of the soul and sea,
Will soon unmask a shape of loveliness
Fit to remind thee of a story old
Which God has in his keeping — of thyself.

But not forgot are children when they sleep.
The darkness lasts all night and clears the eyes;
Then comes the morning and the joy of light.
O, surely madness hideth not from Him!
Nor doth a soul cease to be beautiful
In his sight, that its beauty is withdrawn,
And hid by pale eclipse from human eyes.

6

As the white snow is friendly to the earth,
And pain and loss are friendly to the soul,
Shielding it from the black heart-killing frost ;
So may a madness be one of God's winters,
And when the winter over is and gone,
Then smile the skies, and blooms the earth again,
For the fair time of singing birds is come :
Into the cold wind and the howling night,
God sent for her, and she was carried in
Where there was no more sea.

     What messenger
Ran from the door of heaven to bring her home ?
The sea, her terror.

    In the rocks that stand
Below the cliff, there lies a rounded hollow,
Scooped like a basin, with jagged and pinnacled
   sides :
This, buried low when winds heap up the tide,
Lifts in the respiration of the surge,
Its broken, toothed edge, and deep within
Lies resting water, radiantly clear.
There, on a morn of sunshine, while the wind
Yet blew, and heaved yet the billowy sea

With memories of a night of stormy dreams,
At rest they found her : in the sleep which is
And is not death, she, lying very still,
Gathered the bliss that follows after pain.
O life of love, conquered at last by fate!
O life raised from the dead by savior Death!
O love unconquered and invincible!
The enemy sea had cooled her burning brain;
Had laid to rest those limbs that could not rest;
Had hid the horror of its own dread face.
'Twas but one desolate cry, and then her fear
Became a blessed fact, and straight she knew
What God knew all the time, — that it was well.

   O thou whose feet tread ever the wet sands
And howling rocks along the wearing shore,
Roaming the confines of the sea of death!
Strain not thine eyes, bedimmed with longing tears;
No sail comes climbing back across that line.
Turn thee and to thy work; let God alone;
And wait for Him : faint o'er the waves will come
Far floating whispers from the other shore
To thine averted ears. Do thou thy work,
And thou shalt follow; follow, and find thine own.

And thou who fearest something that may come!
Around whose house the storm of terror breaks
All night! to whose love-sharpened ear, all day,
The Invisible is calling at the door,
To render up a life thou canst not keep,
Or love that will not stay! — open thy door,
And carry forth thy dying to the marge
Of the great sea; yea, walk into the flood,
And lay the bier upon the moaning waves.
Give God thy dead to bury; float it again,
With sighs and prayers to waft it through the gloom,
Back to the spring of life. Say, — "If it die,
Yet thou, the life of life, art still alive,
And thou canst make thy dead alive again."

Ah God! the earth is full of cries and moans,
And dull despair, that neither moans nor cries;
Thousands of hearts are waiting helplessly;
The whole creation groaneth, travaileth
For what it knows not, but with dull-eyed hope
Of resurrection, or of dreamless death!
Raise thou the dead of Aprils past and gone
In hearts of maidens; restore the autumn fruits
Of old men feebly mournful o'er the life

Which scarce hath memory but the mournfulness.

There is no past with thee; bring back once more

The summer eves of lovers, over which

The wintry wind that raveth through the world

Heaps wretched leaves, half tombed in ghastly snow;

Bring back the mother-heaven of orphans lone,

The brother's and the sister's faithfulness;

Bring forth the kingdom of the Son of Man.

They troop around me, children wildly crying;

Women with faded eyes, all spent of tears;

Men who have lived for love, yet lived alone;

And other worse, whose grief cannot be said.

O God, thou hast a work fit for thy strength,

To save these hearts of thine with full content —

Except thou give them Lethe's stream to drink,

And that, my God, were all unworthy thee.

Dome up, O heaven! yet higher o'er my head;

Back, back, horizon! widen out my world;

Rush in, O infinite sea of the Unknown!

For, though He slay me, I will trust in God.

TO LADY NOEL BYRON.

THEY sought and sought, for wealth's dear sake,
  The wizard men of old,
After the secret that should make
  The meaner metals gold.

A nobler alchemy is thine,
  Learned in thy sore distress:
Gold in thy hand becomes divine —
  Grows truth and tenderness.

TO THE SAME.

DEAD, why defend thee, who in life
  Wouldst for thy foe have died?
Who, thy own name the word of strife,
  Hadst silent stood aside.

Grand in forgiveness, what to thee
  The moralizer's prate?
Or thy great heart hath ceased to be,
  Or loveth still its mate.

TO AURELIO SAFFI.

To God and man be simply true;
Do as thou hast been wont to do;
Or, *Of the old more in the new,*
Mean all the same when said to you.

I love thee: thou art calm and strong;
Firm in the right, mild to the wrong;
Thy heart, in every raging throng,
A chamber shut for prayer and song.

Defeat thou know'st not, canst not know;
'Tis that thy aims so lofty go,
They need as long to root and grow
As infant hills to reach the snow.

Press on and prosper, holy friend.
I, weak and ignorant, would lend
A voice, thee, strong and wise, to send
Prospering onward, without end.

THE DISCIPLE

THE DISCIPLE.

---◆---

I.

THE times are changed, and gone the day
    When the high heavenly land,
Though unbeheld, quite near them lay,
    And men could understand.

The dead yet find it, who, when here,
    Did love it more than this;
They enter in, are filled with cheer,
    And pain expires in bliss.

All-glorious gleams the blessed land!
    Ah God! I weep and pray:
The heart thou holdest in thy hand
    Loves more this sunny day.

I see the hundred thousand wait
  Around the radiant throne:
Ah, what a dreary, gilded state!
  What crowds of beings lone!

I do not care for singing psalms;
  I tire of good men's talk;
To me there is no joy in palms,
  Or white-robed, solemn walk.

I love to hear the wild winds meet, —
  The wild old winds at night;
To watch the cold stars flash and beat,
  The feathery snow alight.

I love all tales of valiant men,
  Of women good and fair:
If I were rich and strong, ah! then
  I would do something rare.

But for thy temple in the sky,
  Its pillars strong and white, —
I cannot love it, though I try
  And long with all my might.

Sometimes a joy lays hold on me,
  And I am speechless then;
Almost a martyr I could be,
  To join the holy men.

Straightway my heart is like a clod,
  My spirit wrapt in doubt:
"*A pillar in the house of God,*
  And never more go out!"

No more the sunny, breezy morn;
  No more the glowing noon;
No more the silent heath forlorn;
  No more the waning moon!

My God, this heart will never burn,
  Will never taste thy joy;
Even Jesus' face is calm and stern:
  I am a hapless boy.

   .   .   .   .   .   .

II.

I read good books. My heart despairs.
　In vain I try to dress
My soul in feelings like to theirs, —
　These men of holiness.

My thoughts, like doves, abroad I fling
　To find a country fair:
Wind-baffled, back, they, with tired wing,
　To my poor ark repair.

Or comes a sympathetic thrill
　With long-departed saint,
A feeble dawn, without my will,
　Of feelings old and quaint,

As of a church's holy night,
　With low-browed chapels round,
Where common sunshine dares not light
　On the too sacred ground, —

One glance at sunny fields of grain,
　One shout of child at play, —

A merry melody drives amain
  The one-toned chant away.

My spirit will not enter here,
  To haunt the holy gloom ;
I gaze into a mirror mere, —
  A mirror, not a room.

And as a bird against the pane
  Oft strikes, deceived sore,
So I, who would go in, remain
  Outside some closed door.

O ! it will cost me many a sigh,
  If this be what it claims, —
This book, so unlike earth and sky,
  Unlike my hopes and aims ;

To me a desert parched and bare,
  In which a spirit broods
Whose wisdom I would gladly share
  At cost of many goods.

.   .   .   .   .   .

III.

O hear me, God! O give me joy,
    Such as thy chosen feel;
Have pity on a wretched boy,
    Whose heart is hard as steel.

I have no care for what is good;
    Thyself I do not love;
I relish not this bible-food;
    My heaven is not above.

Thou wilt not hear. I come no more.
    Thou heedest not my woe.
With sighs and tears my heart is sore.
    Thou comest not. I go.

   .   .   .   .

IV.

Once more I kneel. The earth is dark,
    And darker yet the air;
If light there be, 'tis but a spark
    Amid a world's despair —

A hopeless hope there yet may be, —
　A God somewhere to hear ;
A God to whom I bend my knee,
　A God with open ear.

I know that men laugh still to scorn
　The grief that is my lot ;
Such wounds, they say, are hardly borne,
　But easily forgot.

What matter that my sorrows rest
　On ills which men despise !
More hopeless heaves my aching breast,
　Than when a prophet sighs.

Æons of griefs have come and gone, —
　My grief is yet my mark.
The sun sets every night, yet none
　Sees therefore in the dark.

There 's love enough upon the earth,
　And beauty too, they say :

7

There may be plenty, may be dearth,
  I care not any way.

The world has melted from my sight;
  No grace in life is left;
I cry to thee with all my might,
  Because I am bereft.

In vain I cry. The earth is dark,
  And darker yet the air;
Of light there trembles now no spark
  In my lost soul's despair.

.   .   .   .   .

v.

I sit and gaze from window high
  Down on the noisy street.
No part in this great coil have I,
  No fate to go and meet.

My books unopened long have lain;
  In class I am all astray:

The questions growing in my brain
  Demand and have their way.

Knowledge is power, the people cry;
  Grave men the lure repeat:
After some rarer thing I sigh,
  That makes the pulses beat.

Old truths, new facts, they preach aloud, —
  Their tones like wisdom fall:
One sunbeam glancing on a cloud,
  Hints things beyond them all.

    .   .   .   .

VI.

But something is not right within;
  High hopes are all gone by.
Was it a bootless aim — to win
  Sight of a loftier sky?

They preach men should not faint, but pray,
  And seek until they find;

But God is very far away,
  Nor is his countenance kind.

And yet I know my father prayed,
  Withdrawing from the throng ;
I think some answer must have made
  His heart so high and strong.

Once more I'll seek the God of men,
  Redeeming childhood's vow.
I failed with bitter weeping then,
  And fail cold-hearted now.

VII.

Why search for God? A man I tread
  This old life-bearing earth ;
High thoughts arise and lift my head —
  In me they have their birth.

The preacher says a Christian must
  Do all the good he can ;
I must be noble, true, and just,
  Because I am a man.

They say a man must wake, and keep
  Lamp burning, garments white,
Else he shall sit without and weep
  When Christ comes home at night;

I say, his manhood must be free;
  Himself he dares not stain;
He must not soil the dignity
  Of heart and blood and brain.

Yes, I say well! for words are cheap.
  What action have I borne?
What praise will my one talent reap?
  What grapes are on my thorn?

Have high words kept me pure enough?
  In evil have I no part?
Hath not my bosom "perilous stuff,
  That weighs upon the heart?"

I am not that I well may praise;
  I do not that I say;
I sit a talker in the ways,
  A dreamer in the day.

VIII.

The preacher's words are true, I know,
  That man may lose his life ;
That every man must downward go
  Without the upward strife.

'Twere well my soul should cease to roam,
  Should seek and have and hold.
It may be there is yet a home
  In that religion old.

Again I kneel, again I pray:
  Wilt thou be God to me?
Wilt thou give ear to what I say,
  And lift me up to thee?

Lord, is it true? O, vision high!
  The clouds of heaven dispart ;
An opening depth of loving sky
  Looks down into my heart.

There *is* a home wherein to dwell —
  The very heart of light!

Thyself my sun immutable,
  My moon and stars all night !

I thank thee, Lord. It must be so,
  Its beauty is so good.
Up in my heart thou mad'st it go,
  And I have understood.

The clouds return. The common day
  Falls on me like a *No;*
But I have seen what might be — may;
  And with a hope I go.

IX.

I am a stranger in the land,
  It gives no welcome dear;
The lilies bloom not for my hand, —
  The roses for my cheer.

The sunshine used to make me glad,
  But now it knows me not;
This weight of brightness makes me sad, —
  It isolates a blot.

I am forgotten by the hills,
  And by the river's play;
No look of recognition thrills
  The features of the day.

Then only am I moved to song,
  When down the darkening street,
While vanishes the scattered throng,
  The driving rain I meet.

The rain pours down. My thoughts awake,
  Like flowers that languished long
From bare cold hills the night-winds break,
  From me the unwonted song.

x.

I read the Bible with my eyes,
  But hardly with my brain;
Should this the meaning recognize,
  My heart yet reads in vain.

These words of promise and of woe
  Seem but a tinkling sound;

As through an ancient tomb I go,
  With dust-filled urns around.

Or, as a sadly searching child,
  Afar from love and home,
Sits in an ancient chamber piled
  With scroll and musty tome ;

So I, in these epistles old
  From men of heavenly care,
Find all the thoughts of other mould
  Than I can love or share.

No sympathy with mine they show,
  Their world is not the same ;
They move me not with joy or woe,
  They touch me not with blame.

I hear no word that calls my life,
  Or owns my struggling powers ;
Those ancient ages had their strife,
  But not a strife like ours.

O ! not like men they move and speak,
   Those pictures in old panes ;
Nor alter they their aspect meek
   For all the winds and rains.

Their thoughts are filled with figures strange
   Of Jewish forms and rites :
A world of air and sea I range,
   Of mornings and of nights.

XI.

I turn me to the gospel-tale.
   My hope is faint with fear
That neediest search will not avail
   To find a refuge here.

A misty wind blows bare and rude
   From the dead sea of the past ;
And through the clouds that halt and brood,
   Dim dawns a shape at last :

A sad worn man who bows his face,
  And treads a frightful path,
To save an abject hopeless race
  From an eternal wrath.

Kind words He speaks — but all the time
  As from a pathless height
Where human feet can never climb,
  Half swathed in ancient night.

And sometimes, to a gentle heart,
  His words unkindly flow ;
Surely it is no Saviour's part
  To speak to women so.

Much rather would I refuge take
  With Mary, dear to me,
To whom those rough hard words He spake,
  What have I to do with thee ?

Surely I know men tenderer,
  Women of larger soul,
Who need no prayers their hearts to stir,
  Who always would make whole.

Oftenest He looks a weary saint,
　Embalmed in pallid gleam,
Listless and sad, without complaint,
　Like dead men in a dream.

But at the best He is uplift
　A spectacle, a show:
To me, an old, an outworn gift,
　Whose worth I cannot know.

I have no love to pay my debt —
　He leads me from the sun.
Yet it is hard men should forget
　The kindness He has done;

That He, to expiate a curse,
　Upon that altar-hill,
Beneath a sunless universe,
　Did suffer, patient, still.

But what is he, whose pardon slow
　At so much blood is priced?
If such thou art, O Jove, I go
　To the Promethean Christ.

XII.

A word within says I am to blame,
  And therefore must confess ;
Must call my doing by its name,
  And so make evil less.

" I could not his false triumph bear,
  For he was first in wrong."
"Thy own ill-doings are thy care,
  His to himself belong."

"To do it right, my heart should own
  Some sorrow for the ill."
" Plain, honest words will half atone,
  And they are in thy will."

The struggle comes. Evil or I
  Must gain the victory now.
I am unmoved, and yet would try :
  O God, to thee I bow.

The skies are brass ; there falls no aid ;
  No wind of help will blow,

But I bethink me: I am made
   A man: I rise and go.

XIII.

To Christ I needs must come, they say,
   Who went to death for me:
I turn aside; I come, I pray,
   My unknown God, to thee.

He is afar; the story old
   Is blotted, worn, and dim;
With thee, O God, I can be bold —
   I cannot pray to Him.

Pray! At the word a cloudy grief
   Around me folds its pall:
With nothing to be called belief,
   How can I pray at all?

I know not if a God be there
   To heed my crying sore,
If in the great world anywhere
   An ear keep open door.

An unborn faith I will not nurse;
  Nor search — an endless task;
But loud into its universe
  My soul shall call and ask.

Is there no God — earth, sky, and sea
  Are but a chaos wild;
Is there a God — I know that He
  Must hear his calling child.

XIV.

I kneel. But all my soul is dumb
  With hopeless misery:
Is *He* a friend who will not come,
  Whose face I may not see?

It is not fear of broken laws,
  Or judge's damning word;
It is a lonely pain, because
  I call and am not heard.

A cry where no man is to hear,
  Doubles the lonely pain;

Returns in silence on the ear,
  In torture on the brain.

No look of love a smile can bring,
  No kiss wile back the breath
To cold lips : I no answer wring
  From this great face of death.

xv.

Yet sometimes when the agony
  Dies of its own excess,
Unhoped repose descends on me, —
  A rain of gentleness ;

A sense of bounty and of grace,
  A calm within my breast,
As if the shadow of his face
  Did fall on me and rest.

'Tis God, I say, and cry no more —
  Upraised, with strength to stand
And wait unwearied at the door,
  Till comes an opening hand

XVI.

But is it God?   Once more the fear
  Of *No God* loads my breath :
Amidst a sunless atmosphere,
  I rise to fight with death.

This rest may be but such as lulls
  The man who fainting lies :
His bloodless brain his spirit dulls,
  With darkness veils his eyes.

But even this, my heart responds,
  May be the ancient rest
Rising released from frozen bonds
  To flow and fill the breast.

The o'ertasked will falls down aghast,
  In individual death ;
Then God takes up the severed past,
  And breathes the primal breath.

For torture's self can breed no calm,
  Nor death to life give birth ;
8

No labor can create the balm
  That soothes the sleeping earth.

So I will hope it is The One
  Whose peace is life in me,
Who, when my strength is overdone,
  Inspires serenity.

XVII.

When the hot sun's too urgent might
  Hath shrunk the tender leaf,
The dew slides down the blessed night,
  And cools its fainting grief.

When poet's heart is in eclipse,
  A glance from childhood's eye,
A smile from passing maiden's lips,
  Will clear a glowing sky.

 Might not from God such influence come
  A dying hope to lift?
Could He not send, in trouble, some
  Unmediated gift?

My child is moaning.   Far in dreams
  Which her own heart has made,
A world no caring love redeems
  She wanders, much afraid.

I lay my hand upon her breast;
  Her moaning dies away ;
She waketh not ; but, lost in rest,
  Sleeps on into the day.

And when my heart with soft release
  Grows calm as summer-sea,
Shall I not hope the God of peace
  Hath laid his hand on me ?

XVIII.

But why from thought should fresh doubt start —
  An ever-lengthening cord ?
Might He not make my troubled heart
  Right sure it was the Lord ?

God will not give a little boon
  To turn thee from the best ;

A granted sign might all too soon
   Rejoice thee into rest.

Yet could not any sign, though grand
   As hosts of fire about,
Though lovely as a sunset-land,
   Secure thy soul from doubt.

A smile from one thou lovest well
   May glad thee all the day ;
All day afar thy doubt may dwell, —
   Return with twilight gray.

For doubt will come, will ever come,
   Though signs be perfect good,
Till face to face strikes doubting dumb,
   And both are understood.

XIX.

I shall behold Him one day, nigh ;
   Assailed with glory keen,
My eyes shall open wide, and I
   Shall see as I am seen.

Of nothing can my heart be sure
　　Except the highest, best:
When God I see with vision pure,
　　That sight will be my rest.

Therefore I look with longing eye,
　　And still my hope renew;
Still think that comfort from the sky
　　May come like falling dew.

XX.

But if a vision should unfold
　　That I might banish fear;
That I, the chosen, might be bold,
　　And walk with upright cheer;

My heart would cry: But shares my race
　　In this great love of thine?
I pray, put me not in good case,
　　If others lack and pine.

Nor claim I thus a loving heart
　　That for itself is mute:

In such love I desire no part
   As reaches not my root.

If all my brothers thou dost call
   As children to thy knee,
Thou givest me my being's all, —
   Thou sayest *child* to me.

If thou to me alone shouldst give,
   My heart were all beguiled.
It would not be *because* I live,
   And am my Father's child.

XXI.

As little comfort would it bring,
   Amidst a throng to pass ;
To stand with thousands worshipping
   Upon the sea of glass ;

To know that of a sinful world,
   I one was saved as well ;

My roll of ill with theirs upfurled,
　And cast in deepest hell ,

That God looked bounteously on one,
　Because on many men ;
As shone Judæa's earthly sun
　Upon the healed ten.

No ; thou must be a God to me
　As if but me were none ;
I such a perfect child to thee
　As if thou hadst but one.

XXII.

Then, O my Father, hast thou not
　A blessing even for me ?
Shall I be, barely, not forgot ?
　Never come home to thee ?

Hast thou no care for this one child,
　This thinking, living need ?
Or is thy countenance only mild,
　Thy heart not love indeed ?

For some eternal joy I pray,
　To make me strong and free;
Yea, such a friend I need alway
　As thou alone canst be.

Art thou not, by infinitude,
　Able, in every man,
To turn thyself to every mood
　Since ever life began?

Art thou not each man's God — his own,
　With secret words between,
As thou and he lived all alone,
　Insphered in silence keen?
　.

Ah God! my heart is not the same
　As any heart beside;
Nor is my sorrow or my blame,
　My tenderness or pride.

My story too, thou knowest, God,
　Is different from the rest;
Thou knowest — none but thee — the load
　With which my heart is pressed.

Hence I to thee a love might bring,
  By none besides me due;
One praiseful song at least might sing
  Which could not but be new.

XXIII.

Nor seek I thus to stand apart
  In thee, my kind above;
'Tis only that my aching heart
  Must rest ere it can love.

If thou love not, I have no care,
  No power to love, no hope.
What is life here or anywhere?
  Or why with darkness cope?

I scorn love's every motion, sign,
  So feeble, selfish, low,
If thy love give no pledge that mine
  Shall one day perfect grow.

But if thy love were only such,
  As, tender and intense,

As, tested by its human touch,
  Would satisfy my sense

Of what a father never was
  But should be to his son,
My heart would leap for joy, because
  My rescue was begun.

And then my love, by thine set free,
  Would overflow thy men;
In every face my heart would see
  God shining out again.

There are who hold high festival
  And at the board crown Death:
I am too weak to live at all,
  Except I breathe thy breath.

Show me a love that nothing bates,
  Absolute, self-severe,
And at Gehenna's prayerless gates
  "I cannot taint with fear."

XXIV.

I cannot brook that men should say, —
   Nor this for gospel take, —
That thou wilt hear me if I pray,
   Asking for Jesus' sake.

For love to Him is not to me,
   And cannot lift my fate ;
The love is not that is not free,
   Perfect, immediate.

Love is salvation: life without
   No moment can endure.
Those sheep alone go in and out,
   Who know thy love is pure.

XXV.

But what if God requires indeed,
   For cause yet unrevealed,
Assent to moulded form of creed,
   Such as I cannot yield?

The words may have some other sense,
  Or we be different
From what we seem when thought intense
  Is only one way bent.

Or what if all-distorting pride
  Shows me the good thing ill?
For man, they say, hath God defied,
  And walks with stubborn will.

Or God may choose to give a test,
  And try the earnest aim,
That only he may win the best,
  Who conquers pride and shame.

And yet the words I cannot say
  With the responding folk;
I at his feet a heart would lay,
  Not shoulders for the yoke.

"And wilt thou bargain then with Him?"
  Some priest will make reply.
I answer: "Though the sky be dim,
  My hope is in the sky."

XXVI.

But is my will alive, awake?
  The one God will not heed,
If in my lips or hands I take
  A half word or half deed.

Day after day I sit and dream,
  Amazed in outwardness;
The powers of things that only seem
  The things that are oppress;

Till in my soul some discord sounds,
  Till sinks some yawning lack:
I turn me from life's rippling rounds,
  And unto thee come back.

Thou seest how poor a thing am I;
  Yet hear, whate'er I be;
Despairing of my will, I cry,
  Be God enough to me.

My being low, irresolute,
  I cast before thy feet;

And wait, while even prayer is mute,
  For what thou judgest meet.

XXVII.

My safety lies not, any hour,
  In what I generate,
But in the living, healing power
  Of that which doth create.

If He is God to the incomplete,
  Fulfilling lack and need,
Then I *may* cast before his feet
  A half word or half deed.

I bring, Lord, to thy altar-stair,
  To thee, love-glorious,
My very lack of will and prayer,
  Crying, Thou seest me thus

From some old well of life they flow!
  The words my being fill! —
" Of me that man the truth shall know
  Who wills the Father's will "

XXVIII.

What is his will? — that I may go
　　And do it in the hope
That light will rise and spread and grow,
　　As deed enlarges scope.

I need not search the sacred book
　　To find my duty clear;
Scarce in my bosom need I look,
　　It lies so very near.

Henceforward I must watch the door
　　Of word and action too;
There 's one thing I must do no more,
　　Another I must do.

Alas, these are such little things!
　　No glory in their birth!
Doubt from their common aspect springs,
　　If God will count them worth.

But here I am not left to choose,
　　My duty is my lot;

And weighty things will glory lose,
   If small ones are forgot.

I am not worthy high things yet;
   I'll humbly do my own;
Good care of sheep may so beget
   A fitness for the throne.

Ah fool! why dost thou reason thus?
   Ambition's very fool!
Through high and low, each glorious,
   Shines God's all-perfect rule.

'Tis God I need, not rank in good;
   'Tis Life, not honor's meed;
With Him to fill my every mood,
   I am content indeed.

XXIX.

Will do: shall know: I feel the force,
   The fullness of the word;
His holy boldness held its course,
   Claiming divine accord.

What if, as yet, I have never seen
   The true face of the Man?
The named notion may have been
   A likeness vague and wan;

Or bright with such unblended hues
   As on his chamber wall
The humble peasant gladly views,
   And Jesus Christ doth call.

The story I did never scan
   With vision calm and strong;
Have never tried to see the Man,
   The many words among.

Some faces that would never please
   With any sweet surprise,
Gain on the heart by slow degrees
   Until they feast the eyes;

And if I ponder, day by day,
   Over the storied place,

9

Through mists that slowly melt away
　　May dawn a human face.

A face! What face? Exalting thought
　　That face may dawn on me
Which Moses on the mountain sought,
　　God would not let him see.

XXX.

ı read and read the ancient tale.
　　A gracious form I mark ;
But dim and faint as rapt in veil
　　Of Sinai's cloudy dark.

I see a simple, truthful man,
　　Who walks the earth erect,
Nor stoops his noble head to one
　　From fear or false respect.

He seeks to climb no high estate,
　　No low consent secure,
With high and low serenely great,
　　Because his ends are pure ;

Nor walks alone, beyond our reach,
  Our joy and grief beyond:
He counts it joy divine to teach,
  When human hearts respond;

And grief divine oft woke in Him
  O'er souls that lay and slept:
" How often, O Jerusalem!"
  He said, and gazed, and wept.

Hid in his heart, some spring of grace
  Flowed silent through the din;
The sorrow-cloud upon his face,
  Was lighted from within.

Love was his very being's root,
  And healing was its flower;
Love only, root and flower and fruit, —
  Beginning, end, and power.

O Life of Jesus — the unseen,
  Which found such glorious show —
Deeper than death, and more serene!
  How poor am I! how low!

XXXI.

As in a living well I gaze,
   Kneeling upon its brink.
What are the very words He says?
   What did the one man think?

I find his heart was all above ;
   Obedience his one thought ;
Reposing in his Father's love,
   His will alone He sought.

.   .   .   .   .   .

XXXII.

Years have passed o'er my broken plan
   To picture out a strife
Where ancient Death, in horror wan,
   Faced young and fearing Life.

More of the tale I tell not so —
   But for myself would say:
My heart is quiet with what I know,
   With what I hope, is gay.

And where I cannot set my faith,
  Unknowing or unwise,
I say, " If this be what *He* saith,
  Here hidden treasure lies."

Through years gone by since thus I strove,
  Thus shadowed out my strife,
While at my history I wove,
  Thou didst weave in the life.

Through poverty that had no lack,
  For friends divinely good ;
Through pain that not too long did rack ;
  Through love that understood ;

Through light that taught me what to hold,
  And what to cast away ;
Through thy forgiveness manifold,
  And things I cannot say,

Here thou hast brought me — able now
  To kiss thy garment's hem,
Entirely to thy will to bow,
  And trust thee even for them.

Who, lost in darkness, in the mire,
   With ill-contented feet,
Walk trailing loose their white attire,
   For the sapphire-floor unmeet.

Lord Jesus Christ, I know not how —
   With this blue air, blue sea,
This yellow sand, that grassy brow,
   All isolating me —

My words to thy heart should draw near,
   My thoughts be heard by thee ;
But He who made the ear must hear,
   Who made the eye, must see.

Thou mad'st the hand with which I write,
   That sun descending slow
Through rosy gates, that purple light
   On waves that shoreward go,

Bowing their heads in golden spray,
   As if thy foot were near:
I think I know thee, Lord, to-day,
   Have known thee many a year.

I know thy Father — thine and mine —
 Thus thy great word doth go:
If thy great word the words combine,
 I will not say *Not so.*

Lord, thou hast much to make me yet, —
 A feeble infant still:
Thy thoughts, Lord, in my bosom set,
 Fulfill me of thy will,

Even of thy truth, both in and out,
 That so I question free:
The man that feareth, Lord, to doubt,
 In that fear doubteth thee.

THE GOSPEL WOMEN.

THE GOSPEL WOMEN.

I.

THE MOTHER MARY.

I.

MARY, to thee the heart was given
   For infant hand to hold,
Thus clasping, an eternal heaven,
   The great earth in its fold.

He seized the world with tender might
   By making thee his own ;
Thee, lowly queen, whose heavenly height
   Was to thyself unknown.

He came, all helpless, to thy power,
   For warmth, and love, and birth ;
In thy embraces, every hour,
   He grew into the earth.

And thine the grief, O mother high,
    Which all thy sisters share,
Who keep the gate betwixt the sky
    And this our lower air;

And unshared sorrows, gathering slow;
    New thoughts within thy heart,
Which through thee like a sword will go,
    And make thee mourn apart.

For, if a woman bore a son
    That was of angel brood,
Who lifted wings ere day was done,
    And soared from where he stood;

Strange grief would fill each mother-moan,
    Wild longing, dim, and sore:
"My child! my child! he is my own,
    And yet is mine no more!"

So thou, O Mary, years on years,
    From child-birth to the cross,
Wast filled with yearnings, filled with fears,
    Keen sense of love and loss.

His childish thoughts outsoared thy reach;
  Even his tenderness
Had deeper springs than act or speech
  Could unto thee express.

Strange pangs await thee, mother mild!
  A sorer travail-pain,
Before the spirit of thy child
  Is born in thee again.

And thou wilt still forbode and dread,
  And loss be still thy fear,
Till form be gone, and, in its stead,
  The very self appear.

For, when thy son hath reached his goal,
  And vanished from the earth,
Soon shalt thou find Him in thy soul,
  A second, holier birth.

II.

Ah, there He stands! With wondering face
  Old men surround the boy;

The solemn looks, the awful place
    Bestill the mother's joy.

In sweet reproach her joy is hid,
    Her trembling voice is low,
Less like the chiding than the chid:
    "How couldst thou leave us so?"

But will her dear heart understand
    The answer that He gives —
Childlike, eternal, simple, grand,
    The law by which He lives?

"Why sought ye me?"   Ah, mother dear!
    The gulf already opes
That soon will keep thee to thy fear,
    And part thee from thy hopes.

"My Father's business — that ye know,
    I cannot choose but do."
Mother, if He that work forego,
    Not long He cares for you.

Creation's harder, better part
  Is in his willing hand ;
I marvel not the mother's heart
  Not yet could understand.

III.

The Lord of life among them rests ;
  They quaff the merry wine ;
They do not know, those wedding guests,
  The present power divine.

Believe, on such a group He smiled,
  Though He might sigh the while ;
Believe not, sweet-souled Mary's child
  Was born without a smile.

He saw the pitchers high upturned,
  The last red drops to pour ;
His mother's cheek with triumph burned,
  And expectation wore.

He knew the prayer her bosom housed ;
  He read it in her eyes ;

Her hopes in Him sad thoughts have roused,
  Before her words arise.

"They have no wine," her shy lips said,
  With prayer but half begun,
Her eyes went on, "Lift up thy head,
  Show what thou art, my son!"

A vision rose before his eyes,
  The cross, the waiting tomb,
The people's rage, the darkened skies,
  His unavoided doom.

"Ah woman-heart! what end is set
  Common to thee and me?
My hour of honor is not yet, —
  'Twill come too soon for thee."

The word was dark; the tone was kind·
  His heart the mother knew,
And still his eyes more sweetly shined,
  His voice more gentle grew.

Another, on the word intent,
　　Had heard refusal there;
His mother heard a full consent,
　　A sweetly answered prayer.

"Whate'er He saith unto you, do."
　　Fast flowed the grapes divine;
Though then, as now, not many knew
　　Who made the water wine.

IV.

" He is beside himself." Dismayed,
　　His mother, brothers talked:
" He from the well-known path has strayed,
　　In which our fathers walked."

And sad at heart, they sought Him. Loud
　　Some one the message bore;
He stands within, amidst a crowd,
　　They at the open door.

" Thy mother and thy brothers would
　　Speak with thee. Lo, they stand

10

Without and wait thee ! "   Like a flood
  Of sunrise on the land,

A new-born light his face o'erspread ,
  Out from his eyes it poured ;
He lifted up that gracious head,
  Looked round him, took the word :

" My mother — brothers — who are they ? "
  Hearest thou, Mary mild ?
This is a sword that well may slay, —
  Disowned by thy child !

Ah, no ! My brothers, sisters, hear !
  What says our humble Lord ?
O mother, did it wound *thy* ear ?
  We thank Him for the word.

" Who are my friends ? " O ! hear Him say,
  Stretching his hand abroad :
" My mother, sisters, brothers, they
  Who do the will of God."

My brother! Lord of life and me,
  If it might come to this!
Ah! brother, sister, that would be
  Enough for all amiss.

Yea, hear Him, mother, and rejoice:
  No better name hath He,
To give as best of all his choice,
  Than that He gives to thee.

O humble child, O faithful son!
  Of women most forlorn,
She who the Father's will hath done,
  The Son of Man hath borne.

Mary, if in thy coming pain,
  Thou to thy Father bow,
The Christ shall be thy son again,
  And twice his mother thou.

v.

Life's best things crowd around its close,
  To light it from the door;

When woman's aid no further goes,
　　She weeps and loves the more.

Oft, oft, she doubted, in his life,
　　And feared his mission's loss ;
But now she shares the losing strife,
　　And weeps beside the cross.

The dreaded hour is come at last ;
　　The sword has reached her soul ;
The hour of timid hope is past,
　　Unveiled the awful whole.

There hangs the son her body bore,
　　Who in her arms did rest ;
Those limbs the nails and hammer tore
　　Have lain upon her breast.

He speaks.　With torturing joy the sounds
　　Invade her desolate ear ;
The mother's heart, though bleeding, bounds
　　Her dying son to hear

" Woman, behold thy son. — Behold
  Thy mother." Best relief —
That woeful love in hers to fold
  Which next to hers was chief !

Another son, but not instead,
  He gave, lest grief should kill,
While he was down among the dead,
  Doing his Father's will.

No, not *instead;* the coming grace
  Shall make Him hers anew —
More hers than when, in her embrace,
  His life from hers he drew.

II.

THE WOMAN THAT LIFTED UP HER VOICE.

Filled with his words of truth and right,
  Her heart will break or cry :
A woman's cry bursts forth in might
  Of loving agony.

"Blessed the womb, thee, Lord, that bare!
  The bosom that thee fed!"
A moment's silence filled the air,
  When she the word had said.

He turns his face to meet the cry;
  He knows from whence it springs —
A woman's heart that glad would die
  For woman's best of things.

Such son to bear, such son to rear,
  The generations laud.
"Yea, rather, blessed they that hear
  And keep the word of God."

The tone was love and not rebuke;
  But, 'mid the murmured stir,
She, sure, was silent in her nook;
  No answer came from her.

III.

THE MOTHER OF ZEBEDEE'S CHILDREN.

She knelt, she bore a bold request,
   Though shy to speak it out;
Ambition, even in mother's breast,
   Before Him stood in doubt.

"What is it?" — "These my sons, allow
   To sit on thy right hand
And on thy left, O Lord, when thou
   Art ruler in the land."

"Ye know not what ye ask." There lay
   A baptism and a cup
They understood not, in the way
   By which He must go up.

She would have had them lifted high
   Above their fellow-men;
Sharing their pride with mother-eye, —
   Had been blest mother then.

But would she praise for granted quest,
  Counting her prayer well heard,
If of the three on Calvary's crest
  They shared the first and third?

She knoweth neither way nor end;
  There comes a dark despair,
When she will doubt if this great friend
  Can answer any prayer.

Yet higher than her love can dare,
  His love her sons will set.
They shall his cup and baptism share,
  And share his kingdom yet.

They, entering at his palace door,
  Shall shun the lofty seat;
Shall gird themselves, and water pour,
  And wash each other's feet.

For in thy kingdom, lowly Lord,
  Who sit with thee on high
Are those who tenderest help afford
  In most humility

IV.

THE SYRO-PHŒNICIAN WOMAN.

" Grant, Lord, her prayer, and let her go ;
    She crieth after us."
Nay, to the dogs ye cast it so ;
    Serve not a woman thus.

Their pride, by condescension fed,
    He speaks with truer tongue :
" It is not meet the children's bread
    Should to the dogs be flung."

The words, because they were so sore,
    His tender voice did rue ;
His face a gentle sadness wore,
    And showed he suffered too.

He makes her share the hurt of good,
    Takes what she would have lent,
That those proud men their evil mood
    May see, and so repent ;

And that the hidden faith in her
  May burst in soaring flame,
From childhood deeper, holier,
  If birthright not the same.

"Truth, Lord ; and yet the dogs that crawl
  Under the table, eat
The crumbs the little ones let fall —
  And that is not unmeet."

Ill names, of proud religion born —
  She'll wear the worst that comes ;
Will clothe her, patient, in their scorn,
  To share the healing crumbs.

The cry rebuff could not abate
  Was not like water spilt :
"O woman, but thy faith is great !
  Be it even as thou wilt."

O, happy she who will not tire,
  But, baffled, prayeth still !
What if He grant her heart's desire
  In fullness of *her* will !

V.

THE WIDOW OF NAIN.

Forth from the city, with the load
　That makes the trampling low,
They walk along the dreary road
　That dust and ashes go.

The other way, towards the gate,
　Their footsteps light and loud,
A living man, in humble state,
　Brings on another crowd.

Nearer and nearer come the twain;
　He hears the wailing cry
How can the Life let such a train
　Of death and tears go by?

"Weep not," He said, and touched the bier;
　They stand, the dead who bear;
The mother knows nor hope nor fear,
　He waits not for her prayer.

" Young man, I say to thee, arise."
    Who hears, he must obey;
Up starts the form; wide flash the eyes
    With wonder and dismay.

The lips would speak, as if they caught
    Some converse sudden broke,
When the great word the dead man sought,
    And Hades' silence woke.

The lips would speak: the eyes' wild stare
    Gives place to ordered sight;
The murmur dies upon the air —
    The soul is dumb with light.

He bring no news; he has forgot,
    Or saw with vision weak:
Thou seest all our unseen lot,
    And yet thou dost not speak.

Keep'st thou the news, as parent might
    A too good gift, away,
Lest we should neither sleep at night,
    Nor do our work by day?

His mother has not left a trace
  Of triumph over grief;
Her tears alone have found a place
  Upon the holy leaf.

If gratitude our speech benumb,
  And joy our laughter quell,
May not Eternity be dumb
  For things too good to tell?

While her glad arms the lost one hold,
  Question she asketh none;
She trusts for all he leaves untold;
  Enough, to clasp her son.

The ebbing tide is caught and won —
  Borne flowing to the gate;
Death turns him backward to the sun,
  And Life is yet our fate.

VI.

THE WOMAN WHOM SATAN HAD BOUND.

For eighteen years, she, patient soul,
   Her eyes hath graveward sent;
All vain for her the starry pole,
   She is so bowed and bent.

What mighty words! Who can be near?
   What tenderness of hands!
O! is it strength, or fancy mere?
   New hope, or breaking bands?

The pent life rushes swift along
   Channels it used to know;
And up, amidst the wondering throng,
   She rises firm and slow —

To bend again in grateful awe —
   Will, power no more at strife —
In homage to the living Law
   Who gives her back her life.

Uplifter of the drooping head!
Unbinder of the bound!
Thou seest our sore-burdened
Bend hopeless to the ground.

What if they see thee not, nor cry —
Thou watchest for the hour
To raise the forward-beaming eye,
To wake the slumbering power.

I see thee wipe the stains of time
From off the withered face;
Lift up thy bowed old men, in prime
Of youthful manhood's grace.

Like summer days from winter's tomb,
Arise thy women fair;
Old age, a shadow, not a doom,
Lo! is not anywhere.

All ills of life shall melt away
As melts a cureless woe,
When, by the dawning of the day
Surprised, the dream must go.

I think thou, Lord, wilt heal me too.
　　Whate'er the needful cure ;
The great best only thou wilt do,
　　And hoping I endure.

VII.

THE WOMAN WHO CAME BEHIND HIM IN THE CROWD.

Near Him she stole, rank after rank ;
　　She feared approach too loud ;
She touched his garment's hem, and shrank
　　Back in the sheltering crowd.

A shame-faced gladness thrills her frame :
　　Her twelve years' fainting prayer
Is heard at last ; she is the same
　　As other women there.

She hears his voice.　He looks about.
　　Ah ! is it kind or good
To drag her secret sorrow out
　　Before that multitude ?

The eyes of men she dares not meet —
  On her they straight must fall:
Forward she sped, and at his feet
  Fell down, and told Him all.

His presence makes a holy place;
  No alien eyes are there;
Her shrinking shame finds godlike grace
  The covert of its care.

"Daughter," he said, "be of good cheer;
  Thy faith hath made thee whole."
With plenteous love, not healing mere,
  He would content her soul.

VIII.

THE WIDOW WITH THE TWO MITES.

Here *much* and *little* shift and change,
  With scale of need and time;
There *more* and *less* have meanings strange,
  Nor with our reason rhyme.

11

Sickness may be more hale than health,
 And service kingdom high ;
Yea, poverty be bounty's wealth,
 To give like God thereby.

Bring forth your riches, let them go,
 Nor mourn the lost control,
For if ye hoard them, surely so
 Their rust will reach your soul.

Cast in your coins, for God delights
 When from wide hands they fall ;
But here is one who brings two mites,
 And yet gives more than all.

She heard not, she, the mighty praise ;
 Went home to care and need ;
Perhaps the knowledge still delays,
 And yet she has the meed.

IX.

THE WOMEN WHO MINISTERED UNTO HIM.

Enough He labors for his hire ;
  Yea, nought can pay his pain :
But powers that wear, and waste, and tire,
  Need strength to toil again.

They give Him freely all they can ;
  They give Him clothes and food ;
In this rejoicing, that the man
  Is not ashamed they should.

High love takes form in lowly thing ;
  He knows the offering such ;
To them 'tis little that they bring,
  To Him 'tis very much.

X.

PILATE'S WIFE.

Why came in dreams the low-born man
  Between thee and thy rest;

For vain thy whispered message ran,
  Though justice was thy quest?

Did some young ignorant angel dare —
  Not knowing what must be,
Or blind with agony of care —
  To fly for help to thee?

It may be. Rather I believe,
  Thou, nobler than thy spouse,
The rumored grandeur didst receive,
  And sit with pondering brows,

Until thy maidens' gathered tale
  With possible marvel teems ·
.Thou sleepest, and the prisoner pale
  Returneth in thy dreams.

Well mightst thou suffer things not few
  For his sake all the night!
In pale eclipse He suffers, who
  Is of the world the light.

Precious it were to know thy dream
  Of such a one as He !
Perhaps of Him we, waking, deem
  As poor a verity.

XI.

THE WOMAN OF SAMARIA.

In the hot noon, for water cool,
  She strayed in listless mood :
When back she ran, her pitcher full
  Forgot behind her stood.

Like one who followed straying sheep,
  A weary man she saw,
Who sat upon the well so deep,
  And nothing had to draw.

"Give me to drink," He said.   Her hand
  Was ready with reply ;
From out the old well of the land
  She drew Him plenteously.

He spake as never man before ;
   She stands with open ears ;
He spake of holy days in store,
   Laid bare the vanished years.

She cannot still her throbbing heart ;
   She hurries to the town,
And cries aloud in street and mart,
   " The Lord is here : come down."

Her life before was strange and sad,
   Its tale a dreary sound :
Ah ! let it go — or good or bad,
   She has the Master found.

XII.

MARY MAGDALENE.

With eyes aglow, and aimless zeal,
   She hither, thither, goes ;
Her speech, her motions, all reveal
   A mind without repose.

She climbs the hills, she haunts the sea,
  By madness tortured, driven ;
One hour's forgetfulness would be
  A gift from very Heaven.

The night brings sleep, sleep new distress ;
  The anguish of the day
Returns as free, in darker dress,
  In more secure dismay.

The demons blast her to and fro ;
  She has no quiet place ;
Enough a woman still to know
  A haunting dim disgrace.

Hers in no other eyes confide
  For even a moment brief ;
With restless glance they turn aside,
  Lest they betray her grief.

A human touch ! a pang of death !
  And in a low delight
Thou liest, waiting for new breath,
  For morning out of night.

Thou risest up: the earth is fair,
   The wind is cool and free;
Is it a dream of hell's despair
   Dissolves in ecstasy?

Did this man touch thee? Eyes divine
   Make sunrise in thy soul;
Thou seest love and order shine:
   His health hath made thee whole.

What matter that the coming time
   Will stain thy virgin name!
Will call thine agony thy crime,
   And count thy madness blame!

Let the reproach of men abide!
   He shall be well content
To see not seldom by his side
   Thy head serenely bent.

Thou, sharing in the awful doom,
   Shalt help thy Lord to die,
And, mourning o'er his empty tomb,
   First share his victory.

XIII.

THE WOMAN IN THE TEMPLE.

A still dark joy! A sudden face!
  Cold daylight, footsteps, cries!
The temple's naked, shining space,
  Aglare with judging eyes!

All in abandoned guilty hair,
  With terror-pallid lips,
To vulgar scorn her honor bare,
  To vulgar taunts and quips,

Her eyes she fixes on the ground,
  Her shrinking soul to hide;
Lest, at uncurtained windows found,
  Its shame be clear descried.

All-idle hang her listless hands,
  And tingle with the shame;
She sees not who beside her stands,
  She is so bowed with blame.

He stoops, He writes upon the ground,
  Regards nor priests nor wife ;
An awful silence spreads around,
  And wakes an inward strife.

Is it a voice that speaks for thee?
  Almost she hears aghast:
" Let him who from this sin is free,
  At her the first stone cast."

Astonished, waking, growing sad,
  Her eyes bewildered rose ;
She saw the one true friend she had,
  Who loves her though He knows.

Upon her deathlike, ashy face,
  The blushes rise and spread:
No greater wonder sure had place
  When Lazarus left the dead !

He stoops. In every charnel breast
  Dead conscience rises slow:
They, dumb before that awful guest,
  Turn, one by one, and go.

Alone with Him! Yet no new dread
  Invades the silence round;
False pride, false shame, all false is dead;
  She has the Master found.

Who else had spoken on her side,
  Those cruel men withstood?
From Him even shame she would not hide;
  For Him she *will* be good.

He rises — sees the temple bare;
  'They two are left alone.
He turns and asks her, "Woman, where
  Are thine accusers gone?

"Hath none condemned thee?" — "Master, no,"
  She answers, trembling sore.
"Neither do I condemn thee. Go,
  And sin not any more."

She turned and went. To hope and grieve?
  Be what she had not been?
We are not told; but I believe
  His kindness made her clean.

Our sins to thee us captive hale —
  Offenses, hatreds dire;
Weak loves that selfish grow, and fail
  And fall into the mire.

Our conscience-cry with pardon meet;
  Our passion cleanse with pain;
Lord, thou didst make these miry feet—
  O! wash them clean again.

XIV.

MARTHA.

With joyful pride her heart is high:
  Her humble chambers hold
The man prophetic destiny
  Long centuries hath foretold.

Poor, is He? Yes, and lowly born:
  Her woman-soul is proud
To know and hail the coming morn
  Before the eyeless crowd.

At her poor table will He eat?
    He shall be served there
With honor and devotion meet
    For any king that were.

'Tis all she can; she does her part,
    Profuse in sacrifice;
Nor knows that in her unknown heart
    A better offering lies.

But many crosses she must bear;
    Her plans are turned and bent;
Do all she can, things will not wear
    The form of her intent.

With idle hands, and drooping lid,
    See Mary sit at rest!
Shameful it was her sister did
    No service for their guest.

But Martha one day Mary's lot
    Must share with hands and eyes;
Must — all her household cares forgot —
    Sit down as idly wise.

Ere long they both in Jesus' ear
　　Shall make the self-same moan :
" Lord, if thou only hadst been here,
　　My brother had not gone."

Then once will Martha set her word,
　　Yet once, to bar his ways,
Crying, " By this he stinketh, Lord ;
　　He hath been dead four days."

When Lazarus drags his trammeled clay
　　Forth with half-opened eyes,
Her buried best will hear, obey,
　　And with the dead man rise.

XV.

MARY.

I.

She sitteth at the Master's feet
　　In motionless employ ,
Her ears, her heart, her soul complete
　　Drinks in the tide of joy.

Ah! who but her the glory knows
    Of life, pure, high, intense,
Whose holy calm breeds awful shows
    Beyond the realm of sense!

In her still ear, his thoughts of grace
    Incarnate are in voice;
Her thoughts, the people of the place,
    Receive them, and rejoice.

Her eyes, with heavenly reason bright,
    Are on the ground cast low,
It is his words of truth and light
    That sets them shining so.

But see! a face is at the door
    Whose eyes are not at rest;
A voice breaks in on wisest lore
    With petulant request.

"Lord," Martha says, "dost thou not care
    She lets me serve alone?
Tell her to come and take her share."
    Still Mary's eyes shine on.

Calmly she lifts a questioning glance
    To Him who calmly heard,
The merest sign, she'll rise at once,
    Nor wait the uttered word.

The other, standing by the door,
    Waits too what He will say.
His "Martha, Martha" with it bore
    A sense of coming *nay*.

Gently her troubled heart He chid;
    Rebuked its needless care;
Methinks her face she turned and hid,
    With shame that bordered prayer.

What needful thing is Mary's choice,
    Nor shall be taken away?
There is but one — 'tis Jesus' voice;
    And listening she shall stay.

O, joy to every doubting heart,
    Doing the thing it would,
When He, the holy, takes its part,
    And calls its choice the good!

II.

Not now the living words are poured
   Into her single heart ;
For many guests are at the board,
   And many tongues take part.

With sacred foot, refrained and slow,
   With daring, trembling tread,
She comes, with worship bending low
   Behind the godlike head.

The costly chrism, in snowy stone,
   A gracious odor sends.
Her little hoard, so slowly grown,
   In one full act she spends.

She breaks the box, the honored thing !
   And down its riches pour ;
Her priestly hands anoint her king,
   To reign for evermore.

With murmur and nod, they called it waste :
   Their love they could endure ;

12

Hers ached a prisoner in her breast,
  And she forgot the poor.

She meant it for his coming state;
  He took it for his doom.
The other women were too late,
  For He had left the tomb.

XVI.

THE WOMAN THAT WAS A SINNER.

His face, his words, her heart awoke,
  Awoke her slumbering truth;
She judged Him well; her bonds she broke,
  And fled to Him for ruth.

With tears she washed his weary feet;
  She wiped them with her hair;
Her kisses — call them not unmeet,
  When they were welcome *there*.

What saint — a richer crown to throw,
  Could love's ambition teach?

Her eyes, her lips, her hair, down go,
  In love's despair of speech.

His holy manhood's perfect worth
  Owns her a woman still;
It is impossible henceforth
  For her to stoop to ill.

Her to herself his words restore,
  The radiance to the day;
A horror to herself no more,
  Not yet a cast-away!

And so, in kisses, ointment, tears,
  And outspread lavish hair,
Love, shame, and hope, and griefs and fears,
  Mingle in worship rare.

Mary, thy hair thou didst not spread
  About the holy feet;
Didst only bless the holy head
  With spikenard's ointment sweet.

Or if thou didst, as some would hold —
　Thy heart the lesson caught,
The abandonment so humble-bold,
　From her whom pardon taught.

And if thy hair thou too didst wind
　The holy feet around,
Such plenteous tears thou couldst not find
　As this sad woman found.

Let her in grief the first be read —
　And love, the woeful sweet!
Be thou content to bless his head,
　Let this one crown his feet.

Simon, her kisses will not soil;
　Her tears are pure as rain;
Eye not her hair's untwisted coil,
　Baptized in pardoning pain.

For God hath pardoned all her *much*;
　Her iron bands hath burst,

Her love could never have been such,
  Had not his love been first.

But O! rejoice, ye sisters pure,
  Who hardly know her case:
There is no sin but has its cure,
  Its all consuming grace.

He did not leave her soul in hell,
  'Mong shards the silver dove;
But raised her pure that she might tell
  Her sisters how to love.

She gave Him all your best love can.
  Was He despised and sad? —
Yes; and yet never mighty man
  Such perfect homage had.

Jesus, by whose forgiveness sweet,
  Her love grew so intense,
We, sinners all, come round thy feet —
  Lord, make no difference.

A BOOK OF SONNETS.

A BOOK OF SONNETS.

——◆——

THE BURNT OFFERING.

THRICE-HAPPY he, whose heart, each new-
    born night,
When the worn day hath vanished o'er earth's brim,
And he hath laid him down in chamber dim,
Straightway begins to tremble and grow bright,
And loose faint flashes towards the vaulted height
Of the great peace that overshadows him,
Till tongues of fiery hope awake and swim
Through his soul, and touch each point with light!
Then the great earth a holy altar is,
Upon whose top a sacrifice he lies,
Burning in love's response up to the skies
Whose fire descended first and kindled his:
When slow the flickering flames at length expire,
Sleep's ashes only hide the glowing fire.

THE UNSEEN FACE.

"I do beseech thee, God, show me thy face."
"Come up to me in Sinai on the morn:
Thou shalt behold as much as may be borne."
And on a rock stood Moses, lone in space.
From Sinai's top, the vaporous, thunderous place,
God passed in cloud, an earthly garment worn
To hide, and thus reveal. In love, not scorn,
He put him in a cleft of the rock's base,
Covered him with his hand, his eyes to screen —
Passed — lifted it — his back alone appears.
Ah, Moses! had he turned, and hadst thou seen
The pale face crowned with thorns, baptized with
        tears,
The eyes of the true man, by men belied,
Thou hadst beheld God's face, and straightway died.

CONCERNING JESUS

I.

If thou hadst been a sculptor, what a race
Of forms divine had thenceforth filled the land!
Methinks I see thee, glorious workman. stand,
Striking a marble window through blind space;
Thy face's reflex on the coming face,
As dawns the stone to statue 'neath thy hand —
Body obedient to its soul's command,
Which is thy thought informing it with grace!
So had it been. But God, who quickeneth clay,
Nor turneth it to marble — maketh eyes,
Not shadowy hollows, where no sunbeams play,
Would mould his loftiest thought in human guise:
Thou didst appear, walking unknown abroad,
God's living sculpture, all-informed of God.

II.

If one should say, "Lo, there thy statue! take
Possession, sculptor; now inherit it;
Go forth upon the earth in likeness fit;
As with a trumpet-cry at morning, wake
The sleeping nations; with light's terror, shake
The slumber from their hearts, that, where they sit,
They leap straight up, aghast, as at a pit
Gaping beneath;" I hear him answer make:
"Alas for me! for I nor can nor dare
Inform what I revered as I did trace.
'Twere scorn, inspired truth so to impair,
With feeble spirit mocking the enorm
Strength on its forehead." Thou, God's thought thy
    form,
Didst live the large significance of thy face.

III.

Men have I seen, and seen with wonderment,
Noble in form, "lift upward and divine,"[1]

---

[1] Marlowe's *Tamburlaine the Great.*

In whom I yet must search, as in a mine,

After that soul of theirs, by which they went

Alive upon the earth.   And I have bent.

Regard on many a woman, who gave sign

God willed her beautiful, when He drew the line

That shaped each float and fold of beauty's tent :

Her soul, alas! chambered in pygmy space,

Left the fair visage pitiful inane —

Poor signal only of a coming face

When from the penetrale she filled the fane.

Possessed of thee was every form of thine —

Thy very hair replete with the divine.

IV.

If thou hast built a temple, how my eye

Had greedily worshipped, from the low-browed crypt

Up to the soaring pinnacles that, tipt

With stars, made signals when the sun drew nigh!

Dark caverns in and under ; vivid sky

Its home and aim!   Say, from the glory slipt,

And down into the shadows dropt and dipt,

Or reared from darkness up so holy-high?

'Tis man himself, the temple of thy Ghost,

From hidden origin to hidden fate —

Foot in the grave, head in blue spaces great —

From grave and sky filled with a fighting host.

Fight glooms and glory? or does the glory borrow

Strength from the hidden glory of to-morrow?

v.

If thou hadst been a painter, what fresh looks,

What outbursts of pent glories, what new grace

Had shone upon us from the great world's face!

How had we read as in new-languaged books,

Clear love of God in loneliest shyest nooks!

A lily, if thy hand its form did trace,

Had plainly been God's child, of lower race; —

How strong the hills, how sweet the grassy brooks!

To thee all nature open lay, and bare,

Because thy soul was nature's inner side;

Clear as the world on the dawn's golden tide,

Its vast idea in thy soul did rise;

Thine was the earth, thine all her meanings rare —

The ideal Man, with the eternal eyes!

VI.

But I have seen pictures the work of man,
In which at first appeared but chaos wild:
So high the art transcended, they beguiled
The eye as formless, and without a plan.
Not soon the spirit, brooding o'er, began
To see a purpose rise, like mountain isled,
When God said, Let the Dry appear! and, piled
Above the waves, it rose in twilight wan.
So might thy pictures then have been too strange
For us to pierce beyond their outmost look;
A vapor and a darkness; a sealed book;
An atmosphere too high for wings to range;
Where gazing must our spirits pale and change,
And tremble as at a void thought cannot brook.

VII.

But earth is now thy living picture, where
Thou shadowest truth, the simple and profound
By the same form in vital union bound:
Where one can see but the first step of thy stair,

Another sees it vanish far in air.
When thy king David viewed the starry round,
From heart and fingers broke the psaltery-sound:
Lord, what is man, that thou shouldst mind his
      prayer!
But when the child beholds the heavens on high,
He babbles childish noises — not less dear
Than what the king sang praying — to the ear
Of Him who made the child, and king, and sky.
Earth is thy picture, painter great, whose eye
Sees with the child, sees with the kingly seer.

VIII.

If thou hadst built some mighty instrument,
And set thee down to utter ordered sound,
Whose faithful billows, from thy hands unbound,
Breaking in light, against our spirits went,
And caught, and bore above this earthly tent,
The far-strayed back to their prime natal ground,
Where all roots fast in harmony are found,
And God sits thinking out a pure concent;
If — ah! how easy that had been for thee!

Our broken music thou must first restore —
A harder task than think thine own out free;
But till thou hast done it, no divinest score,
Though rendered by thine own angelic choir,
Could lift a human soul from foulest mire.

IX.

If thou hadst been a poet! On my heart
The thought flashed sudden, burning through the weft
Of life, and with too much I sank bereft.
Up to my eyes the tears, with sudden start,
Thronged blinding: would the veil now rend and
      part?
The husk of vision — would that in twain be cleft,
Its hidden soul in naked beauty left,
And I behold thee, Nature, as thou art?
O poet Jesus! at thy holy feet
I should have lien, sainted with listening;
My pulses answering ever, in rhythmic beat,
The stroke of each triumphant melody's wing,
Creating, as it moved, my being sweet;
My soul thy harp, thy word the quivering string.

X.

Thee had we followed through the twilight land
Where thought grows form, and matter is refined
Back into thought of the eternal mind,
Till, seeing them one, lo, in the morn we stand!
Then start afresh and follow, hand in hand,
With sense divinely growing, till, combined,
We heard the music of the planets wind
In harmony with billows on the strand!
Till, one with earth and all God's utterance,
We hardly knew whether the sun outspake,
Or a glad sunshine from our spirits brake;
Whether we think, or winds and blossoms dance!
Alas, O poet leader! for such good,
Thou wast God's tragedy, writ in tears and blood.

XI.

Hadst thou been one of these, in many eyes,
Too near to be a glory for thy sheen,
Thou hadst been scorned; and to the best hadst been
A setter forth of strange divinities;

But to the few construct of harmonies,

A sudden sun, uplighting the serene

High heaven of love; and, through the cloudy screen

That 'twixt our souls and truth all wretched lies

Dawning at length, hadst been a love and fear,

Worshipped on high from magian's mountain-crest,

And all night long symboled by lamp-flames clear;

Thy sign, a star upon thy people's breast,

Where now a strange mysterious token lies,

That once barred out the sun in noontide skies.

XII.

But as thou camest forth to bring the poor,

Whose hearts are nearer faith and verity,

Spiritual childhood, thy philosophy —

So taught'st the A, B, C of heavenly lore;

Because thou sat'st not lonely evermore,

With mighty thoughts informing language high,

But, walking in thy poem continually,

Didst utter deeds, of all true forms the core —

Poet and poem one indivisible fact;

Because thou didst thine own ideal act,

And so for parchment, on the human soul
Didst write thine aspirations, at thy goal
Thou didst arrive with curses for acclaim,
And cry to God up through a cloud of shame.

XIII.

For three-and-thirty years, a living seed,
A lonely germ, dropt on our waste world's side,
Thy death and rising thou didst calmly bide;
Sore companied by many a clinging weed
Sprung from the fallow soil of evil and need;
Hither and thither tossed, by friends denied;
Pitied of goodness dull, and scorned of pride;
Until at length was done the awful deed,
And thou didst lie outworn in stony bower
Three days asleep — O, slumber godlike brief
For man of sorrows and acquaint with grief!
Heaven's seed thou diedst, that out of thee might
        tower
Aloft with rooted stem and shadowy leaf,
Of all humanity the crimson flower.

XIV.

When dim the ethereal eye, no art, though clear
As golden star in morning's amber springs,
Can pierce the fogs of low imaginings
Painting and sculpture are but mockery mere.
When dull to deafness is the hearing ear,
Vain too the poet. Nought but earthly things
Have credence. When the soaring skylark sings
How shall the stony statue strain to hear?
Open the deaf ear, wake the sleeping eye,
And lo, musicians, painters, poets — all
Trooping unsent for, come without a call;
As winds that where they list blow evermore;
As waves from silent deserts roll to die
In mighty voices on the peopled shore.

XV.

Our ears thou openedst; mad'st our eyes to see
All they who work in stone or color fair,
Or build up temples of the quarried air,
Which we call music, scholars are of thee.
Henceforth in might of such the earth shall be

Truth's temple-theatre, where she shall wear
All forms of revelation, and they bear
Tapers in acolyte humility.
O Master-maker! thy exultant art
Goes forth in making makers. Pictures? No ;
But painters, who in love and truth shall show
Glad secrets from thy God's rejoicing heart.
All-unforetold, green grass and corn up start,
When through dead sands thy living waters go.

XVI.

From the beginning good and fair are one ;
But men the beauty from the truth will part,
And, though the truth is ever beauty's heart,
After the beauty will, short-breathed, run,
And the indwelling truth deny and shun.
Therefore, in cottage, synagogue, and mart,
Thy thoughts came forth in common speech, not art ;
With voice and eye in Jewish Babylon
Thou taughtest — not with pen or carved stone,
Nor in thy hand the trembling wires didst take ;
Thou of the truth not less than all wouldst make ;
For her sake even her forms thou didst disown :

Ere beauty cause the word of truth to fail,
The light behind shall burn the broidered veil.

XVII.

Holy of holies ! — Lord, let me come nigh !
For, Lord, thy body is the shining veil
By which I look on God and am not pale.
Forgive me, if in these poor verses lie
Mean thoughts, for see, the thinker is not high.
But were my song as loud as saints' all-hail,
As pure as prophet's cry of warning wail,
As holy as thy mother's ecstasy,
I know a better thing — for love or ruth,
To my weak heart a little child to take.
Nor thoughts nor feelings, art nor wisdom seal
The man who at thy table bread shall break.
Thy praise was not that thou didst know, or feel,
Or show, or love, but that thou didst the truth.

XVIII.

Despised ! Rejected by the priest-led roar
Of multitudes ! The imperial purple flung

Around the form the hissing scourge had wrung!
To the bare truth dear witnessing, before
The false, and trembling true! As on the shore
Of infinite love and truth, I kneel among
The blood-prints, and with dumb adoring tongue,
Cry to the naked man who erewhile wore
The love-wove garment, — " Witness to the truth,
Crowned by thy witnessing, thou art the King!
With thee I die, to live in worshipping.
O human God! O brother, eldest born!
Never but thee was there a man in sooth!
Never a true crown but thy crown of thorn!"

A MEMORIAL OF AFRICA.

I.

Upon a rock I sat — a mountain-side,
Far, far forsaken of the old sea's lip;
A rock where ancient waters' rise and dip,
Recoil and plunge, and backward eddying tide
Had worn and worn, while races lived and died,
Involved channels. Where the sea-weed's drip
Followed the ebb, now crumbling lichens sip
Sparse dews of heaven, that down with sunset slide.
I sat and gazed southwards. A dry flow
Of withering wind sucked up my drooping strength,
Slow gliding from the desert's burning length.
Behind me piled, away and upward go
Great sweeps of savage mountains — up, away,
Where snow gleams ever — panthers roam, they say.

II.

This infant world has taken long to make !
Nor hast Thou done the making of it yet,
But wilt be working on when death has set
A new mound in some church-yard for my sake.
On flow the centuries without a break ;
Uprise the mountains, ages without let ;
The lichens suck the rock's breast — food they get ·
Years more than past, the young earth yet will take.
But in the dumbness of the rolling time,
No veil of silence shall encompass me —
Thou wilt not once forget and let me be ;
Rather wouldst thou some old chaotic prime
Invade, and, with a tenderness sublime,
Unfold a world, that I, thy child, might see.

A. M. D.

METHINKS I see thee, lying straight and low,
Silent and darkling, in thy earthy bed,
The mighty strength in which I trusted, fled,
The long arms lying careless of kiss or blow;
On thy tall form I see the night robe flow
Down from the pale, composed face — thy head
Crowned with its own dark curls: though thou wast
      dead,
They dressed thee as for sleep, and left thee so.
My heart, with cares and questionings oppressed,
Seldom since thou didst leave me, turns to thee;
But wait, my brother, till I too am dead,
And thou shalt find that heart more true, more free,
More ready in thy love to take its rest,
Than when we lay together in one bed.

TO GARIBALDI.

WITH A BOOK — WHEN HE VISITED ENGLAND.

WHEN, at Philippi, he who would have freed
Great Rome from tyrants, for the season brief
That lay 'twixt him and battle, sought relief
From painful thoughts, he in a book did read,
That so the death of Portia might not breed
Too many thoughts, and cloud his mind with grief:
Brother of Brutus, of high hearts the chief,
When thou in heaven receiv'st the heavenly meed,
And I shall find my hoping not in vain,
Tell me my book has wiled away one pang
That out of some lone sacred memory sprang,
Or wrought an hour's forgetfulness of pain,
And I shall rise, my heart brimful of gain,
And thank my God amid the golden clang.

TO S. F. S.

THEY say that lonely sorrows do not chance.
It may be true ; one thing I think I know :
New sorrow joins a gliding funeral slow
With less jar than it shocks a merry dance.
But if griefs troop, why, joy doth joy enhance
As often, and the balance levels so.
If quick to see flowers by the way-side blow,
As quick to feel the lurking thorns that lance
The foot that walketh naked in the way, —
Blest by the lily, white from toils and fears,
Oftener than wounded by the thistle-spears,
We should walk upright, bold, and earnest-gay ;
And when the last night closed on the last day,
Should sleep like one that far-off music hears.

ORGAN SONGS.

TO A. J SCOTT.

WITH THE FOLLOWING POEM

I WALKED all night the darkness did not yield.
   Around me fell a mist, a weary rain,
Enduring long At length the dawn revealed

A temple's front, high-lifted from the plain.
Closed were the lofty doors that led within ;
But by a wicket one might entrance gain.

'Twas awe and silence When I entered in,
The night, the weariness, the rain were lost
In hopeful spaces First I heard a thin

Sweet sound of voices low, together tossed,
As if they sought some harmony to find
Which they knew once, but none of all that host

Could wile the far-fled music back to mind.
Loud voices, distance-low, wandered along
The pillared paths, and up the arches twined

14

With sister-arches, rising, throng on throng,
Up to the roof's dim height. At broken times
The voices gathered to a burst of song,

But parted sudden, and were but single rhymes
By single bells through Sabbath morning sent,
That have no thought of harmony or chimes.

Hopeful confusion! Who could be content
Looking and listening only by the door?
I entered further. Solemnly it went —

Thy voice, Truth's herald, walking the untuned roar,
Calm and distinct, powerful and sweet and fine ·
I loved and listened, listened and loved more.

If the weak harp may, tremulous, combine
Faint ghostlike sounds with organ's loudest tone,
Let my poor song be taken in to thine.

Thy heart, with organ-tempests of its own,
Will hear æolian sighs from thin chords blown.

1850.

LIGHT.

FIRST-BORN of the creating Voice !
Minister of God's Spirit, who wast sent
Waiting upon Him first, what time He went
Moving about 'mid the tumultuous noise
Of each unpiloted element
Upon the face of the void formless deep !
Thou who didst come unbodied and alone,
Ere yet the sun was set his rule to keep,
Or ever the moon shone,
Or e'er the wandering star-flocks forth were driven !
Thou garment of the Invisible, whose skirt
Sweeps, glory-giving, over earth and heaven !
Thou comforter, be with me as thou wert
When first I longed for words, to be
A radiant garment for my thought, like thee.

We lay us down in sorrow,
Wrapt in the old mantle of our mother Night ;

In vexing dreams we strive until the morrow;
Grief lifts our eyelids up — and lo, the light!
The sunlight on the wall! And visions rise
Of shining leaves that make sweet melodies;
Of wind-borne waves with thee upon their crests;
Of rippled sands on which thou rainest down;
Of quiet lakes that smooth for thee their breasts;
Of clouds that show thy glory as their own;
O joy! O joy! the visions are gone by!
Light, gladness, motion, are reality!

Thou art the god of earth. The skylark springs
Far up to catch thy glory on his wings;
And thou dost bless him first that highest soars.
The bee comes forth to see thee; and the flowers
Worship thee all day long, and through the skies
Follow thy journey with their earnest eyes.
River of life, thou pourest on the woods,
And on thy waves float out the wakening buds.
The trees lean towards thee, and, in loving pain,
Keep turning still to see thee yet again.
And nothing in thine eyes is mean or low:
Where'er thou art, on every side,

All things are glorified;
And where thou canst not come, there thou dost
    throw
Beautiful shadows, made out of the dark,
That else were shapeless ; now it bears thy mark.

  And men have worshipped thee.
The Persian, on his mountain-top,
Waits kneeling till thy sun go up,
God-like in his serenity.
All-giving, and none-gifted, he draws near ;
And the wide earth waits till his face appear —
Longs patient. And the herald glory leaps
Along the ridges of the outlying clouds,
Climbing the heights of all their towering steeps ;
Till a quiet multitudinous laughter crowds
The universal face, and, silently,
Up cometh he, the never closing eye.
Symbol of Deity ! men could not be
Farthest from truth when they were kneeling unto
    thee,

  Thou plaything of the child,
When from the water's surface thou dost spring,

Thyself upon his chamber ceiling fling,

And there, in mazy dance and motion wild,

Disport thyself — ethereal, undefiled,

Capricious, like the thinkings of the child!

I am a child again, to think of thee

In thy consummate glee

Or, through the gray dust darting in long streams,

How I would play with thee, athirst to climb

On sloping ladders of thy moted beams!

How marvel at the dusky glimmering red,

With which my closed fingers thou hadst made

Like rainy clouds that curtain the sun's bed!

And how I loved thee always in the moon!

But most about the harvest-time,

When corn and moonlight made a mellow tune,

And thou wert grave and tender as a cooing dove!

And then the stars that flashed cold, deathless love!

And the ghost-stars that shimmered in the tide!

And more mysterious earthly stars,

That shone from windows of the hill and glen —

Thee prisoned in with lattice-bars,

Mingling with household love and rest of weary men!

And still I am a child, thank God! — to spy

Thee starry stream from bit of broken glass,
Upon the brown earth undescried,
Is a found thing to me, a gladness high,
A spark that lights joy's altar-fire within,
A thought of hope to prophecy akin,
And from my spirit fruitless will not pass.

Thou art the joy of age :
Thy sun is dear when long the shadow falls.
Forth to its friendliness the old man crawls,
And, like the bird hung out in his poor cage
To gather song from radiance, in his chair
Sits by the door ; and sitteth there
His soul within him, like a child that lies
Half dreaming, with half-open eyes,
At close of a long afternoon in summer —
High ruins round him, ancient ruins, where
The raven is almost the only comer ;
Half dreams, half broods, in wonderment
At thy celestial descent,
Through rifted loops alighting on the gold
That waves its bloom in many an airy rent :
So dreams the old man's soul, that is not old,
But sleepy 'mid the ruins that enfold.

What soul-like changes, evanescent moods,

Upon the face of the still passive earth,

Its hills, and fields, and woods,

Thou with thy seasons and thy hours art ever call-
    ing forth !

Even like a lord of music bent

Over his instrument,

Who gives to tears and smiles an equal birth !

When clear as holiness the morning ray

Casts the rock's dewy darkness at its feet,

Mottling with shadows all the mountain gray ;

When, at the hour of sovereign noon,

Infinite silent cataracts sheet

Shadowless through the air of thunder-breeding
    June ;

And when a yellower glory slanting passes

'Twixt longer shadows o'er the meadow grasses ;

When now the moon lifts up her shining shield,

High on the peak of a cloud-hill revealed,

Now crescent, low, wandering sun-dazed away,

Unconscious of her own star-mingled ray,

Her still face seeming more to think than see,

Makes the pale world lie dreaming dreams of thee !

No mood of mind, no melody of soul,
But lies within thy silent soft control.

  Of operative single power,
And simple unity the one emblem,
Yet all the colors that our passionate eyes devour,
In rainbow, moonbow, or in opal gem,
Are the melodious descant of divided thee.
Lo thee in yellow sands! lo thee
In the blue air and sea!
In the green corn, with scarlet poppies lit,
Thy half souls parted, patient thou dost sit.
Lo thee in speechless glories of the west!
Lo thee in dew-drop's tiny breast!
Thee on the vast white cloud that floats away,
Bearing upon its skirt a brown moon-ray!
Regent of color, thou dost fling
Thy overflowing skill on everything!
The thousand hues and shades upon the flowers,
Are all the pastime of thy leisure hours;
And all the jeweled ores in mines that hidden be,
Are dead till touched by thee.

  Everywhere,
Thou art lancing through the air;

Every atom from another
Takes thee, gives thee to his brother ;
Continually.
Thou art wetting the wet sea,
Bathing its sluggish woods below,
Making the salt flowers bud and blow;
Silently,
Workest thou, and ardently,
Waking from the night of nought
Into being and to thought:
Influences
Every beam of thine dispenses,
Potent, subtle, reaching far,
Shooting different from each star.
Not an iron rod can lie
In circle of thy beamy eye,
But thy look doth change it so
That it cannot choose but show
Thou, the worker, hast been there ;
Yea, sometimes, on substance rare,
Thou dost leave thy ghostly mark
Even in what men call the dark.
Doer, shower, mighty teacher !
Truth-in-beauty's silent preacher !

Universal something sent
To shadow forth the Excellent!

When the first-born affections —
Those winged seekers of the world within,
That search about in all directions,
Some bright thing for themselves to win —
Through pathless forests, gathering fogs,
Through stony plains, treacherous bogs,
Long, long, have followed faces fair, —
Fair soulless faces which have vanished into air;
And darkness is around them and above,
Desolate, with nought to love;
And through the gloom on every side,
Strange dismal forms aie dim descried;
And the air is as the breath
From the lips of void-eyed Death;
And the knees are bowed in prayer
To the Stronger than despair;
Then the ever-lifted cry,
Give us light, or we shall die,
Cometh to the Father's ears,
And He hearkens, and He hears;

And slow, as if some sun would glimmer forth
From sunless winter of the north,
They, hardly trusting happy eyes,
Discern a dawning in the skies.
'Tis Truth awaking in the soul;
Thy Righteousness to make them whole.
What shall men, this Truth adoring,
Gladness giving, youth-restoring,
Call it but Eternal Light?—
'Tis the morning, 'twas the night.
Even a misty hope that lies on
Our dim future's far horizon,
We call a fresh aurora, sent
Up the spirit's firmament,
Telling, through the vapors dun,
Of the coming, coming sun.

All things most excellent
Are likened unto thee, excellent thing!
Yea, He who from the Father forth was sent,
Came like a lamp, to bring,
Across the winds and wastes of night,
The everlasting light;

The Word of God, the telling of his thought,
The Light of God, the making-visible;
The far-transcending glory brought
In human form with man to dwell;
The dazzling gone; the power not less
To show, irradiate, and bless;
The gathering of the primal rays divine,
Informing chaos, to a pure sunshine!

Dull horrid pools no motion making!
No bubble on the surface breaking!
The heavy dead air gives no sound,
Asleep and moveless on the marshy ground.

Rushing winds and snow-like drift,
Forceful, formless, fierce, and swift!
Hair-like vapors madly riven!
Waters smitten into dust!
Lightning through the turmoil driven,
Aimless, useless, yet it must!

Gentle winds through forests calling!
Bright birds through the thick leaves glancing!

Solemn waves on sea-shores falling!
White sails on blue waters dancing!
Mountain streams glad music giving!
Children in the clear pool laving!
Yellow corn and green grass waving!
Long-haired, bright-eyed maidens living!
Light, O Radiant! it is thou!
And we know our Father now.

Forming ever without form;
Showing, but thyself unseen;
Pouring stillness on the storm;
Making life where death had been!
Light, if He did draw thee in,
Death and Chaos soon were out,
Weltering o'er the slimy sea,
Riding on the whirlwind's rout,
In unmaking energy!
Thou art round us, God within,
Fighting darkness, slaying sin.

Father of Lights, high-lost, unspeakable
On whom no changing shadow ever fell!

Thy light we know not, aie content to see;
And shall we doubt because we know not thee?
Or, when thy wisdom cannot be expressed,
Fear lest dark vapors brood within thy breast?
It shall not be;
Our hearts awake and speak aloud for thee.
The very shadows on our souls that lie,
Good witness to the light supernal bear;
The something 'twixt us and the sky
Could cast no shadow if light were not there.
If children tremble in the night,
It is because their God is light.
The shining of the common day
Is mystery still, howe'er it ebb and flow
Behind the seeing orb, the secret lies;
Thy living light's eternal play,
Its motions, whence or whither, who shall know?—
Behind the life itself, its fountains rise.

Enlighten me, O Light!—why art thou such?
Why art thou awful to our eyes, and sweet?
Cherished as love, and slaying with a touch?
Why in thee do the known and unknown meet?

Why swift and tender, strong and delicate?
Simple as truth, yet manifold in might?
Why does one love thee, and another hate?
Why cleave my words to the portals of my speech,
When I a goodly matter would indite?
Why fly my thoughts themselves beyond my reach?
In vain to follow thee, I thee beseech,
For God is light.

TO A. J. SCOTT.

THUS, once, long since, the daring of my youth
Drew nigh thy greatness with a little thing.
Thou didst receive me ; and thy sky of truth

Has domed me since, a heaven of sheltering,
Made homely by the tenderness and grace
Which round thy absolute friendship ever fling

A radiant atmosphere. Turn not thy face
From that small part of earnest thanks, I pray,
Which, spoken, leaves much more in speechless case.

I see thee far before me on thy way
Up the great peaks, and striding stronger still
Thy intellect unrivaled in its sway,

15

Upheld and ordered by a regnant will ;
Thy wisdom, seer and priest of holy fate,
Searching all truths, its prophecy to fill ;

But, O my friend, throned in thy heart so great,
High Love is queen, and hath no equal mate.

May, 1857.

I WOULD I WERE A CHILD.

I WOULD I were a child,
That I might look, and laugh, and say, My Father!
And follow thee with running feet, or rather
  Be led through dark and wild.

How I would hold thy hand,
My glad eyes often to thy glory lifting!
Should darkness 'twixt thy face and mine come
    drifting,
  How hearken thy command!

If an ill thing came near,
I would but creep within thy mantle's folding,
Shut my eyes close, thy hand yet faster holding,
  And thus forgot my fear.

O soul, O soul, rejoice!
Thou art God's child indeed, for all thy sinning·
A poor weak child, yet his, and worth the winning
  With savior eyes and voice.

Who spoke the words?   Didst Thou?
They are too good, even for such a giver:
Such water drinking once, I must feel ever
    As I had drunk but now.

Yet sure He taught us so,
Teaching our lips to say with his, Our Father!
Telling the tale of wanderer who did gather
    His goods to him, and go!

Ah! thou dost lead me, God;
But it is dark; no stars! the way is dreary;
Almost I sleep, I am so very weary
    Upon this rough hill-road.

Almost!   Nay, I *do* sleep;
There is no darkness save in this my dreaming;
Thy fatherhood above, around, is beaming;
    Thy hand my hand doth keep.

Cast on my face one gleam;
I have no knowledge but that I am sleeping;
Lost in its lies, my life goes out in weeping;
    Wake me from this my dream.

How long shall heavy night
Deny the day? How long shall this dull sorrow
Say in my heart that never any morrow
   Will bring the vanished light?

   Lord, art thou in the room?
Come near my bed; O! draw aside the curtain;
A child's heart would say *Father*, were it certain
   The word would not presume.

   But if this dreary sleep
May not be broken, help thy helpless sleeper
To rest in thee; so shall his sleep grow deeper —
   For evil dreams too deep.

   Father! I dare at length;
My childhood sure will shield me from all blaming:
Sinful, yet hoping, I to thee come, claiming
   Thy tenderness, my strength.

A PRAYER FOR THE PAST.

ALL sights and sounds of day and year,
All groups and forms, each leaf and gem,
Are thine, O God, nor will I fear
To talk to thee of them.

Too great thy heart is to despise;
Thy day girds centuries about;
From things we little call, thine eyes
See great things looking out.

Therefore the prayerful song I sing
May come to thee in ordered words;
Its low-born echo shall not cling
In terror to the chords.

I think that nothing made is lost;
That not a moon has ever shone,
That not a cloud my eyes hath crossed,
But to my soul is gone.

That all the lost years garnered lie
In this thy casket, my dim soul;
And thou wilt, once, the key apply,
And show the shining whole.

But were they dead in me, they live
In thee, whose Parable is — Time,
And Worlds, and Forms, and Sounds that give
Thee back the offered rhyme.

And after what men call my death,
When I have crossed the unknown sea,
Some heavenly morn, on hopeful breath,
Shall rise this prayer to thee.

O let me be a child once more,
To dream the glories of the gloom,
The climbing suns and starry store
That ceiled my little room.

O call again the moons that crossed
Blue gulfs, behind gray vapors crept ;
Show me the solemn skies I lost
Because in thee I slept.

Once more let gathering glory swell,
And lift the world's dim eastern eye;
Once more in twilight's bosoming spell
The western close and die.

But show me first —O, blessed sight!
The lowly house where I was young;
There winter sent wild winds at night,
And up the snow-heaps flung,

Or soundless built a chaos, fair
With lovely wastes and lawless forms,
With ghostly trees and sparkling air—
New sport for white-robed storms.

But, lo! there dawned a dewy morn;
A man was turning up the mould;
And in our hearts the spring was born,
Crept hither through the cold.

On with the glad year let me go,
With troops of daisies round my feet;
Flying my kite, or, in the glow
Of arching summer heat,

Outstretched in fear upon the bank,
Lest, gazing up on awful space,
I should fall down into the blank,
From off the round world's face.

And let my brothers come with me
To play our old games yet again,
Children on earth, more full of glee
That we in heaven are men.

If over us the shade of death
Pass like a cloud across the sun,
We'll tell a secret, in low breath :
" Soon will the *dream* be done.

" ''Tis in the dream our brother 's gone
Up stairs · he heard our Father call ;
For one by one we go alone,
Till He has gathered all."

Father, in joy our knees we bow ;
This earth is not a place of tombs :
We are but in the nursery now ;
They in the upper rooms.

For are we not at home in thee,
And all this world a visioned show,
That, knowing what Abroad is, we
What Home is, too, may know?

And at thy feet I sit, O Lord,
As once I sat, in moonlight pale,
Hearing my father's measured word
Read out a lofty tale.

Then in the vision let me go
On, onward through the gliding years;
Gathering great noontide's joyous glow,
Eve's love-contented tears;

One afternoon sit pondering
In that old chair in that old room,
Where passing pigeon's sudden wing
Flashed lightning through the gloom;

There try once more, with effort vain,
To mould in one perplexed things,
There find the solace yet again
Faith in the Father brings;

Or mount and ride in sun and wind,
Through desert moors, hills bleak and high :
There wandering vapors fall, and find
In me another sky.

For so thy Visible grew mine,
Though half its power I could not know ;
And in me wrought a work divine,
Which thou hadst ordered so ;

Filling my heart with shape and word
From thy full utterance unto men ;
Forms that with ancient truth accord,
And find it words again.

But if thou give me thus the past —
Spring to thy summer leading in,
I now bethink me at the last —
O Lord, leave out the sin.

On what I loved my thoughts I bent ;
Green leaves unfolding to their fruits,
Expanding flowers, aspiring scent —
Forgot the writhing roots.

For Spring, in latest years of youth,
Became the form of every form;
Now bursting joyous into truth,
Now sighing in the storm.

Then far from my old northern land,
I lived where gentle winters pass;
Saw green seas lave a wealthy strand,
From hills of unsown grass.

Saw gorgeous sunsets claim the scope
Of gazing heaven, to spread their show;
Hang scarlet clouds i' th' topmost cope,
With fringes flaming low.

Saw one beside me in whose eyes
Once more old Nature found a home;
There treasured up her changeful skies,
Gray rocks and bursting foam.

But life lies dark before me, God.
Shall I throughout desire to see
And walk once more the hilly road
By which I went to thee?

O'er a new joy this day we bend,
Of lovely power the soul to lift —
A wondering wonder thou dost lend
With loan outpassing gift :

'A little child beholds the sun ;
Once more incarnates thy old law —
One born of two, two born in one,
All into one to draw.

But is there no day creeping on
Which I should tremble to renew ?
I thank thee, Lord, for what is gone —
Thine is the future too.

And are we not at home in thee,
And all this world a visioned show ;
That knowing what Abroad is, we
What Home is too may know ?

LONGING.

My heart is full of inarticulate pain,
  And beats laborious. Cold ungenial looks
Invade my sanctuary. Men of gain,
  Wise in success, well-read in feeble books,
No nigher come, I pray: your air is drear;
'Tis winter and low skies when ye appear.

Beloved, who love beauty and fair truth!
  Come nearer me; too near ye cannot come;
Make me an atmosphere with your sweet youth;
  Give me your souls to breathe in, a large room;
Speak not a word, for see, my spirit lies
Helpless and dumb; shine on me with your eyes.

O all wide places, far from feverous towns!
  Great shining seas! pine forests! mountains wild!

Rock-bosomed shores! rough heaths! and sheep-
    cropt downs!
Vast pallid clouds! blue spaces undefiled!
Room! give me room! give loneliness and air!
Free things and plenteous in your regions fair.

White dove of David, flying overhead,
    Golden with sunlight on thy snowy wings,
Outspeeding thee my longing thoughts are fled
    To find a home afar from men and things;
Where in his temple, earth o'erarched with sky,
God's heart to mine may speak, my heart reply.

O God of mountains, stars, and boundless spaces!
    O God of freedom and of joyous hearts!
When thy face looketh forth from all men's faces,
    There will be room enough in crowded marts;
Brood thou around me, and the noise is o'er;
Thy universe my closet with shut door.

Heart, heart, awake! The love that loveth all
    Maketh a deeper calm than Horeb's cave.

God in thee, can his children's folly gall?

  Love may be hurt, but shall not love be brave?—

Thy holy silence sinks in dews of balm;

Thou art my solitude, my mountain-calm.

I KNOW WHAT BEAUTY IS.

I KNOW what beauty is, for Thou
    Hast set the world within my heart;
    Of me thou madest it a part;
I never loved it more than now.

I know the Sabbath afternoons;
    The light asleep upon the graves;
    Against the sky the poplar waves;
The river murmurs organ tunes.

I know the spring with bud and bell;
    The hush in summer woods at night;
    Autumn, when leaves let in more light;
Fantastic winter's lovely spell.

I know the rapture music gives,
    The power that dwells in ordered tones;
    Dream-muffled voice, it loves and moans,
And half alive, comes in and lives.

The charm of verse, where, love-allied,
  Music and thought, in concord high,
  Show many a glory sailing by,
Borne on the Godhead's living tide.

And Beauty's regnant All I know,
  The imperial head, the starry eye;
  The fettered fount of harmony,
That makes the woman radiant go.

But I leave all, thou man of woe!
  Put off my shoes, and come to thee,
  Most beautiful of all I see,
Most wonderful of all I know.

As child forsakes his favorite toy,
  His sisters' sport, his wild bird's nest;
  And, climbing to his mother's breast,
Enjoys yet more his former joy —

I lose to find. On white-robed bride
  Fair jewels fairest light afford;
  So, gathered round thy glory, Lord,
All glory else is glorified.

SYMPATHY.

GRIEF held me silent in my seat;
  I neither moved nor smiled
Joy held her silent at my feet,
  My shining lily-child.

She raised her face and looked in mine;
  It seemed she was denied;
The door was shut, there was no shine;
  Poor she was left outside.

Once, twice, three times, with infant grace,
  Her lips my name did mould;
Her face was pulling at my face, —
  She was but ten months old.

She called the thoughts into the sighs;
  And soon I asked, — Does God
Need help from his poor children's eyes,
  To ease him of his load?

Rarely from love our looks arise —
  Sometimes from needy woe :
If comfort lay in loving eyes,
  He seldom found it so ;

But when we cry in evil case
  From comfort's weary lack,
The weakest hope that seeks his face
  A stronger hope comes back.

Nor waits He, moveless, till we cry,
  But wakes the sleeping prayer ;
Not Father only in the sky,
  But servant everywhere.

I looked *not* up , nor comfort slid
  Downward, my grief to wile .
It was his present face that did
  Smile upward in her smile.

THE THANK-OFFERING.

My Lily snatches not my gift ;
  Hungry she would be fed,
But to her mouth she will not lift
  The piece of broken bread,
Till on my lips, unerring, swift,
  The morsel she has laid.

This is her grace before her food,
  This her libation poured ;
Even thus his offering, Aaron good,
  Heaved up to thank the Lord,
When for the people all he stood,
  And with a cake adored.[1]

Our Father, every gift of thine
  I offer at thy knee ;

[1] Numbers xv. 19, 20.

Not else I take the love divine
  With which it comes to me;
Not else the offered grace is mine
  Of being one with thee.

Yea, all my being I would lift,
  An offering of me;
Not yet my very own the gift,
  Till heaved again to thee :
Draw from this dry and narrow clift
  Thy boat upon thy sea.

PRAYER.

WE doubt the word that tells us : Ask,
   And ye shall have your prayer ;
We turn our thoughts as to a task,
   With will constrained and rare.

And yet we have ; these scanty prayers
   Yield gold without alloy :
O God ! but he that trusts and dares
   Must have a boundless joy.

REST.

I.

WHEN round the earth the Father's hands
    Have gently drawn the dark ;
Sent off the sun to fresher lands,
    And curtained in the lark ;
'Tis sweet, all tired with glowing day,
    To fade with fading light ;
To lie once more, the old weary way,
    Upfolded in the night.

If mothers o'er our slumbers bend,
    And unripe kisses reap,
In soothing dreams with sleep they blend,
    Till even in dreams we sleep.
And if we wake while night is dumb,
    'Tis sweet to turn and say,
It is an hour ere dawning come,
    And I will sleep till day.

II.

There is a dearer, warmer bed,
　Where one all day may lie,
Earth's bosom pillowing the head,
　And let the world go by.
There come no watching mother's eyes ;
　The stars instead look down ;
Upon it breaks, and silent dies,
　The murmur of the town.

The great world, shouting, forward fares ;
　This chamber, hid from none,
Hides safe from all, for no one cares
　For him whose work is done.
Cheer thee, my friend ; bethink thee how
　A certain unknown place,
Or here or there, is waiting now,
　To rest thee from thy race.

III.

Nay, nay, not there the rest from harms,
　The slow composed breath !

Not there the folding of the arms!
    Not there the sleep of death!
It needs no curtained bed to hide
    The world with all its wars;
No grassy cover to divide
    From sun and moon and stars.

There is a rest that deeper grows
    In midst of pain and strife;
A mighty, conscious, willed repose,
    The death of deepest life.
To have and hold the precious prize
    No need of jealous bars;
But windows open to the skies,
    And skill to read the stars.

IV.

Who dwelleth in that secret place,
    Where tumult enters not,
Is never cold with terror base,
    Never with anger hot.

For if an evil host should dare
   His very heart invest,
God is his deeper heart, and there
   He enters in to rest.

When mighty sea-winds madly blow,
   And tear the scatteied waves,
Peaceful as summer woods, below
   Lie darkling ocean caves
The wind of words may toss my heart,
   But what is that to me !
'Tis but a surface storm — thou art
   My deep, still, resting sea.

O DO NOT LEAVE ME.

O DO not leave me, mother, lest I weep ;
   Till I forget, be near me in that chair.
The mother's presence leads her down to sleep —
   Leaves her contented there.

O do not leave me, lover, brother, friends,
   Till I am dead, and resting in my place.
Love-compassed thus, the girl in peace ascends,
   And leaves a raptured face.

Leave me not, God, until — nay, until when ?
   Not till I have with thee one heart, one mind ;
Not till the Life is Light in me, and then
   Leaving is left behind.

BLESSED ARE THE MEEK, FOR THEY SHALL INHERIT THE EARTH.

A QUIET heart, submissive, meek,
  Father, do thou bestow,
Which more than granted will not seek
  To have, or give, or know.

Each little hill then holds its gift
  Forth to my joying eyes ;
Each mighty mountain will uplift
  My spirit to the skies.

Lo, then the running water sounds
  With gladsome, secret things !
The silent water more abounds,
  And more the hidden springs.

Sweet murmurs then the trees will send
  To hold the birds in song ;

The waving grass its tribute lend
  Low music to prolong.

The sun will cast great crowns of light
  On waves that anthems roar;
The dusky billows break at night
  In flashes on the shore.

Yea, every lily's shining cup,
  The hum of hidden bee,
The odors floating mingled up,
  With insect revelry, —

All hues, all harmonies divine,
  The holy earth about,
Their souls will send forth into mine,
  My soul to widen out.

And thus the great earth I shall hold,
  A perfect gift of thine;
Richer by these, a thousandfold,
  Than if broad lands were mine.

HYMN FOR A SICK GIRL.

FATHER, in the dark I lay,
  Thirsting for the light ;
Helpless, but for hope alway
  In thy father-might.

Out of darkness came the morn,
  Out of death came life ;
I and faith and hope, new-born,
  Out of moaning strife.

So, one morning yet more fair,
  I, alive and brave,
Sudden breathing loftier air,
  Triumph o'er the grave.

Though this feeble body lie
  Underneath the ground,
Wide awake, not sleeping, I
  Shall in Him be found.

But a morn yet fairer must
  Quell this inner gloom ;
Resurrection from the dust
  Of a deeper tomb.

Father, wake thy little child ;
  Give me bread and wine.
Till my spirit undefiled
  Rise and live in thine.

A CHRISTMAS CAROL FOR 1862.

THE YEAR OF THE TROUBLE IN LANCASHIRE.

THE skies are pale, the trees are stiff,
  The earth is dull and old;
The frost is glittering as if
  The very sun were cold.
And hunger fell is joined with frost,
  To make me thin and wan:
Come, babe, from heaven, or we are lost;
  Be born, O child of man.

The children cry, the women shake,
  The strong men stare about;
They sleep when they should be awake,
  They wake ere night is out.
For they have lost their heritage —
  No sweat is on their brow:
Come, babe, and bring them work and wage;
  Be born, and save us now.

17

Across the sea, beyond our sight,
　　Roars on the fierce debate ,
The men go down in bloody fight,
　　The women weep and hate.
And in the right be which that may,
　　Surely the strife is long:
Come, Son of Man, thy righteous way
　　And right will have no wrong.

Good men speak lies against thine own, —
　　Tongue quick, and hearing slow;
They will not let thee walk alone,
　　And think to serve thee so.
If they the children's freedom saw
　　In thee, the children's king,
They would be still with holy awe,
　　Or only speak to sing.

Some neither lie, nor starve, nor fight,
　　Nor yet the poor deny ,
But in their hearts all is not right, —
　　They often sit and sigh

We need thee every day and hour,
   In sunshine and in snow :
Child king, we pray with all our power —
   Be born, and save us so.

We are but men and women, Lord ;
   Thou art a gracious child ;
O fill our hearts, and heap our board,
   Of grace, this winter wild.
And though the trees be sad and bare,
   Hunger and hate about,
Come, child, and ill deeds and ill fare
   Will soon be driven out.

A CHRISTMAS CAROL.

Babe Jesus lay in Mary's lap ;.
  The sun shone on his hair ;
And this was how she saw, mayhap,
  The crown already there.

For she sang : "Sleep on, my little king,
  Bad Herod dares not come ;
Before thee sleeping, holy thing,
  The wild winds would be dumb.

"I kiss thy hands, I kiss thy feet,
  My child, so long desired ;
Thy hands shall never be soiled, my sweet ;
  Thy feet shall never be tired.

"For thou art the king of men, my son ;
  Thy crown I see it plain ;
And men shall worship thee, every one,
  And cry, Glory ! Amen."

Babe Jesus opened his eyes so wide!
   At Mary looked her Lord.
And Mary stinted her song and sighed.
   Babe Jesus said never a word.

THE SLEEPLESS JESUS.

'Tis time to sleep, my little boy;
　Why gaze thy bright eyes so?
At night our children, for new joy,
　Home to thy father go,
But thou are wakeful. Sleep, my child,
　The moon and stars are gone;
The wind is up and raving wild;
　But thou art smiling on.

My child, thou hast immortal eyes
　That see by their own light;
They see the children's blood — it lies
　Red-glowing through the night.
Thou hast an ever open ear
　For sob, or cry, or moan.
Thou seemest not to see or hear,
　Thou only smilest on.

When first thou camest to the earth,
　All sounds of strife were still;

A silence lay about thy birth,
  And thou didst sleep thy fill.
Thou wakest now — why weep'st thou not?
  Thy earth is woe-begone ;
Both babes and mothers wail their lot,
  But still thou smilest on.

I read thy face like holy book ;
  No hurt is pictured there ;
Deep in thine eyes I see the look
  Of one who answers prayer.
Beyond pale grief and wild uproars,
  Thou seest God's will well done ;
Low prayers, through chambers' closed doors,
  Thou hear'st — and smilest on.

Men say: " I will arise and go."
  God says: " I will go meet."
Thou seest them gather, weeping low,
  About the Father's feet.
And all must, each for others, bear,
  Till all are homeward gone.
Answered, O eyes, ye see all prayer :
  Smile, Son of God, smile on.

THE CHILDREN'S HEAVEN.

THE infant lies in blessed ease
    Upon his mother's breast;
No storm, no dark, the baby sees
    Invade his heaven of rest
He nothing knows of change or death —
    Her face his holy skies;
The air he breathes his mother's breath,
    His stars, his mother's eyes.

Yet half the sighs that wander there
    Are born of doubts and fears;
The dew slow falling through that air —
    It is the dew of tears
And ah! my child, thy heavenly home
    Hath rain as well as dew,
Black clouds fill sometimes all its dome,
    And quench the starry blue.

Her smile would win no smile again,
  If baby saw the things
That ache across his mother's brain,
  The while she sweetly sings.
Thy faith in us is faith in vain —
  We are not what we seem.
O dreary day, O cruel pain,
  That wakes thee from thy dream !

No ; pity not his dream so fair,
  Nor fear the waking grief ;
O, safer he than though we were
  Good as his vague belief !
There is a heaven that heaven above,
  Whereon he gazes now ;
A truer love than in thy kiss ;
  A better friend than thou.

The Father's arms fold like a nest
  His children round about ;
His face looks down, a heaven of rest,
  Where comes no dark, no doubt.

Its mists are clouds of stars that move
  In sweet concurrent strife ;
Its winds, the goings of his love ;
  Its dew, the dew of life.

We for our children seek thy heart,
  For them the Father's eyes:
Lord, when their hopes in us depart,
  Let hopes in thee arise.
When childhood s visions them forsake,
  To women grown and men,
Thou to thy heart their hearts wilt take,
  And bid them dream again.

REJOICE.

"REJOICE," said the Sun; "I will make thee gay
With glory and gladness and holiday;
I am dumb, O man, and I need thy voice."
But man would not rejoice.

"Rejoice in thyself," said he, "O Sun,
For thy daily course is a lordly one;
In thy lofty place, rejoice if thou can:
For me, I am only a man."

"Rejoice," said the Wind; "I am free and strong;
I will wake in thy heart an ancient song;
Hear the roaring woods, my organ noise!"
But man would not rejoice.

"Rejoice, O Wind, in thy strength,' said he,
"For thou fulfillest thy destiny;
Shake the forest, the faint flowers fan:
For me, I am only a man."

"Rejoice," said the Night, "with moon and star;
The Sun and the Wind are gone afar;
I am here with rest and dreams of choice."
But man would not rejoice.

For he said, — "What is rest to me, I pray,
Whose labor brings no gladsome day?
He only should dream who has hope behind.
Alas for me and my kind!"

Then a voice that came not from moon or star,
From the sun, or the wind roving afar,
Said, "Man, I am with thee — hear my voice."
And man said, "I rejoice."

THE GRACE OF GRACE.

HAD I the grace to win the grace
 Of some old man in lore complete;
My face would worship at his face,
 And I sit lowly at his feet.

Had I the grace to win the grace
 Of childhood, loving shy, apart;
The child should find a nearer place,
 And teach me resting on my heart.

Had I the grace to win the grace
 Of maiden living all above;
My soul would trample down the base,
 That she might have a man to love.

A grace I had no grace to win
 Knocks now at my half-open door:
Ah! Lord of glory, come thou in;
 Thy grace divine is all, and more!

ANSIPHONY.

DAYLIGHT fades away.
  Is the Lord at hand,
In the shadows gray
  Stealing on the land?

    Gently from the east
      Come the shadows gray;
    But our lowly priest
      Nearer is than they.

It is darkness quite.
  Is the Lord at hand,
In the cloak of night
  Stolen upon the land?

    But I see no night,
      For my Lord is here;
    With Him dark is light,
    ' With Him far is near.

List ! the cock 's awake.
  Is the Lord at hand?
Cometh He to make
  Light in all the land?

    Long ago He made
      Morning in my heart;
    Long ago He bade
      Shadowy things depart.

Lo, the dawning hill!
  Is the Lord at hand,
Come to scatter ill,
  Ruling in the land?

    He hath scattered ill,
      Ruling in my mind.
    Growing to his will,
      Freedom comes, I find.

We will watch all day,
  Lest the Lord should come;
All night waking stay,
  In the darkness dumb.

I will work all day,
   For the Lord hath come,
Down my head will lay,
   All night glad and dumb.

For we know not when
   Christ may be at hand,
But we know that then
   Joy is in the land.

For I know that where
   Christ hath come again,
Quietness without care
   Dwelleth in his men.

DORCAS.

If I might guess, then guess I would:
  Amid the gathered folk,
This gentle Dorcas one day stood,
  And heard what Jesus spoke.

She saw the woven, seamless coat —
  Half envious for his sake:
"O, happy hands," she said, "that wrought
  That honored thing to make!"

Her eyes with longing tears grow dim
  She never can come nigh
To work one service poor for Him
  For whom she glad would die!

But hark! He speaks a mighty word:
  She hearkens now indeed!
"When did we see thee naked, Lord,
  And clothed thee in thy need?

"The King shall answer, Inasmuch
  As to my brothers ye
Did it — even to the least of such —
  Ye did it unto me."

Home, home she went, and plied the loom
  And Jesus' poor arrayed.
She died — they wept about the room,
  And showed the coats she made.

MARRIAGE SONG.

"THEY have no more wine," she said.
But they had enough of bread;
And the vessels by the door
Held for thirst a plenteous store;
Yes, *enough,* but Love divine
Turned the water into wine.

When should wine not water flow,
But when home two glad hearts go,
And in sacred bondage bound,
Soul in soul hath freedom found?
Meetly then, a holy sign,
Turns the water into wine.

Good is all the feasting then,
Good the merry words of men;
Good the laughter and the smiles,
Good the wine that grief beguiles;—

Crowning good, the Word divine
Turning water into wine.

Friends, the Master with you dwell;
Daily work this miracle;
When fair things too common grow
Wake again the heavenly show,
Ever at your table dine,
Turning water into wine.

So at last you shall descry
All the patterns of the sky:
Earth a heaven of short abode,
Houses temples unto God,
Waterpots, to vision fine,
Brimming full of heavenly wine.

BLIND BARTIMÆUS.

As Jesus went into Jericho town,
'Twas darkness all, from toe to crown,
    About blind Bartimæus.
He said, "When eyes are so very dim,
They are no use for seeing Him;
    No matter — He can see us..

"Cry out, cry out, blind brother — cry;
Let not salvation dear go by.
    Have mercy, Son of David."
Though they were blind, they both could hear, —
They heard, and cried, and He drew near;
    And so the blind were saved.

O Jesus Christ, I am very blind,
Nothing comes through into my mind;
    'Tis well I am not dumb:

Although I see thee not, nor hear,
I cry because thou may'st be near :
   O son of Mary, come.

I hear it through the all things blind :
Is it thy voice, so gentle and kind —
   "Poor eyes, no more be dim"?
A hand is laid upon mine eyes ;
I hear, and hearken, see, and rise —
   'Tis He: I follow Him.

COME UNTO ME.

Come unto me, the Master says.
But how? I am not good;
No thankful song my heart will raise,
Nor even wish it could.

I am not sorry for the past,
Nor able not to sin;
The weary strife would ever last
If once I should begin

Hast thou no burden then to bear?
No action to repent?
Is all around so very fair?
Is thy heart quite content?

Hast thou no sickness in thy soul?
No labor to endure?

Then go in peace, for thou art whole,
    Thou needest not his cure.

Ah! mock me not. Sometimes I sigh;
    I have a nameless grief, —
A faint sad pain, — but such that I
    Can look for no relief.

Come, come to Him who made thy heart;
    Come weary and oppressed,
To come to Jesus is thy part,
    His part to give thee rest.

New grief, new hope He will bestow,
    Thy grief and pain to quell,
Into thy heart Himself will go,
    And that will make thee well.

MORNING HYMN.

O LORD of life, thy quickening voice
   Awakes my morning song;
In gladsome words I would rejoice
   That I to thee belong.

I see thy light, I feel thy wind;
   Earth is thy uttered word,
Whatever wakes my heart and mind,
   Thy presence is, my Lord

The living soul which I call me
   Doth love, and long to know;
It is a thought of living thee,
   Nor forth of thee can go.

Therefore I choose my highest part,
   And turn my face to thee;

Therefore I stir my inmost heart
To worship fervently.

Lord, let me live and act this day,
Still rising from the dead ;
Lord, make my spirit good and gay, —
Give me my daily bread.

Within my heart, speak, Lord, speak on,
My heart alive to keep,
Till the night comes, and, labor done,
In thee I fall asleep.

NOONTIDE.

I LOVE thy skies, thy sunny mists,
  Thy fields, thy mountains hoar,
Thy wind that bloweth where it lists, —
  Thy will, I love it more.

I love thy hidden truth to seek
  All round, in sea, on shore ;
The arts whereby like gods we speak, —
  Thy will to me is more.

I love thy men and women, Lord,
  The children round thy door,
Calm thoughts that inward strength afford, —
  Thy will, O Lord, is more.

But when thy will my life shall hold
  Thine to the very core,
The world, which that same will did mould,
  I shall love ten times more.

EVENING HYMN.

O GOD, whose daylight leadeth down
   Into the sunless way,
Who with restoring sleep dost crown
   The labor of the day!

What I have done, Lord, make it clean
   With thy forgiveness dear ;
That so to-day what might have been,
   To-morrow may appear.

And when my thought is all astray,
   Yet think thou on in me ;
That with the new-born innocent day
   My soul rise fresh and free.

Nor let me wander all in vain
   Through dreams that mock and flee ;
But even in visions of the brain,
   Go wandering towards thee.

THE HOLY MIDNIGHT.

Aн, holy midnight of the soul,
  When stars alone are high;
When winds are resting at their goal,
  And sea-waves only sigh !

Ambition faints from out the will;
  Asleep sad longing lies ,
All hope of good, all fear of ill,
  All need of action dies;

Because God is ; and claims the life
  He kindled in thy brain ;
And thou in Him, rapt far from strife,
  Diest and liv'st again.

LaVergne, TN USA
28 October 2009

162242LV00007B/3/P

9 781115 848206